The North Country Trail

The Best Walks, Hikes, and
Backpacking Trips on America's
Longest National Scenic Trail

Ron Strickland *with the*
North Country Trail Association

The University of Michigan Press
Ann Arbor

Published in the United States of America by
The University of Michigan Press
Printed and bound by CPI Group (UK) Ltd, Croydon, CR0 4YY
⊚ Printed on acid-free paper

2017   2016   2015   2014   5   4   3   2

Photographs courtesy of the North Country Trail Association

A CIP catalog record for this book is available from the British Library.

Library of Congress Cataloging-in-Publication Data

Strickland, Ron.
    The North Country Trail : the best walks, hikes, and backpacking trips on
America's longest national scenic trail / Ron Strickland with the North Country Trail
Association.
        pages   cm
    Includes bibliographical references and index.
    ISBN 978-0-472-07184-5 (cloth : alk. paper) — ISBN 978-0-472-05184-7
(pbk. : alk. paper) — ISBN 978-0-472-02872-6 (e-book)
    1. Hiking—North Country National Scenic Trail—Guidebooks. 2. Walking—
North Country National Scenic Trail—Guidebooks. 3. Trails—North Country
National Scenic Trail—Guidebooks. 4. North Country National Scenic Trail—
Guidebooks. I. Title.
GV199.42.N67S87 2013
796.5109756—dc23   2013000020

To Thomas J. Gilbert,

first National Park Service superintendent of the
North Country National Scenic Trail (1981–2011),
for his unerring dedication and unswerving vision
in service to the trail and its family of builders and
community of users—present and future—
and to God and his country

I live for those who love me,
For those who know me true,
For the Heaven that smiles above me,
And awaits my spirit too;
For the cause that lacks assistance,
For the wrong that needs resistance,
For the future in the distance,
And the good that I can do.

       George Linnaeus Banks (1821–81)

Acknowledgments

So many hundreds of people helped in the creation of this book that I feel inadequate to express my gratitude. First and always foremost, I am greatly indebted to Tom Gilbert, retired National Park Service superintendent of the North Country and Ice Age National Scenic Trails. Tom was part of the North Country Trail even before its 1980 enabling legislation. In recent years, he was the instigator and guiding force behind this book project.

The North Country Trail Association's executive director, Bruce Matthews, deftly guided my manuscript through many hoops. NCTA's staff cartographer and GIS specialist, Matt Rowbotham, performed his legerdemain with impressive skill and imagination.

In traveling from the Vermont border to western North Dakota, I learned anew that the North Country Trail is truly a grassroots project. I was assisted by volunteers wherever I went. I developed a deep sense of affection for them and a feeling of great admiration for their dedication and talent.

A trail guidebook is a snapshot in time of a footpath that inevitably is in constant flux. I hope that readers will not hesitate to voice their suggestions for improvements to future editions of this guide. In the meantime, I am both responsible for its faults and delighted to imagine the joy it may inspire in some unknown hearts.

Special thanks are given to the following people, who were instrumental to the creation of this guide and comprise only a few of the many volunteers dedicated to the project.

Brent Anslinger
Joyce Appel
Loren Bach
Andrew Bashaw
Anne Billiard
Katie Blau
Steve Boller
Ryan Bowles
Eugene Branigan
Dave Brewer
Devin and Ashley Callihan

Mary Coffin
Joe Dabes
Matt Davis
Dennis Fay
Kellie Flannery
Melanie Fullman
Chris Grupenhof, Regional Park
    Manager, Ohio State Parks,
    Hocking Hills Region
Paul Haan
Mary Hamilton

Joe Hardisky

Tim Hass

Mick Hawkins

Nelda B. Ikenberry

Lorana Jinkerson

Bruce and Linda Johnson

Keith Klos

Charles Krammin

Kay and Stan Kujawa

John Kwapinski, Park Manager,
    Fort Ransom State Park

Duane Lawton

Eric and Cheryl Longman

Richard Lutz

Bill Menke

Andy Mytys

Lynne Nason

Theresa Neal

Peter Nordgren

Steve Perecini

Darrel Rodekuhr

Lynda Rummel

Sigi and Horst Schwinge

John and Alic Stehle

Peter Stotts

Bryan Stotts, District Ranger,
    Sheyenne National Grasslands

Marty and Vickie Swank

Dick Swanson

Jerry and Beth Trout

Santiago Utsumi, W. K. Kellogg
    Biological Station

Ray Vlasak

Lynette Webber

Doug Welker

Greg Wisniewski

Quinn Wright

Chuck Zosel

—*Ronald G. Strickland, PhD*

In addition to those thoughtfully acknowledged by Dr. Strickland, folks listed and those who were not, I need to add the North Country Trail Association's great thanks to the following people:

The members of NCTA's Guidebook Committee, who conceived and led this effort with great foresight and commitment. Led by chair David Cornell, they are Joan Young, Matt Rowbotham, Tom Gilbert, Tom Moberg, and Lynda Rummel.

Joan Young, the indefatigable "Spirit of the NCT." She has given so much of herself to the notion of a national hiking trail connecting our nation's rugged red-plaiders and to promoting long-distance hiking accomplishments.

Tom Gilbert, to whom this book is dedicated. His career, his legacy, and a significant part of his heart are indubitably painted Nelson Boundary Blue.

The membership of the North Country Trail Association, without whom, simply, there is no trail. A finer, more bootstrapping, freethinking cadre of citizen stewards does not exist this side of heaven.

Matt Rowbotham, NCTA's staff cartographer and GIS specialist. "Above and beyond" is far too anemic a description of not only his effort but his interest, enthusiasm, expertise, and insights, which contributed immeasurably to this book.

NCTA's staff. They collectively shoved aside priorities in order to see this project through.

Rose Ann M. Davis. She stepped in with her organizational skills to help at the last minute in tracking all the data, versions, documents, and details.

The surprisingly and delightfully diverse Red Plaid Nation, whose members are united by their toughness, perseverance, independence, and occasionally perverse and always crusty pride. In his fine book, *The Windward Shore*, author Jerry Dennis describes how the term *sisu*—a basically nontranslatable Finnish term often used to describe what it means to be Finnish—relates to the residents of Michigan's Upper Peninsula:

> It is the Yoopers' humble anthem, adopted by those who have survived a single winter as readily as those whose ancestors immigrated to work in the copper and iron mines. It is stoicism stripped of its philosopher's robe and dressed in a Woolrich coat and Packers' cap, with a chainsaw in the back of the pickup and a snowmobile rusting all summer in the yard. It means sticking to a job until it is finished, no matter how difficult it is or how long it takes, and one of those jobs, the one that requires the greatest endurance and the most courage, is life itself. In a harsh climate and inhospitable land, *sisu* helps a person get by with dignity.

These are also the traits of the Red Plaid Nation, defined by their rugged individualism in meeting the challenges of eking out a livelihood in the unforgiving north.

—*Bruce Matthews, Executive Director,*
North Country Trail Association

Contents

Introduction   1

Planning Your Hike on the NCT   13

New York   21

1. Onondaga Loop   25
2. Sugar Hill State Forest and Watkins Glen State Park   30
3. Mitchellsville Gorge   38
4. Allegany State Park   43

Pennsylvania   47

1. Henry's Mills   50
2. Cook Forest State Park   56
3. Hell's Hollow   61
4. Wampum   66

Ohio   73

1. Beaver Creek State Park   77
2. Zoar Village and the Ohio and Erie Canal Towpath Trail   81
3. Hocking Hills State Park/State Forest   85
4. Shawnee State Forest   90
5. Dayton   94
6. Snaketown   101

Michigan   107

1. Yankee Springs State Recreation Area and
   Barry State Game Area   111
2. Lowell   116
3. Birch Grove Trail Loop   122
4. Bowman Lake Loop   127
5. Manistee River Loop   130
6. Traverse City   139

7. Jordan River Pathway Loop   147

8. Wilderness State Park Loop   152

9. Tahquamenon Falls State Park   156

10. Lake Superior Shoreline   161

11. Marquette   166

12. Old Victoria Overlooks   172

13. Black River Falls   181

Wisconsin   187

1. Wren Falls   190

2. Porcupine Lake Wilderness   195

3. Historic Portage and Brule Bog Round-Trips   200

Minnesota   207

1. Milton Lake Esker   210

2. Wetland Wonders   214

3. Shingobee-Anoway   217

4. The Itasca Moraine Chain of Lakes   221

5. Itasca State Park   227

North Dakota   231

1. Sheyenne National Grasslands   234

2. Sheyenne State Forest   238

3. Lake Ashtabula   242

4. Lonetree Wildlife Management Area   245

5. Lake Sakakawea State Park   249

Chronology of the NCT   252

Bibliography   255

Index   257

Introduction

On October 2, 1968, the US Congress ratified the National Trails System Act, legislation designed to promote the preservation and enjoyment of America's natural areas and historic resources and to provide for the population's increasing need for trails-based outdoor recreation. Two trails—the Appalachian and the Pacific Crest National Scenic Trails—were designated as the first in the National Trails System, but the act also provided for the study of additional trails for possible future inclusion, including one that traversed and linked America's "Great North Woods." Congress authorized the North Country National Scenic Trail in 1980. Today, there are eleven National Scenic Trails.

The North Country National Scenic Trail (colloquially, the North Country Trail, or NCT) is the longest of these trails, spanning 4,600 miles in seven states. But it's not only its length that distinguishes the NCT. The diversity of the places and people connected by the trail is another highlight—as is its accessibility. More than twice the length of the Appalachian Trail, the NCT is within a day's drive of fully 40 percent of all Americans.

There are places along the NCT where it navigates pristine wilderness, expansive wildflower meadows, virgin stands of timber, extraordinary overlooks, and the third largest waterfall east of the Mississippi; other segments take hikers on strolls through towns, past tempting ice cream parlors and aromatic bakeries. Throughout, the NCT is deeply connected with American history, following the footsteps of the country's first peoples, voyageurs, surveyors, soldiers, canal boaters, sailors, lumbermen, runaway slaves, miners, and aeronauts, as well as a few less savory characters here and there. America's greatest scenic trail is a national treasure, a peoples' trail, linking and celebrating our natural heritage and the cultural and historic diversity of our northern heartlands. The featured hikes found in this guide are just a sample of what's waiting to be discovered on the NCT.

How to Use This Guide

A comprehensive covering of all 4,600 miles of the NCT isn't possible in a single guidebook. For one thing, the NCT is a work in progress; a little less than half of the trail still needs to be located off-road, which makes keeping a guidebook up to date pretty problematic. Instead, this book is designed to introduce readers to the sport of hiking and initiate a relationship with the NCT and its community of trail builders and maintainers—

the Red Plaid Nation, as they enjoy calling themselves. It's an invitation to get out on the trail and celebrate the heritage of the North Country and its mythical "Great North Woods." It's also an invitation to join fellow red-plaiders to help bootstrap the trail into being in its entirety.

Local experts have selected 40 hikes from within the NCT that represent a range of geographic locations, difficulties, distances, and terrains. These hikes are some of the gems on a 4,600-mile necklace encircling America's northern heartlands. The NCT contains hikes suitable for novice and experienced hikers alike, and this guide will help readers choose and match the experience most suitable for their particular interests and ability levels. Many of these featured hikes begin and end at the same place (i.e., they are loop trails or "out-and-back" trails), and many have easy or even flat grades, making them perfect for families with young hikers.

This guide is divided into seven chapters—one for each of the seven states through which the NCT runs. After reviewing the introductory material, pick a state, find its chapter, and skim through the featured hikes. Each has information about mileage and ease of hiking and navigation, where to start and finish, and so on. GPS coordinates are provided because so many today have access to this technology—even on cell phones.

Local information sources are provided for each featured hike, as well as the contact for the local chapters who maintain that section of the trail. Hikers are strongly encouraged to use these contacts and to check the North Country Trail Association (NCTA) website (www.northcountry trail.org) for current trail conditions, up-to-date maps, and other information helpful in planning a successful hike. As with any outdoor activity, trail conditions are influenced by the weather; to avoid disappointment, always get the latest info before going.

The trail guide provided for each hike briefly describes what to look for and how to get from one end of the hike to the other. Waypoints are often provided for key landmarks. All of this guidebook's hikes are labeled as easy, moderate, or challenging. This rating is anecdotal and based solely on the author's observations. The factors include length of the hike, terrain and elevation changes, navigation difficulty, and suitability for families and younger children. Strenuous hikes requiring good physical conditioning, located in remote areas, and calling for higher levels of experience, skills, and judgment are identified as challenging. Hikes lending themselves to a leisurely saunter with young children are rated as easy. Of course, there are variables such as temperature, weather, bug prevalence, and so on that hikers need to factor in on the spot. Any of these can change an easy hike into a more difficult one.

Where Exactly Does the NCT Go?

The NCT traverses seven states. From east to west, they are New York, Pennsylvania, Ohio, Michigan, Wisconsin, Minnesota, and a good bit of North Dakota. From the eastern terminus at Crown Point on Lake Champlain at New York's border with Vermont, the trail meanders through the Adirondack Mountains, traverses the Mohawk Valley, and skirts the southern end of the Finger Lakes before heading southwest into the Allegheny Mountains. Cutting off the northwest corner of Pennsylvania, the trail enters Ohio just north of Pittsburgh and continues south into the Wayne National Forest, connecting with the Buckeye Trail. After looping farther south through the Shawnee State Forest, the NCT heads north through Dayton into Ohio's canal country. From there, it wanders into Michigan, which hosts more of the NCT than any other state (1,150 miles). After the farmlands and forests of southwestern Michigan give way to larger wooded tracts, the trail moves into the big timber country of northern Michigan, crossing the Straits of Mackinac into Michigan's wild Upper Peninsula, where it turns west again, blazing its way through Pictured Rocks National Lakeshore all the way to the Porcupine Mountains before heading into Wisconsin's portion of the Great North Woods. At Duluth, Minnesota, the NCT again follows the Lake Superior shoreline, this time northeast on the Superior Hiking Trail all the way to the Canadian border, which it then follows after again turning west. From the Boundary Waters, the NCT heads ever westward through Minnesota's Iron Range to the lakes region and then stretches out on the prairies into North Dakota, where it finds its western terminus at Lake Sakakawea State Park near the Garrison Dam, which creates Lake Sakakawea on the Missouri River.

What Can You See on the NCT?

The NCT climbs mountains in the Adirondacks, Alleghenies, Porcupines, and Sawtooths; it crosses the Iron Range of Minnesota and the Laurentian Shield. The NCT passes through major watersheds, including the mighty Hudson, Susquehanna, Allegheny, Ohio, Mississippi, and Missouri Rivers. NCT-touched waters eventually flow into the Atlantic Ocean via the St. Lawrence, Hudson, and Susqehanna Rivers and the Gulf of Mexico, through the mighty Mississippi (which the NCT leaps across at its source). It touches Lake Champlain, New York's Finger Lakes, and the Allegheny Reservoir. It spans Lakes Michigan and Huron on the Mighty Mac—Michigan's Mackinac Bridge. It leaves over 40 miles of footprints on Lake Superior's shoreline beaches. It pauses at Tahquamenon Falls and many smaller waterfalls and cascades along the way. The NCT traverses 10 national forests.

The NCT shares towpaths with the historic Erie Canal in New York as well as Ohio's Miami and Erie Canal. It follows historic railways, including the famed Wabash Cannonball. Winding its way through the Great North Woods, the NCT retraces the footsteps of America's first peoples—portage paths used by indigenous Americans, missionaries, and voyageurs and, later, by the lumbermen, miners, oilmen, and farmers who tried to eke out a living from the North Country's natural resources. Escaped slaves made their way north along the Underground Railroad. More recently, there are the vacationers immortalized in Gordon Lightfoot's "Wreck of the Edmund Fitzgerald"; "the islands and bays are for sportsmen," as well as the rivers, streams, fields, and mountains. The North Country epitomized by Hemingway, Zane Grey, and many others is a recreation destination and unique experience. The NCT experience aggregates and links the best of America's Great North Woods and its hardy peoples. A hike anywhere along the trail is an immersion in the natural and cultural landscapes of the region.

Because of its length and diversity, there's no single thing that sums up the NCT experience, unlike the case with most of its sister trails in the National Scenic Trails System. With the Appalachian, Pacific Crest, or Continental Divide National Scenic Trails, for example, it's immediately apparent what they're about—they follow mountain ranges. The NCT is about mountains as well as river bottoms, people as well as places, all connected by the sweat of human endeavor, the essence of the NCT experience. Even so, the trail is full of surprises.

You expect big skies while hiking Dakota prairies on the NCT, but not a lush, wildflower-filled river valley and even a waterfall. You expect solitude in North Woods wilderness, but not day after day without seeing another soul. You expect vineyards during a saunter on the trail through New York's Finger Lakes region, but not the intoxicating perfumes of spring blooming or fall harvest. You might expect evidence of America's North Country past along the trail, but not the birthplace of the United States

Navy. Hikers can sense the presence of Algonquin and Ojibway, Jesuit and voyageur, escaped slaves reaching for freedom, miner, logger, sailor, or canal boat driver, all sharing their stride. You expect an occasional interesting character when you hike the North Country Trail, but never the number of folks offering tired hikers a hot shower, cold drinks, warm meals, a backyard in which to pitch a tent, or a blessing from the heart. With the NCT, you learn to expect the unexpected. Wherever you are in America's northern heartlands, when following the blue blazes of the NCT, you are getting to know the Red Plaid Nation. Your adventure always starts nearby.

Is the NCT Complete?

Although the NCT spans two-thirds of the North American continent, from great eastern forests to tall grass prairies, the entire trail is not yet "on the ground." About half of it is physically completed—signed, blazed, and mapped accordingly. The rest of it is a series of road walks and connector trails that get hikers from one point on the completed trail to the next. Hikers *can* hike the entire NCT, and at this writing, 11 intrepid folks have either segment-hiked or thru-hiked the entirety. The hardworking volunteers of the NCTA and partners are putting more trail on the ground

Status of the Eastern and Western Extensions of the NCT

Extending the NCT eastward has proved much easier than going in the opposite direction. Only about 40 new miles of trail need to be located and constructed between Lake Champlain and the crest of the Green Mountains to link the NCT with the Appalachian Trail. The feasibility study is completed, and public meetings have concluded, with a preferred corridor approved by the National Park Service. The task that remains is getting congressional authorization of the terminus extension into Vermont.

The NCT's current western terminus at North Dakota's Lake Sakakawea State Park may eventually be moved to the Rocky Mountains. This extension will never become a reality without significant local support—difficult to imagine in that empty landscape stretching through western North Dakota and eastern Montana. Volunteers and donations are needed to make this happen in time for the 50th anniversary of the National Trails System. It would create something really exciting for that 2018 celebration.

every year (see more later in this introduction about the NCTA and how to help). Furthermore, plans are afoot to expand east into Vermont to connect with the Appalachian Trail. Eventually, hiking enthusiasts hope to extend the trail west into Montana to connect with the Continental Divide and Pacific Northwest Trails and thus forge a link going from sea to shining sea. But the NCT continues to be a work in progress and will not be fully completed for many years to come. Progress in trail construction is recorded at NCTA headquarters, and the most current maps and trail conditions can be found at www.northcountrytrail.org.

What Is the North Country Trail Association?

The NCT is administered by the National Park Service, but building, maintaining, and telling the story of this national park that is 4,600 miles

End-to-Enders

Though the hikes featured in this guide were selected primarily to please day hikers, the North Country Trail is wonderfully well suited for long-distance walking. Thru-hikers typically hike 500 miles or more at a stretch. They go farther (and often faster) than anyone else. Though they constitute only a tiny minority of all hikers, their dedication, curiosity, and adventurousness set a high standard. Their feats are inspirational, and their effects are aspirational— they make the rest of us want to be able to do the same. As of this publication, the following end-to-ender (E2E) pioneers have completed the entire North Country Trail:

Peter Wolfe (E2E 1974–80)

Carolyn Hoffman (E2E trip 1978)

Chet Frome (E2E 1992–95)

Ed Talone (E2E 1994)

Andrew Skurka (E2E 2004–5)

Don Beattie (E2E 1980-2005)

Allen Shoup (E2E 1995–2005)

Bart Smith (E2E completed 2007)

M. J. "Eb" Eberhart (E2E 2009)

Joan Young (E2E 1991–2010)

Judy Geisler (E2E trip completed 2011)

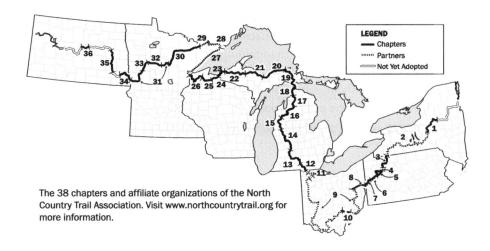

The 38 chapters and affiliate organizations of the North Country Trail Association. Visit www.northcountrytrail.org for more information.

long by 4 feet wide is mainly a volunteer effort. The NCT, like most long-distance hiking trails, would be nothing without volunteers. Erecting signs, painting blazes, clearing brush, constructing bridges, cutting weeds, maintaining shelters, and removing all-too-frequent storm debris are just some examples of the sweat equity volunteers invest over many thousands of hours each year so that hikers can experience the NCT at its best. These volunteers are members of the North Country Trail Association and its partner and affiliate organizations.

The NCTA is a private, membership-based, nonprofit 501(c)(3) organization, whose mission is *to develop, maintain, protect, and promote the NCT as the premier hiking path across the northern tier of the United States through a trail-wide coalition of volunteers and partners.* Building the trail is impossible without the grassroots mobilization of talent, money, and ideas supported through the partnership of the National Park Service with the NCTA. The NCTA has a small professional staff headquartered in Lowell, Michigan, as well as regional trail coordinators in Minnesota and Wisconsin. At its Lowell headquarters, the NCTA manages the association's finances, engages in fund-raising and marketing programs, provides training and mapping expertise, advocates for the NCT in Congress and at the capitols of the seven states through which the trail travels, and builds the capacity of chapters and affiliate/partner organizations doing grassroots work where it matters most.

It is the grassroots work in chapters and several additional affiliate and partner organizations along the entire length of the NCT that gets the trail built and keeps it maintained. Each chapter's charter defines its assigned length of trail for building, maintaining, and monitoring. Many sections of the NCT within a chapter's boundaries are "adopted" by members, who regularly patrol them, report on conditions, and conduct routine maintenance. Trail adopters usually take their responsibilities very seriously. They are among the many unsung heroes devoted to bringing a quality hiking experience to all.

Partner and Affiliate Organizations

The NCT has benefited from visionary leaders in the hiking community who pioneered regional trails, such as the Finger Lakes, Buckeye, Superior Hiking, Kekekabic, and Border Route Trails, which now host portions of the NCT on their tread. These preexisting trails were built by dedicated volunteers before the NCT was authorized by Congress, and their existence likely contributed to the effort to obtain authorization. In agreeing to cohost the NCT with the NCTA, these partner and affiliate organizations maintain their own trail and their own identity—and in some cases, their own trail maps, waypoints, guidebooks, and other resources. From east to west, these groups include:

Finger Lakes Trail Conference (www.fltconference.org), which maintains the 420 miles of the Finger Lakes Trail shared with the NCT in New York);

Join the NCTA

With local chapters in communities scattered along the trail, as well as many at-large members elsewhere, the NCTA unites individuals as well as local and regional trail organizations in a legacy effort to give the trail to America. NCTA members not only provide sweat equity; they contribute time, talent, and treasure toward building the trail and telling its story, from local trail towns to Washington, DC. To apply for membership, visit www.northcountrytrail .org/get-involved/become-a-member/ online or contact NCTA Headquarters at 229 East Main Street, Lowell, MI 49331, 866-445-3628 (toll-free).

Buckeye Trail Association (www.buckeyetrail.org), which maintains the 800-plus miles of the Buckeye Trail shared with the NCT in Ohio;

Superior Hiking Trail Association® (www.shta.org), which maintains the 300 miles of the Superior Hiking Trail shared with the NCT in Minnesota;

Kekekabic Trail Association (www.kek.org), which maintains the 41 miles of the Kekekabic Trail shared with the NCT in Minnesota; and

Border Route Trail Association (www.borderroutetrail.org), which maintains the 65 miles of the Border Route Trail shared with the NCT in Minnesota.

The National Park Service

Like the better-known Appalachian and Pacific Crest Trails, the NCT is managed by a federal agency and built and maintained by a nonprofit organization. In the case of the NCT, that agency is the National Park Service. A National Park Service superintendent and trail manager provide financial, technical, and planning support as well as set standards that determine when sections of the trail can be formally certified as NCT, as opposed to temporary connectors or uncertified trail.

Who Owns the NCT?

Neither the NCTA nor the National Park Service actually own or manage most of the land on which the NCT is located. Yet every inch does belong to somebody. By comparison, the Appalachian Trail is almost entirely protected via public ownership or easements. The NCT is more complicated. As much as possible, the NCT uses public lands, and the National Park Service and the NCTA work with government partners to ensure the quality of the NCT experience. However, private property (corporate or individual) accounts for a very significant percent of the NCT's mileage.

This means that different sections may have different regulations. For instance, some managers and owners may forbid camping, hunting, or open fires. There may be closures for certain hunting seasons on private lands leased for that purpose. Often, signs alert hikers about what is permitted and where. When in doubt, be extra careful to behave in a considerate manner. One hiker's "commando camping" could lead to the loss of access for all.

Today's hikers have a responsibility to travel lightly on the land, whether it be public or private. Most people understand the importance of not only taking care of their own trash but also picking up after the more thoughtless. However, if the actions of even a few people impact a site, its managers and owners may react against the entire trail community. The NCTA endorses the principles of the Leave No Trace Center for Outdoor Ethics (www.lnt.org/programs/principles.php).

Leave No Trace

Plan Ahead and Prepare

Know the regulations and special concerns for the area you'll visit.

Prepare for extreme weather, hazards, and emergencies.

Schedule your trip to avoid times of high use.

Visit in small groups when possible. Consider splitting larger groups into smaller groups.

Repackage food to minimize waste.

Use a map and compass to eliminate the use of marking paint, rock cairns or flagging.

Travel and Camp on Durable Surfaces

Durable surfaces include established trails and campsites, rock, gravel, dry grasses or snow.

Protect riparian areas by camping at least 200 feet from lakes and streams.

Good campsites are found, not made. Altering a site is not necessary.

In popular areas: Concentrate use on existing trails and campsites. Walk single file in the middle of the trail, even when wet or muddy. Keep campsites small. Focus activity in areas where vegetation is absent.

In pristine areas, disperse use to prevent the creation of campsites and trails.

Avoid places where impacts are just beginning.

Dispose of Waste Properly

Pack it in, pack it out. Inspect your campsite and rest areas for trash or spilled foods. Pack out all trash, leftover food, and litter.

Deposit solid human waste in catholes dug 6 to 8 inches deep at least 200
feet from water, camp, and trails. Cover and disguise the cathole when
finished.

Pack out toilet paper and hygiene products.

To wash yourself or your dishes, carry water 200 feet away from streams or
lakes and use small amounts of biodegradable soap. Scatter strained
dishwater.

Leave What You Find

Preserve the past: examine, but do not touch, cultural or historic structures
and artifacts.

Leave rocks, plants and other natural objects as you find them.

Avoid introducing or transporting non-native species.

Do not build structures, furniture, or dig trenches.

Minimize Campfire Impacts

Campfires can cause lasting impacts to the backcountry. Use a lightweight
stove for cooking and enjoy a candle lantern for light.

Where fires are permitted, use established fire rings, fire pans, or mound fires.

Keep fires small. Only use sticks from the ground that can be broken by hand.

Burn all wood and coals to ash, put out campfires completely, then scatter
cool ashes.

Respect Wildlife

Observe wildlife from a distance. Do not follow or approach them.

Never feed animals. Feeding wildlife damages their health, alters natural
behaviors, and exposes them to predators and other dangers.

Protect wildlife and your food by storing rations and trash securely.

Control pets at all times, or leave them at home.

Avoid wildlife during sensitive times: mating, nesting, raising young, or winter.

Be Considerate of Other Visitors

Respect other visitors and protect the quality of their experience.

Be courteous. Yield to other users on the trail.

Step to the downhill side of the trail when encountering pack stock.

Take breaks and camp away from trails and other visitors.

Let nature's sounds prevail. Avoid loud voices and noises.

(© Leave No Trace)

Planning Your Hike on the NCT

This book offers an overview of hiking opportunities and a series of featured hikes along the NCT. While each featured hike includes a map, it may be helpful to access additional online resources when planning day hikes or more extended backpacking trips.

Maps

For many parts of the NCT, excellent maps are available from the NCTA. Two categories of maps are available: the overview series, at 1:100,000 or 1:63,360, and the technical series, at 1:24,000.

The 1:24,000 technical series of annotated topographic maps include many of the hikes recommended in this book, except those maintained by affiliates/partners, such as the Finger Lakes Trail Conference. A good example is the Manistee River Loop in Michigan's Manistee National Forest. Avid hikers will appreciate such features as data tables and latitude/longitude waypoints for campsites, water sources, stream crossings, and trailheads. Visit www.northcountrytrail.org to order these maps.

The NCTA's 1:100,000 overview series includes all sections of the NCT that are not covered separately by one of the affiliates/partners. For instance, the aforementioned Manistee River Loop is a small part of the "MI-05: Freesoil Trailhead to M-186" map. This series lacks the waypoint notations mentioned earlier. However, used with a Universal Trans Mercator (UTM), a grid-based map-reading aid marked with predefined measurement ticks based on common map scales, these maps make NCT navigation a breeze.

In addition, the NCTA plans to continue to offer access to digital trail information in the latest formats. Currently, each of the "Explore by Section" pages at www.northcountrytrail.org offers a Google Maps mashup of the trail and select features.

Online Aids and Additional Resources

Web-based resources are increasingly becoming the norm for obtaining the most current information, and hikers on the NCT are no exception. There's no substitute for a detailed paper route map that can be pored over when planning the hike and then carried along as an essential piece of gear, notwithstanding GPS units, phone and computer apps, and other high-tech gizmos. No map ever failed for lack of battery recharge or loss of signal. However, online resources do offer the benefit of being easily and (when it comes to the best resources) frequently updated, which is why the NCTA seeks to provide current hiker support on its website. Referencing support on www.northcountrytrail.org is a critical step in hike planning.

Equipment

Two common barriers to getting outdoors can be (1) not knowing where to go and (2) not knowing what to take. This book helps address the first of these obstacles, but the second—an understanding of what and how much should be carried on a hike—can be equally critical for a successful experience. Things can go wrong in this area before one even sets foot on the trail, as it's all too easy to walk out of a sporting goods store or trail shop much lighter in the wallet yet overburdened with unnecessary weight. The end result can be a disappointing—and even painful—experience on the trail, potentially souring what could have been a lifetime love affair with hiking the NCT.

On the first thru-hike of the NCT's 4,600 miles, Andrew Skurka carried gear weighing a total of ten pounds (summer base weight, not including food, water, and fuel). By paring his belongings down to such an absolute minimum, Skurka was able to pull down big daily miles and thoroughly enjoy the experience. Every item in his pack (and indeed the pack itself) was conceived and constructed to save weight. So what relevance might this have for a day hiker or a weekender? "It doesn't matter whether you go fast and far or slow and short," explains Skurka, "If you carry less stuff, you'll enjoy the hiking substantially more."

Comfort on the NCT is directly related to equipment selection and weight, but this is not just a matter of purchasing the newest, ultralight gear. The best advice is to use a scale and weigh every item. Add up the ounces and the pounds, and weed out the least necessary items until a comfortable weight is reached. This book weighs just less than one pound, by the way.

Serious backpackers may want to move beyond this guidebook for detailed resources supporting their planning efforts. Chris Townsend's *The Backpacker's Handbook* or Andrew Skurka's *The Ultimate Hiker's Gear Guide* are recommended.

Navigation

Getting lost is no fun. The consequences can range from inconvenience and lost time to serious trouble, especially in remote wild country. The NCTA's self-explanatory maps and online resources have taken the guesswork out of staying found.

Of course, the first navigation challenge is to arrive at the trailhead. This guidebook lists the latitude and longitude coordinates of each hike's beginning and end points, which can be input to GPS units or smartphone applications. However, old-fashioned navigation skills using a map and compass are still the default knowledge needed for smart trail navigation. GPS navigation is a great supplement to but not a substitute for map and compass skills.

For the GPS-using hiker and hike planner, the NCTA makes available on its website the free downloading of all the trail's centerline and related waypoint data (at www.northcountrytrail.org/trail/data/), with the exception of sections maintained by the Buckeye Trail Association and the Finger Lakes Trail Conference. To add the NCTA's waypoints to your GPS unit, follow the instructions on the website.

When navigating the NCT, it is also advisable to use trail registers where available. A trail register is usually a loose-leaf binder or other note-

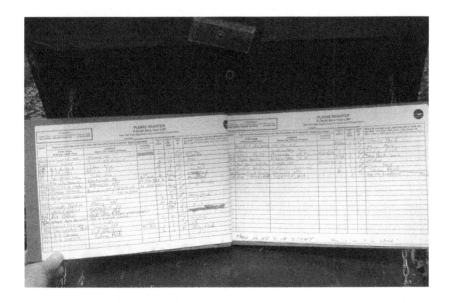

book in which hikers write diary-like entries to mark their passing. Trail registers are typically located in wooden boxes at trailheads and in plastic bags at hiker shelters. Registers primarily serve as a means of communication not only between hikers but also between hikers and trail maintainers. Registers can also be helpful for locating individuals on the trail in emergency situations.

Blazes and Signs

Traditionally, trails are marked with blazes, a practice originating with the historic practice of using an ax to cut away tree bark to expose the white—and more visible—inner layer of a tree. These marks enabled hikers to follow the trails thus blazed. Today on the NCT, a simple six-by-two-inch blue-painted blaze replaces the axed mark. The blue blaze—applied in Nelson Boundary Blue according to National Park Service standards, denotes the NCT and differentiates between the NCT and other trails. These dollar-bill-sized blue paint marks are the standard marking of the NCT except for where the trail shares the 420 miles of the white-blazed Finger

Lakes Trail. As of today, more of the NCT has been blazed than the entire length of the famed Appalachian Trail.

Signs are another classic way of marking a route. The signing standards of the National Park Service are used throughout the NCT. However, despite the best intentions of volunteer trail adopters and land managers, signs sometimes fall prey to vandals, decay, storms, and animals. For instance, on the treeless prairies of North Dakota and western Minnesota, NCT signs, visible for miles when first erected, provide the best scratching posts for the thousand-pound cows that call the region home. These cows can quickly destroy even the most deeply set post on the prairie.

Ron Strickland's Annotated "Ten Essentials" for Hiking

1. **MAPS:** Always carry the most current map. Double-check with www. northcountrytrail.org and its partner websites for recent updates. Know how to use the map.

2. **FIRST AID KIT:** Whether self-assembled or store bought, a first aid kit is not optional. Be sure to personalize it with whatever might be needed for the conditions likely to be encountered.

3. **COMPASS:** There is no substitute for having a good sighting compass, such as one of the Silva Ranger or Brunton Eclipse models, and knowing how to use it. (Regard a GPS unit as merely a useful supplement to your compass.)

4. **RAIN GEAR:** Weather conditions can change *very* fast, and even minimal rain gear can help prevent becoming a statistic. Ultraexpensive gear is nice but not really necessary. For rain protection, hikers need some combination (depending on the circumstances) of jacket, pants, poncho, hat, gaiters, umbrella, pack cover, and garbage bag.

5. **EXTRA CLOTHES:** A sudden drop in temperature or an unexpected overnight bivouac can be life threatening without extra clothes. Always carry enough extra clothes for warmth.

6. **MATCHES.** This might seem like a no-brainer, but many unprepared people hit the trail without a fire starter. Impromptu warming or drying out and/or signal fires may be the key to survival.

7. **KNIFE:** Fires are much easier to start with a little shaved kindling. A simple blade is lightweight, supremely versatile, and should be in every hiker's pack.

8. **SIGNALING DEVICE:** A whistle and a mirror are traditional means of communicating location and distress. A flashlight or headlamp can also fill this role, as well as coming in handy in many other ways. Day hikers often don't think to carry flashlights.

9. **EXTRA FOOD:** Hiking is not the time to involuntarily diet.

10. **GIZMOS:** Traditional lists of the "ten essentials" never mentioned electronic gear. With cell phone coverage more and more a possibility, even in remote locations, take a fully charged cell phone. Take a GPS and extra batteries. In remote areas, consider taking an emergency position-

indicating radio beacon (EPIRB). Being prepared electronically is not wimping out or lessening the delights of nature.

11. **INSECT PROTECTION:** While bug protection is not a problem during much of the year, it definitely is a seasonally devastating factor in the North Country. Unprepared hikers stand not only to lose a lot of blood but also to miss a lot of fun. Insect repellant is a necessity, often along with head nets and clothing that covers every inch of skin. Tucking pants into boots or socks helps deter ticks.

This "Ten Essentials" list expanded to eleven items doesn't even include conveniences such as toilet paper. Prepared hikers will make their own lists and be certain to carry every item on them.

People who don't carry the minimal essentials can endanger both themselves and the people around them. Hiking is one of life's greatest gifts—with the preparation to enjoy it.

New York

The Big Apple and the Statue of Liberty might define the Empire State for some, but for NCT hikers, the focus is definitely "upstate," where the trail's trans-state route launches at Crown Point on the Vermont border. Crown Point is on Lake Champlain; from there, the NCT stretches about 625 miles to far southwestern New York in Allegany State Park, a hefty hike in its own right. But it's just the beginning—there's still 4,000 miles to go!

The NCT begins at its eastern terminus on the southern end of Lake Champlain, famous for its strategic importance in colonial times and the focus of a series of Revolutionary War battles at Ticonderoga, Saratoga, and Crown Point. Threading its way southwest through the Adirondack Mountains, the trail then crosses the Mohawk Valley, showcases 19th-century canals, skirts the Leatherstocking Region, then shares a magnificent pathway known as the Finger Lakes Trail before dipping into Pennsylvania. For this book, we feature four outstanding hikes in New York.

As the map indicates, these selected hikes are located from mid-state westward. None are in the Adirondack Park—New York's wildest landscape—because, as of this writing, the NCT's Adirondack route has not yet been approved by the state of New York. Please check the NCTA website, www.northcountrytrail.org, for the most current information on the NCT route in the Adirondacks.

So, why isn't there an NCT route yet in the Adirondacks? The answer to that question takes a bit of explanation. The plans for a long-distance trail across America's northern heartlands crystallized in the 1970s, after years of discussion extending at least as far back as the 1963 report of the Outdoor Recreation Resources Review Commission. In 1980, Congress added the NCT to the National Trails System, anticipating that it would be routed through New York's Adirondack Park. The 1982 comprehensive plan for the NCT confirmed it.

The Adirondacks are special to New Yorkers, who have given an elevated level of protection to the more than 6 million acres (larger than Yellowstone National Park) encompassed by the "Blue Line" boundary. A "forever wild" designation for the area was incorporated into New York's constitution in 1895. With the regulatory oversight of the Adirondack Park Agency today, development of any kind is scrutinized thoroughly and never speedily accomplished. Such has been the case with efforts to route the NCT inside the Blue Line boundary of the Adirondack Park.

Various proposed routes for the NCT eventually coalesced around three corridors: north, central, and southern. Concerns that the northern route would impact the already heavily used trail systems of the High Peaks Region focused efforts on the central and southern routes. After years of discussion and planning, the state of New York appears close to approving a plan that includes features of both the southern and central route proposals. NCTA's volunteers anxiously await the green light to start blue blazing the Adirondacks. When they do, there will be more than 200 miles of outstanding hiking added to the NCT. Future editions of this guidebook will detail this new section's charms.

Crown Point is located strategically in southern Lake Champlain where the lake narrows significantly in width, enabling 18th-century military control of waterborne travel and commerce between Montreal and Quebec in the north and New York City in the south (overland to the Hudson River until the Champlain Canal was completed in 1823). A fort was first built at Crown Point by the French in the 1730s. After the British chased the French forces north in 1759 during the French and Indian War, they built a larger fort at Crown Point, which they occupied until 1775, when the legendary Green Mountain Boys captured Crown Point for the unified colonies and forced the British north in the wake of their French counterparts 16 years earlier. The British, however, returned.

This area of Lake Champlain saw the birth of the American Navy, which, under the unlikely leadership of Benedict Arnold, proceeded to lose its first battle to the British invading forces attacking south in 1776 on Lake Champlain from Quebec. In doing so, however, the plucky Yanks delayed the British such that the weather prevented further advances until the spring of 1777, which enabled the Americans to strengthen forces enough to eventually stop the British advance permanently at Saratoga, thus thwarting the British intent to drive to New York City and divide the colonies.

Today, NCT hikers start their westward journey from the earthworks and embankments that remain at Crown Point, perhaps pausing to reflect on the role that the ground beneath their feet played long ago in the birth of a nation.

In the meantime, the four New York hikes featured here range in length from 2 to almost 10 miles. They include loop hikes, rivers, and numerous lakes and vistas. Attractions range from immersion in nature to posthike shopping, dining, wine tasting, and lodging. For exercise, views, history, or just plain fun, it's clear why NCT hikers love New York.

Fans of the NCT are often puzzled as to why the trail doesn't just go the extra 30 miles or so into Vermont and connect with the Appalachian National Scenic Trail. What's the point of ending at Crown Point, New York?

Actually, the original proposal in the legislation that eventually led to the 1980 congressional authorization for the NCT did show the two connected. However, during the 1970s, there was an increase in use of hiking trails in the northeast, due in part to the designation of the Appalachian Trail in 1968. With this growing popularity, members of Vermont's Green Mountain Club became concerned that the addition of another national scenic trail in Vermont might create an overuse situation, particularly for the venerable 270-mile Long Trail, the first long-distance hiking trail in the United States. As a consequence of the Green Mountain Club's opposition, the proposed bill was changed to show the current eastern terminus as Crown Point.

In the more than 30 years intervening, minds have changed. The Green Mountain Club has reversed its position, and there is growing support in Vermont and elsewhere for completing the trail according to the original vision. Planning is under way that may eventually lead to the congressional action needed to connect the two National Scenic Trails. The NCT would most likely head east from Crown Point to Middlebury. From there, it would head up into the Green Mountains using existing trail systems, connecting with the Long Trail and veering south until it linked with the Appalachian Trail at Maine Junction in Sherburne Pass.

For more on the Long Trail and the Green Mountain Club, visit www.greenmountainclub.org.

New York's Featured Hikes

1. **Onondaga Loop** (Shackham Road)

2. **Sugar Hill State Forest and Watkins Glen State Park**
   (Sugar Hill Fire Tower to State Park South Entrance Campground)

3. **Mitchellsville Gorge** (County Route 13 to State Highway 54)

4. **Allegany State Park** (Access 5 on ASP 1 to Access 8 on ASP 2)

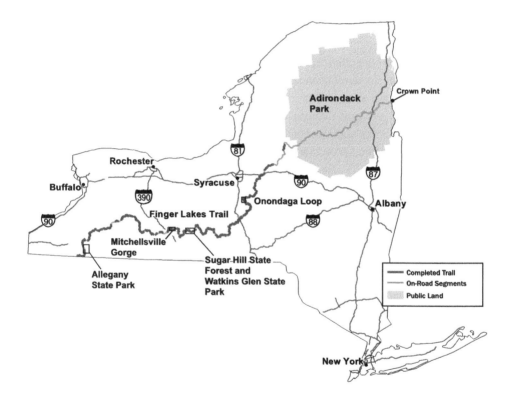

1. Onondaga Loop (Shackham Road)

Distance: 7.6 miles (loop hike: 6.1 trail miles plus 1.5 miles on
Shackham Road)
Physical difficulty: Potentially challenging because of a few steep spots
Navigation difficulty: Moderate
Highlights: Great views, three ponds, a waterfall, local history, an
ecologically unique area, the Syracuse metropolitan area
Nearest towns: Fabius, Truxton, Cuyler, and Tully, NY

The Onondaga Trail is a branch of the Finger Lakes Trail System shared
with and marked with the blue blazes of the NCT. Built and maintained
by the Adirondack Mountain Club–Onondaga Chapter, the Onondaga
Loop is a family-friendly (ages 10+) circuit hike that delivers a delightful woods walk, a fine view, a splendid waterfall, three ponds, swimming,
camping, and the natural history enticements of Labrador Hollow State
Unique Area and Morgan Hill State Forest. It traverses landforms and geological features unique to the landscape of New York's central and southern
tiers, including glacier-carved deep gouges that form "fingers" oriented
from north to south, many of which are filled with water and known as
New York's Finger Lakes. Labrador Hollow is an unfilled finger lake.

The Onondaga Loop follows the ridge formed by Labrador Hollow's
eastern "shore." The valley below, sweeping steeply downward to the west,
contains the remnant Labrador Pond. This is a particularly fine hike during
peak fall foliage season in mid- to late September. If you desire a shorter
hike, Tinker Falls, Spruce Pond, Shackham Pond, and Labrador Pond are
each accessible from nearby roads.

Trip Planner

Map: O1 (Onondaga 1), available from www.fingerlakestrail.org
Parking: Shoulder parking along Shackham Road
Beginning access: Shackham Road (OL-001)
Ending access: Same
Contact information:
HQ@northcountrytrail.org
Onondaga Chapter of the Adirondack Mountain Club (maintains the
Onondaga Trail): www.adk-on.org
State Forest Office (NY Department of Environmental Conservation
Region 7: 607-753-3095 ext. 217 or www.dec.ny.gov/about/615.html

Forest Ranger (Law Enforcement/Emergencies, NY Department of
Environmental Conservation Region 7): 607-283-1159 or
www.dec.ny.gov/about/681.html

Trail Guide

Park along the shoulder at the lower (southern) trail crossing at Shackham
Road (OL-001), just north of the intersection on State Route 91. Though
the shoulder pavement is narrow, there is firm grass offering enough extra
space to get cars off the road. Cross the little bridge and head into the conifers. Don't forget to sign the trail register. Pass several newish skid roads
and continue upward steeply into the mixed forest.

Stroll northwest (often level, sometimes up) under the tall canopy of
maple, oak, and ash. (In late August, look for blackberries.) Soon the trail
ascends high enough to treat hikers with fine views of the valley named
Labrador Hollow, particularly visible in nonleafy seasons. In summer,
peekaboo views merely hint at the delights waiting up the trail.

Continue to follow the charming trail as it contours along the heights
of Jones Hill. Walk the wooded bluff's edge in ground covers of ferns, flowers, and seedlings of beech and striped maple (some prefer the common
name *goosefoot maple*—look at the leaf shape).

Labrador Pond anchors the Labrador Hollow State Unique Area. It is a narrow and shallow 100-acre pond with a north-south orientation. Steep hills
both east and west shade the valley much of each day, creating a minicli-
mate marked by the presence of plant and animal life more likely found in
ecosystems farther north or at higher elevations. After the retreat of the last
glacier (only about 10,000 years ago), this high mountain bog ecosystem has
stabilized and flourished in the narrow confines of these valley walls. The
1,990-foot Labrador Pond interpretive boardwalk trail is a wonderful way to
explore the interesting ecosystem found here. The Department of Environmental Conservation's cabin provides information about the area's trails and
natural history.

Hikers wishing to extend their hike can begin or end their trip with an
overnight stay in an Adirondack-style shelter, the Hemlock Glen Lean-to on
Hemlock Brook. The shelter is located only 0.9 miles east of the Shackham
Road trailhead. Small waterfalls and splash pools make this a favorite for
families with small children.

After a gradual descent, the trail reaches a junction (OL-002). Keep to the right (straight ahead) and avoid the closed, steep trail. (The new route substitutes more easily hikable and far more environmentally sensitive switchbacks for the old path's steepness.)

Descend the two-tiered, wooden stairway to the creek (OL-003) near the top of Tinker Falls, which cascades 80 feet down, including one 50-foot drop. The lip of the falls is only a few steps downstream of the trail's crossing. Climbing down to traverse beneath the lip behind the falls makes for an interesting side trip but is definitely not advised, due to the loose shale offering very poor footing.

From the top of Tinker Falls, climb switchbacks until the Onondaga Trail and the NCT become an old logging skid road. Ascend it to a junction (OL-004) with the orange-blazed access road from the falls parking lot. Turn right and walk steeply uphill. After a long climb, turn right on the access road (OL-005). Climb through open stands of ash and maple.

Turn off the road and onto the trail tread (OL-006). The trail here offers a woodsy feeling.

Cross the road again (OL-007) and hug the rim of the Jones Hill bluff. The trail soon arrives at a splendid opening (1,964 ft.) where the Labrador Valley spreads out in a grand vista to the west and north (OL-008). The highlight of this view is Labrador Pond.

Jones Hill offers one of New York State's most spectacular views, overlooking a glacial valley 720 feet below. Hikers and hang gliders both enjoy this special spot on the trail. Labrador Pond is situated in the remains of a glacial kettle hole at the Labrador Hollow Unique Area. Though there is no direct trail down to the pond, be sure to visit it on the way home. Its nature trail boardwalk showcases this wetland's unique combination of plants evolving after the retreat of the last glacier about 12,000 years ago.

Cross a large, rectangular open area (sometimes used as a staging area for hang gliding) (OL-009), and begin a long descent. Cross a small creek and an old logging road (OL-010). Soon afterward, cross another old skid road. Very soon, cross another little creek. Begin a long climb through young, mixed woods, ending at a height of land in an open, more mature forest.

Descend again, this time heading northeast. Drop down very steeply to Spruce Pond (OL-011), named, aptly enough, for the spruce trees rimming its banks. The official "bivouac area" (OL-012) has water, parking, and plenty of level, grassy places to pitch a tent. Though signs forbid camping and fires, camping is available with a permit from the Department of Environment Conservation, Division of Lands and Forests (1285 Fisher Ave., Cortland, NY 13045; 607-753-3095).

Soon after turning south at the NCT kiosk, the trail crosses a dirt extension off Herlihy Road. The trail parallels a small brook and follows its serpentine watercourse as it gurgles through mossy glades and a cool hemlock forest. Ford the brook (OL-013); at low water, hikers may not even get their feet wet. Those wishing to linger will find flat spots on either side of the stream and a great spot for lunch.

Pass another little brook and some old logging tracks in the spacious, open forest. Exit on Shackham Road at a point north of the parking area, and turn right to find your car about 1.5 miles south along bucolic Shackham Road, passing a few buildings along the way to the original trailhead.

For a delightful side trip, be sure to cross the road at the exit point and continue on the NCT, descending 0.1 miles to Shackham Pond (OL-014). Camping is permitted 150 feet or more from the water, but not near the gravestones that survive from the early nineteenth century, when this area was actively farmed. Look for Lydia Hodgson's tombstone, especially poignant as it is overshadowed by the trunk of a giant white pine.

A side trip to the Labrador Pond boardwalk is only 1.2 miles north via Shackham Road and State Highway 91. Drive south on Shackham Road, then go right (north) via Highway 91 and look for the entrance on the left, just north of Labrador Pond.

New York—Onondaga Loop

Waypoint ID	Description	Mileage	Latitude	Longitude
OL-001	Shackham Road	0.0	42.76970	−76.01923
OL-002	Junction	1.2	42.78181	−76.02998
OL-003	Creek	1.7	42.78334	−76.03275
OL-004	Junction	1.9	42.78316	−76.03394
OL-005	Access Road	2.2	42.78557	−76.03665
OL-006	Trail Junction	2.5	42.78906	−76.04056
OL-007	Road Crossing	2.6	42.79076	−76.04200
OL-008	Jones Hill	2.8	42.79231	−76.04330
OL-009	Open Area	3.2	42.79494	−76.03964
OL-010	Logging Road	3.4	42.79420	−76.03632
OL-011	Spruce Pond	5.7	42.79888	−76.02693
OL-012	Bivouac Area	5.9	42.79689	−76.02526
OL-013	Brook	6.5	42.79057	−76.02278
OL-014	Shackham Pond	7.6	42.79030	−76.00838

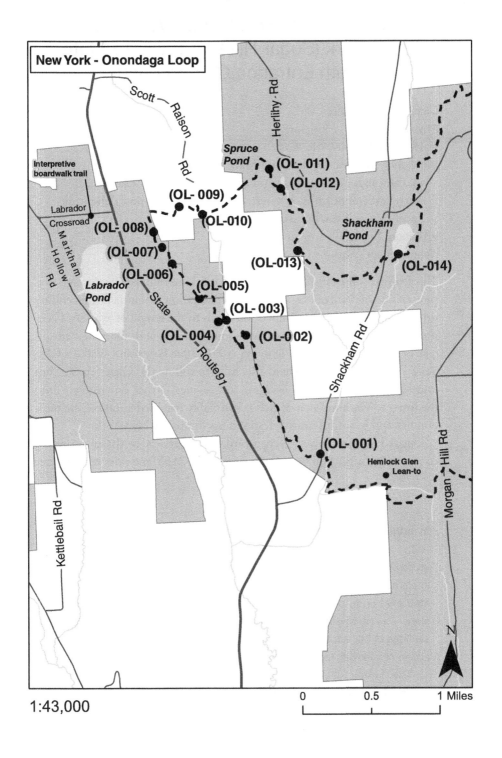

2. Sugar Hill State Forest and Watkins Glen State Park (Sugar Hill Fire Tower to State Park South Entrance Campground)

Distance: 10.1 miles
Physical difficulty: Moderate
Navigation difficulty: Moderate
Highlights: This mostly downhill hike (west to east) delivers plenty of camping, primo views from the fire tower, rustic lean-tos, early settlement ruins, a waterfall, and one of the most delightful creekside walks in the state of New York.
Visitation: Seasonally low to high
Nearest town: Watkins Glen, NY

This featured hike samples the delights of hiking rolling hills through mature stands of hardwoods and a pine plantation, eventually descending through intimate, hemlock-lined waterfalls to the gorges of Watkins Glen. It offers classic hiking for New York's southern tier, with the added advantage of nearby family camping in Sugar Hill State Forest and Watkins Glen State Park. Hikers may extend this hike to follow the Glen's classic (but more crowded) waterfalls, bridges, and ravines farther downstream into the town of Watkins Glen, which is justifiably regarded as one of the most popular and beautiful tourist destinations in upstate New York.

Sugar Hill Fire Tower offers a bird's-eye overview of the surrounding countryside. Sugar Hill State Forest (607-776-2165) provides seasonal free

In authorizing the NCT, Congress designated the Department of the Interior as the lead agency in administering the trail. The National Park Service was given the task of planning the NCT and developing partnerships needed to implement the plan. As part of the planning, the National Park Service created a vision to describe what the trail would look like in its desired future state. This vision offers policy guidance as the National Park Service certifies sections of trail according to standard and works with landowners and management agencies regarding appropriate use of the trail.

The desired future condition for the NCT is a primitive footpath, whose use is primarily for hiking and backpacking.

tent camping complete with flush toilets (note that hikers are likely to be outnumbered by equestrians). Backpack tent camping is also free and is allowed anywhere in the state forest with the following restrictions:

Camping is prohibited within 150 feet of any road, trail, spring, stream, or other body of water unless an area is designated by a "Camp Here" disk/sign.
Groups of 10 or more persons or stays of more than three days in one place require a permit from the state forest ranger in the area.

Additional camping information is available by contacting Sugar Hill forest ranger Bill Meehan at 607-292-6822.

Farther along the trail through Sugar Hill State Forest, hikers and backpackers will find lean-tos (with privies) at several locations. At the South Entrance to Watkins Glen State Park, there is a (fee) campground in the park itself (for info, call 607-535-4511).

Of course, accommodations in such a tourist mecca as Watkins Glen include a wide range of motels and bed-and-breakfasts. On August 17, 2009, NCT thru-hiker Nimblewill Nomad wrote, "Our camp last night was a delightful, old two-room cabin at Seneca Lodge. . . . Supper was in the rustic lodge dining room. The place was packed with auto racing drivers and fans. We had a great stay." For info on Seneca Lodge, call 607-535-2014.

Trip Planner

Map: M14 (Main Trail 14), available from www.fingerlakestrail.org
Beginning access: Sugar Hill Fire Tower
Parking: Off Tower Hill Road, near the Sugar Hill Fire Tower (SH-001)
Ending access: Camping access road

Parking: South Entrance, Watkins Glen State Park

Contact information:

Finger Lakes Trail Conference Center: 585-658-9320 or
 FLTinfo@frontiernet.net

Forestry Office (NY Department of Environmental Conservation Region 8):
 607-776-2165 or www.dec.ny.gov/about/683.html

Trail Guide

Parking is at the north end of Sugar Hill State Forest, just off Tower Hill Road near the fire tower. For a superb 360-degree view of the central Finger Lakes region, climb the stairs of the Sugar Hill Fire Tower (SH-001). The tower's stairs are open to the public to climb, but the observation deck

The **Finger Lakes Trail** shares its on- and off-road tread with the NCT for about 420 miles, from the Pennsylvania border in western New York's Allegany State Park to a point just south of DeRuyter where the NCT/Onondaga Trail branches to the north. The Finger Lakes Trail is lovingly built and maintained by the volunteers of the Finger Lakes Trail Conference and its 13 affiliated hiking clubs and associated scout troops.

The Conference's stated mission is "to build, protect, enhance, and promote a continuous footpath across New York State. Forever!" First envisioned by Wallace D. "Wally" Wood, the Finger Lakes Trail was initially proposed in 1961. Founded the following year, the Conference predates the NCTA by almost 20 years, pioneering the way and leading the effort to build the trail hikers now so value and enjoy in southern New York. The Conference partners with the NCTA in cooperating with the National Park Service to maintain and promote the portion of the trail that carries the NCT. Maps of the Finger Lakes Trail and the NCT are available through the Finger Lakes Trail Conference.

Each year, the Finger Lakes Trail Conference provides three hike programs designed primarily for new hikers. First, the monthly Cross-County Hike Series zeroes in on the trail in a particular county. Second, Finger Lakes Trail Passport Hikes introduce the new hiker to the trail by offering awards from program sponsors if he or she completes at least 4 of the 12 easy hikes. Go to www.fltconference.org for current information. Third, the Sampler Hike Series—Hiking 101 and Hiking 201—offers novice hikers a series of easy, fun, guided hikes. For information, call 585-658-9320 to leave a message.

is not accessible. On a clear day, Lamoka and Waneta Lakes (known as the Little Lakes) are visible to the west, and Seneca Lake (the largest of the Finger Lakes) can be seen to the east. The aerial view also gives a 10-mile radius preview of the terrain to the east, soon to be traversed on trail.

To reach the trail, take the roundabout connector path routed safely away from the field archery site. From the fire tower, walk 300 feet south and pass to the right of a low horse stable. Go 50 feet to the right, angle left, and descend to an old woods road that is now the Seneca Horse/Snowmobile Trail. Turn left and continue to signs for the Finger Lakes Trail and Mohawk Trail. The trail can be directly accessed by turning right onto the Mohawk Horse/Snowmobile Trail and then left where the NCT/Finger Lakes Trail crosses the horse path. To instead access the lean-tos, continue past the signs for the Finger Lakes Trail and Mohawk Trail until the two lean-tos (and a privy) come into view on the left. To access the trail from the lean-tos, turn right (south) onto a blue-blazed side trail, passing to the right side of a small pond, until you reach the junction with the white-blazed NCT/Finger Lakes Trail (SH-002), and turn left at a large red oak. From here, descend to a seasonal brook and continue through mixed hardwood forest. Soon the trail crosses a wet area on rustic puncheon, formed by flattened logs placed side by side. After crossing some private land, reenter the state forest.

Cross County Route 21 (SH-003) and sign the trail register. Cross a private parcel. Pass through a pine plantation on level ground, descend the hill, and continue past an old foundation to Old Locust Lane.

Cross Old Locust Lane (SH-004) and continue east. Initially there will be a small meadow on your left. After a few minutes, follow a white-blazed, overgrown road (SH-005) for a short distance, then revert to the trail tread, descending to a path along a very low bluff. Where the bluff peters out at a wooded hill, climb above the stony valley bottom of North Branch Glen Creek. Descend switchbacks on private land to the wooded flats, cross a seasonal creek's little ravine, and continue on a bluff high above Glen Creek. Back on state forest land, soon the trail takes hikers downstream very near the creek itself. (In summer, the water may be a mere trickle.) At the Wegman's Passport Program mailbox (SH-006), sign the register and do the passport rubbing on top of the post. For more information on getting involved with this fun passport program, go to www.fltconference.org.

Note the large, mysterious stone structure (once part of a thriving early community called Buck Settlement) out of which grow huge maple trees.

Why is it there? What was its function? No one alive today can say for sure.

A hundred yards farther, the tidy, well-constructed Buck Settlement Shelter (SH-007) occupies a pleasant opening in the airy forest of tall ash and walnut trees. There is water, a fire ring, and a privy there. Obtain and treat water from the North Branch of Glen Creek.

Climb the gradual ascent to a height of land, pass a small wetland, enter private land, and walk an old track westward. The trail crosses a ravine and goes left at a junction (SH-008). Follow the woodsy road downhill parallel to the ravine. Pass the 19th-century Buck Settlement Cemetery (SH-009), whose cracked and listing gravestones are intermingled with huge ash trees, a testament to both the finiteness and the resilience of all life.

Reenter the state forest. Follow an old road down to the west branch of Glen Creek, where there is a campsite, hitching rack, and lovely falls. This ford, known as Ebenezer's Crossing, is a perfect example of the flat slate that defines and characterizes the ledges and gorges of the southern Finger Lakes tributaries. Use care, as this area between Buck Settlement Cemetery and Ebeneezer's Crossing sees some equestrian traffic. If horses are present, fording the stream or getting a drink, stand aside, move slowly, and ask permission should you wish to come closer to the horses.

Cross Templar Road (SH-010) and ascend through an extensive red pine plantation. Cross paved Van Zandt Road (SH-011) and follow the bluff top parallel to Van Zandt Road for a short distance through the woods. Reemerge on the road and walk uphill a short distance. At the end-of-road guardrail (SH-012), turn left off the road onto grass. Go obliquely left on the mowed approach to the woods. (This private land is closed during New York's deer hunting season, typically mid-October to near the end of December.) Hikers are urged to check the Finger Lakes Trail Conference maps and especially the trail conditions section on the website at www.fingerlakestrail.org for latest conditions/closures information and additional advice for hikers. Note the posted warning about upcoming Julie's Crossing: "Townsend Creek Conditions Change Frequently—Potentially Dangerous High Water." The sign gives directions for an alternative, 3-mile route in case of flooding. For current creek conditions, contact the New York Department of Environmental Conservation at 607-776-2165.

The trail soon opens up to a view of the heavily wooded valley across a gas pipeline corridor. Continue walking along the edge of a fenced meadow. Enter the pines at a "No Hunting" sign. Enjoy peekaboo views and grand trees as you follow the bluff (SH-013). Cross a small ravine and continue south, away from Glen Creek. Continue through the woods along the bluff to Watkins Glen State Park's boundary, where a seasonal seep may appear.

Continue 0.2 miles from the boundary to Townsend Creek, through open stands of grand trees.

Make a long, very steep descent ending on a hemlock-shaded hogback ridge. At the Townsend Creek valley, cross the brush and sycamore floodplain, following stone cairns. This is Julie's Crossing, for which hikers were warned about high water by the sign encountered earlier on the trail. Please note that sturdy footgear and hiking poles are highly recommended on this crossing, and beware that flooding can displace cairns and signage.

The trail in the park is a lovely tour of hemlock woods and creek views. In drier months, the creek's volume is reduced considerably. The trail passes a dammed-up part of Glen Creek. Hikers descending the pond's access road reach an excellent three-sided shelter located beside the water; however, a sign prohibits camping.

Follow the trail along the bluff to a point above the long fall of the dam's spillway. Pass several cabins and an amphitheater at a bridge over a seasonal stream. Follow the trail to a stone walkway beside a tributary. The water has eroded layers of shale in lovely patterns of rock, moss, and fern. Another charming pool greets hikers above the bridge. Follow closed-off and grassy Riley's Road to paved Whites Hollow Road.

Go right 300 feet on Whites Hollow Road. At the gas pipeline, turn left onto Punch Bowl Road.

Turn off Punch Bowl Road at the junction (SH-014) and hug the bluff edge. This section introduces the famous pools and "gorges" wonders of Watkins Glen.

Watkins Glen State Park is justly renowned for its spectacular gorge experience. With Glen Creek dropping 400 feet over 19 different waterfalls between 200-foot cliffs, visitors inevitably come away deeply impressed. In addition to hosting the NCT and the Finger Lakes Trail, Watkins Glen State Park offers overnight campgrounds as well as day activities such as swimming (pool), picnicking, educational activities, and gorge tours. Look for the Leedy's roseroot wildflower, listed on the federal threatened species list. For more information and campground reservations, visit nysparks.com/parks/142/details .aspx or call 607-535-4511.

Pass a picnic pavilion (SH-015) beside a eutrophic, marshy pond. This is a great picnic spot, complete with grills and rhododendrons. The trail soon comes to the long pool beyond the picnic area and the second gorge dam.

The trail keeps to the top of the bluff as it twists and loops with the bends of the creek below, from which a welcome, cooling breeze sometimes wafts on hot summer afternoons. Walk under the railroad overpass; listen for an oncoming train overhead for a different twist. After passing a 1930s Civilian Conservation Corps side trail down to the creek, hikers reach a defunct shelter (SH-016), where camping is no longer permitted.

At a trail junction (SH-017), turn right toward the park's South Entrance, where hikers exit via a service road at a beautiful stone pavilion (SH-018). The park's large campground is a sharp oblique turn up to your right. Motel accommodations are available at nearby Seneca Lodge, due south out the park entrance road.

New York—Sugar Hill State Forest and Watkins Glen State Park

Waypoint ID	Description	Mileage	Latitude	Longitude
SH-001	Sugar Hill Fire Tower	0.0	42.38601	−77.00255
SH-002	White–Blazed FLT/NCT	0.3	42.38114	−77.00308
SH-003	Cross County Route 21	1.2	42.37786	−76.99031
SH-004	Cross Old Locust Lane	2.8	42.37942	−76.96541
SH-005	Overgrown Road	2.9	42.37975	−76.96259
SH-006	Passport Program Mailbox	3.6	42.37396	−76.95579
SH-007	Buck Settlement Shelter	3.7	42.37297	−76.95559
SH-008	Junction	4.1	42.37061	−76.96196
SH-009	Buck Settlement Cemetery	4.3	42.36934	−76.96053
SH-010	Cross Templar Road	4.7	42.36856	−76.95825
SH-011	Cross Van Zandt Road	5.2	42.36860	−76.95241
SH-012	End–of–Road Guardrail onto Grass	5.3	42.36764	−76.95161
SH-013	Bluff	5.5	42.36762	−76.94871
SH-014	Punch Bowl Road at Junction	8.3	42.36574	−76.90593
SH-015	Picnic Pavilion	8.6	42.36904	−76.90021
SH-016	Defunct Shelter	9.6	42.37199	−76.88437
SH-017	Trail Junction	9.9	42.37309	−76.87966
SH-018	Stone Pavilion	10.1	42.37247	−76.87549

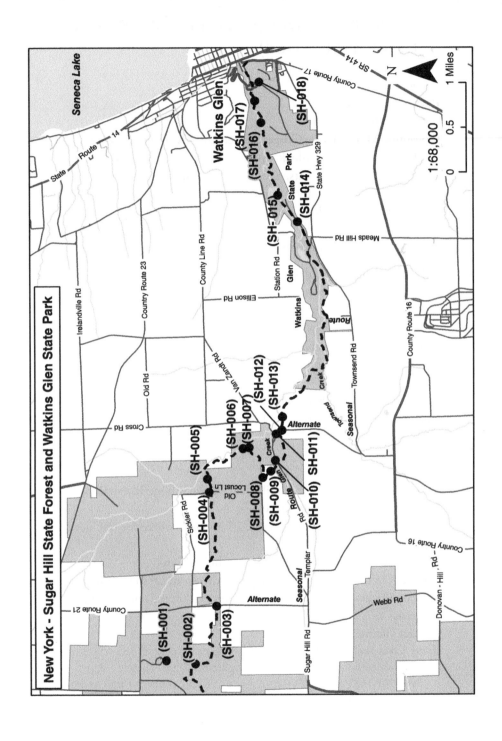

New York - Sugar Hill State Forest and Watkins Glen State Park

3. Mitchellsville Gorge (County Route 13 to State Highway 54)

Distance: 2.4 miles
Physical difficulty: Easy
Navigation difficulty: Easy
Highlights: Mitchellsville Gorge, located entirely on private land, showcases a pine/hemlock woods along a beautiful creek. The waterfalls, forest retreats, and vineyards make for a stunning introduction to the aptly named Pleasant Valley and to the local area's many attractions.
Visitation: Moderate
Nearest town: Hammondsport, NY

This hike delivers the delightful one-two punch of an ultrascenic hike combined with convenient lodging, dining, and shopping. Mitchellsville Gorge is especially rich in woodsy beauty (especially when leaves do not obstruct the views). After a hike, bonus activities range from a great museum to wine tasting and fine eating. Be sure to visit the quaint and historic village of Hammondsport and lovely Keuka Lake in the heart of New York's wine country. Find maps for winery locations at most tourist outlets in the area. Wine trails and cheese trails (tours of local wineries and cheese makers) add a new twist to "trail recreation"!

Trip Planner

Map: M12 (Main Trail 12), available from www.fingerlakestrail.org
Beginning access: County Route 13
Parking: Shoulder of County Route 13 opposite where the trail goes straight across the field
Ending access: State Highway 54 (Vinehurst Motel)
Parking: On the south side of the gravel driveway, off the shoulder of State Highway 54. The trail continues east on the one-lane gravel drive.
Contact information:
Finger Lakes Trail Conference: FLTinfo@fingerlakestrail.org; 585-658-9320
More information: Hickory Hill Camping Resort (7531 Co. Rte. 13, Bath, NY 14810; 800-760-0947) has a half-mile connector trail to the Finger Lakes Trail. Approximately 200 yards north of the junction of

the connector with the Finger Lakes Trail, there is a new lean-to and outhouse.

Trail Guide

Begin at County Route 13 (MV-001) by parking on the shoulder opposite the field. Go east across the field along the mowed path, toward the woods. Cross the fence stile, note the imposing sign on the right, and continue following the white blazes into the woods. Soon the trail traverses a hemlock and red oak forest where there are occasional views of Mitchellsville Gorge from its western rim.

At a junction (MV-002), the bluff-top trail becomes a logging skid road. At a meadow where the logging road curves left at a "Posted" sign, walk straight south-southeast along the east edge of the meadow, following the white blazes, and reenter the woods. Mitchellsville Creek's inviting pools and ripples will be far below on the left.

Continue to follow the trail along the edge of the bluff, enjoying its occasional gorge views. The trail descends and reaches the valley bottom, continuing on a two-track path alongside the shale-layered streambed.

At a junction (MV-003), turn left (east) away from the two-track path, following the white blazes. Go 300 yards through the woods to the unused tracks of the B&H Rail Corporation. Turn left and walk 100 feet along the tracks. Turn right off the tracks (MV-004) and follow the mowed path under the power line and into the woods. This bottomland is characterized by its stately giant sycamore trees and understory of horsetail (*Equisetum*) plants.

The Empire State's astonishing history of innovation is symbolized in Hammondsport by the Glenn H. Curtiss Museum (8419 St. Rte. 54, Hammondsport, NY 14840; 607-569-2160; www.glennhcurtissmuseum.org/). Originally a bicycle mechanic like the Wright brothers, this famed aircraft inventor not only set many land and air speed records but also pioneered the modern aircraft industry. Hikers visiting the museum before setting out will find its fascinating exhibits resonating throughout their hike over the ridges and valleys where Curtiss pioneered flying.

Cross Keuka Inlet on a wooden bridge (MV-005). This creek's banks were riprapped for erosion control. Follow the trail a short distance back upstream to a rock dam, and turn left into a vineyard (MV-006). At this point, a showroom for wine tasting is visible due south in the distance; look up the hill to see two hang glider launch sites on Mount Washington. Look for hang gliders overhead, riding the same air currents on which Glenn Curtiss flew his aircraft in the first 20 years of the 20th century.

Walk east along the edge of the vineyard. Hikers fortunate enough to be here during spring blooming or the fall harvest will find the aroma intoxicating. Nearing the road, cross left between vineyards, following the white blazes painted on the vineyard posts. Walk its edge straight toward a yellow house.

Turn right on County Route 88 (Pleasant Valley Road) (MV-007), where hikers can spot cars on the shoulder should they wish to avoid the short road walk that remains. Pass the Urbana Town Hall and walk the road toward the Pleasant Valley Inn. Cross State Highway 54 opposite the Vinehurst Inn and a red barn, where parking is available on the south side of the gravel driveway off the shoulder of State Highway 54. The hike beginning at County Route 13 totals 2.4 miles to this point.

Hikers can sample local wines at the Pleasant Valley Winery (607-569-6111) or dine, in the evening, at the Pleasant Valley Inn (877-567-7546). Lodging can be found at the Vinehurst Inn (607-569-2300) or any number of other establishments in the Hammondsport area. The Hammondsport Chamber of Commerce is here (www.hammondsport.org/; 607-569-2989).

New York—Mitchellsville Gorge

Waypoint ID	Description	Mileage	Latitude	Longitude
MV-001	County Route 13	0.0	42.40238	−77.29054
MV-002	Bluff−Top Trail Junction	0.8	42.39606	−77.28273
MV-003	Junction	1.8	42.39033	−77.26735
MV-004	Tracks	1.9	42.39064	−77.26608
MV-005	Wooden Bridge	2.0	42.39132	−77.26397
MV-006	Vineyard	2.1	42.39072	−77.26418
MV-007	Pleasant Valley Road	2.4	42.39071	−77.25911

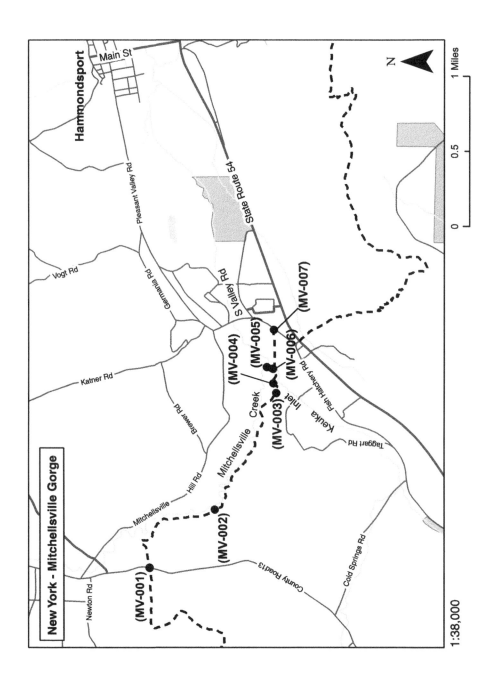

New York - Mitchellsville Gorge

4. Allegany State Park (Access 5 on Allegany State Park 1 to Access 1 on Allegany State Park 2)

Distance: 5.8 miles

Physical difficulty: Easy (Note: To avoid this segment's 700-ft. southbound elevation gain, be sure to walk south to north; i.e., begin at Access 5 on ASP 1 [ALG-001].)

Navigation difficulty: Easy

Highlights: About a mile north from Access 5, there is a long stretch of old-growth forest with immense hemlocks. Beck Hollow Lean-to at mileage point 3.4 is a great place to camp.

Visitation: Moderate

Nearest town: Salamanca, NY

Allegany State Park is New York's largest state park. Within the park, over 20 miles of the NCT/Finger Lakes Trail are maintained by the Foothills Trail Club in cooperation with the Finger Lakes Trail Conference. This beautiful hike will appeal to anyone who loves quiet northern forests and appealing natural surroundings.

Trip Planner

Map: M1 (Main Trail 1), available from www.fingerlakestrail.org
Beginning access: Access 5 (ALG-001)

In 1962, Mabel James and other hiking enthusiasts developed a trail from Allegany State Park to Lake Ontario. Their then-new Foothills Trail Club created the Conservation Trail to connect 177 miles from Pennsylvania through western New York to Niagara Falls. Connecting there with Canada's Bruce Trail, the Conservation Trail showed what people with vision and dedication could achieve.

The Foothills Trail Club's project was so successful that its southernmost 50 miles became part of the Finger Lakes Trail and were eventually shared with the NCT. Mabel James and her volunteers pioneered a major link in North America's long-distance trails network.

Parking: Access 5 has roadside parking, but there is a real parking lot 0.1 miles downhill to the northeast, on Allegany State Park 1

Ending access: On Finger Lakes Trail Map M1, look for Access 1 (near the intersection of Bay State Road and the park entrance road [ASP 2]).

Parking: Shoulder parking is available.

Contact information:

Trail Steward Coordinator, Foothills Trail Club:
webmaster@foothillstrailclub.org

Genesee West Finger Lakes Trail Conference Regional Trail Coordinator:
www.fingerlakestrail.org

Trail Guide

This featured hike begins on the park's paved road, Allegany State Park 1, at trailhead access number 5 (ALG-001). Look for the familiar white blazes of the Finger Lakes Trail. Climb through the mature beech, maple, and oak forest. After a short distance, cross the gravel Bay State Road. Continue a little way over the height of land, soon descending briefly to a junction (ALG-002). Turn left, following the white blazes downhill. Follow the flat trail to a junction (ALG-003) with the Eastwood Meadow Trail (marked with blue, circular medallions).

Turn right and walk the trail's gentle grade. Eventually descend a long ridge and ease through a parklike setting of tall hemlocks. At a junction (ALG-004) 2 miles from this segment's start, there is a dilapidated, old shelter (located 100 ft. east of the junction) (ALG-005). Although the structure is in extreme need of repair, there is a campsite, complete with a seasonal stream/trickle. Do not take the trail located to the right of the shelter. Follow the white blazes heading northwest from the junction.

The trail ascends gradually through an open, mixed forest of large ash, beech, and hemlock. After crossing a height of land, the abrupt descent that follows may be a welcome change of pace. Walk through the ensuing brushy, hemlock flat. At a junction (ALG-006) with the Conservation Loop Trail, turn left northwest to continue following the NCT/Finger Lakes Trail.

Beside a small stream, camping is permitted at the small, attractive Beck Hollow Lean-to, with its fire pit, grate, and privy. After crossing a height of land (ALG-007) and descending a very long, pleasant grade, the trail emerges from the forest and down a set of wooden steps into an

overgrown field. Interstate 86 is visible (and audible) to the left. Follow the mowed path across and into the next woods and then downhill toward the traffic sounds. Emerge at Access 1 (ALG-008) near the intersection of Bay State Road and Allegany State Park 2, the park entrance road.

New York—Allegany State Park

Waypoint ID	Description	Mileage	Latitude	Longitude
ALG-001	Trailhead Number 5	0.0	42.05299	−78.76552
ALG-002	Junction	0.3	42.05544	−78.76582
ALG-003	Junction	0.7	42.05928	−78.77265
ALG-004	Junction	2.3	42.07739	−78.76977
ALG-005	Old Shelter	2.3	42.07756	−78.76958
ALG-006	Junction	3.0	42.08546	−78.76942
ALG-007	Height of Land	3.5	42.08543	−78.77837
ALG-008	Access 1 on Allegany State Park 2	5.8	42.10646	−78.77779

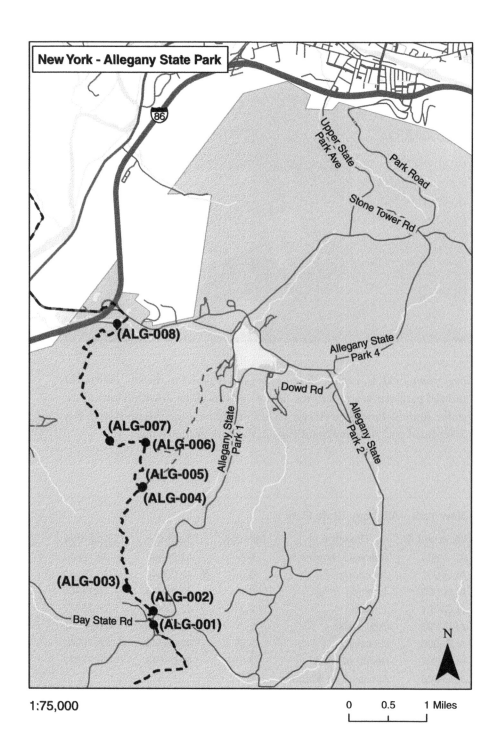

Pennsylvania

New York hands off the NCT to the Keystone State as the trail continues south and westward through the rugged Allegheny Plateau toward Ohio. Pennsylvania's rich history and even greater natural resources offer hikers an invitation to immerse themselves in the rugged hollows of the Alleghenies and follow the river south. There, abundant trout streams and unlimited solitude mix with passages through working landscapes, including the region where oil was first discovered in America in 1859. Wildlife abounds in the deciduous forests, with the possibility of seeing bald eagles, wild turkeys, river otters, beavers, black bears, and white-tailed deer. Other states may boast of more challenging mountains or longer sections of trail, but the charms of the Quaker State will captivate all.

Pennsylvania has about 265 miles of the NCT slicing off its northwest corner, from the Allegheny Reservoir at the New York State line to the Ohio border just west of Darlington and Wampum. Much of the trail is currently completed, with four NCTA chapters and a number of other trail-building affiliate groups working diligently to finish and protect it. With its proximity to the Pittsburgh metropolitan area, there's a standing invitation for a lot of folks to experience the NCT, a short drive away.

Although this chapter highlights five hikes on the NCT in Pennsylvania, the entire trail is well worth a visit. For instance, where the NCT leaves New York's Allegany State Park, it enters Pennsylvania's differently spelled Allegheny National Forest (which hosts the trail for 96 miles). Visitors can hike along the scenic shoreline of the Allegheny Reservoir and through the Heart's Content and the Tionesta Scenic Areas and can enjoy scenic trout streams, such as the Clarion River, coursing through Cook Forest State Park's white pines and eastern hemlocks. Local footpaths offer quality hiking, including the Rachel Carson Trail and the Baker Trail, which connects Pittsburgh to the Allegheny National Forest. Southwest of Cook Forest State Park, the NCT crosses private lands in the Toby Creek watershed. Following the scenic Clarion River corridor, the trail continues southwest through Pennsylvania state game lands.

Only 90 miles north of Pittsburgh, the minicity of Parker is an urban island in the vast, forested landscape. After crossing the hills and wetlands of State Game Lands Number 95, the NCT reaches the Old Stone House on Pennsylvania State Route 8, where local hikers celebrate George

Washington's 1753 expedition to the area with an annual gastronomic extravaganza known as the Cherry Pie Hike (held on the Saturday closest to the president's February 22 birthday). The NCT wends west through the Jennings Environmental Education Center and Moraine State Park, with its scenic views of Lake Arthur. Lodging is available at the historic Davis Hollow Cabin, operated as a hostel by NCT volunteers.

After Moraine State Park, the NCT reaches McConnells Mill State Park, site of a working 19th-century gristmill. McConnells Mill State Park hosts one of the featured hikes, which is 7.7 miles long from Alpha Pass to Hell's Run Slippery Rock Gorge, a steep-walled ravine formed by the draining of ancient glacial lakes. For a family-friendly listing of local attractions, check out Butler County's tourism website at www.visitbutler-county.com/attractions/festivals-events.

Between State Game Lands Numbers 148 and 285, there is a long road walk through private lands where the NCT has not yet been established. A midway resupply is possible at historic Darlington, PA (zip code 16115). Continuing westerly through State Game Lands Number 285, hikers will find the final Adirondack shelter in Pennsylvania located along the north fork of Little Beaver Creek.

NCTA Wampum Chapter's Dave Brewer says, "The general public doesn't know that a long trail such as the NCT is primarily the product of local volunteers. For instance, in our group, we have 39 dues-paying members and a supporting cast (comers and goers and once-a-year volunteers like Student Conservation Association and church groups) of over a hundred people. All of them have diverse interests and abilities. Each person contributes his or her time in a variety of ways: some weekly, some once a year; some out on the trail and others who contribute mightily by handling the finances, correspondence, and PR. Some plan and attend meetings. Others provide ideas and input, financial support, cooking, and spreading the word to kids and families. Our goal is to have fun and to make and maintain the best trail that we possibly can. Anyone who attends one of our activities will find that we are a very welcoming bunch."

Pennsylvania's Featured Hikes

1. **Henry's Mills** (State Route 666 to Forest Road 116 [Bob's Creek Road])

2. **Cook Forest State Park** (Cook Forest Fire Tower to Highland Drive trailhead)

3. **Hell's Hollow** (Alpha Pass to Hell's Hollow)

4. **Wampum** (Sankey Hill Road to Edwards Road)

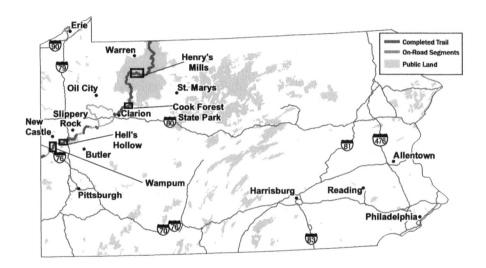

1. Henry's Mills (State Route 666 to Forest Road 116 [Bob's Creek Road])

Distance: 13.4 miles
Physical difficulty: Moderate
Navigation difficulty: Easy
Highlights: Fine hiking, dispersed camping, old railroad grades, and Hunter Station's three-sided shelter (including tent platforms and reliable water)
Visitation: Light
Nearest town: Sheffield, PA

Henry's Mills is a delightful hike showcasing the diversity of the Allegheny National Forest. Located on century-old railroad grades, built to haul logs from forest to mill, the trail provides pleasant walking and illustrates the landscape of picturesque mountains and forests. Once out of the Tionesta Creek valley (Henry's Mills trailhead), the trail traverses gentle, rolling hills that encourage hikers to stay forever.

The trail here passes through areas where the nation's first oil wells were drilled in the mid-1800s and where the devastated landscape was subsequently reforested. Since 1923, the Allegheny National Forest, through careful planning and stewardship, has become a beautiful eastern forest including oak, cherry, hemlock, and white pine. Wildlife abounds in the form of white-tailed deer, bobcats, turkey, and ruffed grouse. (Note: after crossing Minister Road, the trail transects a proposed wilderness area until it reaches FR 116.)

Whether one is passing through the Allegheny Reservoir or the Tionesta Scenic Area, part of the NCT's lure is its deep-woods charm. Old-growth stands of eastern hemlock and black cherry sometimes include trees that are more than 150 feet in height.

The Allegheny National Forest is not managed without controversy, however. Mineral rights in this still oil- and gas-rich region were not automatically acquired by the US Forest Service, and recent court decisions have affirmed the oil industry's access to exploit mineral resources. Hikers as well as the trail itself can be impacted by the activities of the oil and gas industry.

Camping is permitted throughout Allegheny National Forest, which also features hiking, backpacking, swimming, biking, fishing, and more.

Trip Planner

Map: PA-01 (Pennsylvania 01), available from www.northcountrytrail.org
Beginning access: Henry's Mills trailhead (HM-001)
Parking: Go 4 miles south on State Route 666 from Sheffield. Make a
right turn (still on Rte. 666) and continue another 3 miles. Cross
the bridge and find parking for 8 to 10 cars on the left.
Ending access: Forest Road 116 trailhead
Parking: From Warren, go south about 12 miles on Pleasant Drive
(St. Rte. 337); at the sign for Heart's Content Campground, go
straight (Rte. 337 turns right) another 7 miles to Forest Road 116,
on the right; turn right on Forest Road 116 and go half a mile.
From Sheffield, turn at the Uni-Mart in downtown Sheffield (there
is only one way to turn), go across the bridge veering left, and
follow the road for 11 miles; turn left on Forest Road 116 and go
half a mile. There is room to park six cars.
Contact information:
PA Regional Trail Coordinator: HQ@northcountrytrail.org
Allegheny National Forest Chapter, NCTA: anf@northcountrytrail.org,
www.northcountrytrail.org/anf
Allegheny National Forest, US Department of Agriculture Forest Service:
814-723-5150

Trail Guide

The Henry's Mills hike begins at the concrete bridge over Tionesta Creek
(HM-001), a good soaking spot on hot days. After passing the kiosk at the
Henry's Mills trailhead, continue south for 150 yards on State Route 666.
To the right is a routed wooden sign. Follow the blue blazes from here.

In this area, the NCT alternates from trail tread to abandoned oil lease
roads and two-track paths to old logging railroad grades. At the first abandoned pump jack, there is a pipe to avoid, sticking up in the middle of the
trail. This pipe is a plugged oil well.

At the top of the long hill, go left on Forest Service Road 410. Go
southwest 0.1 miles on FR 410.

Turn off northwest into the woods at the blue blazes. About a half mile
from the trailhead at Henry's Mills, an old locomotive tender (HM-002)
lies beside the trail as a silent memorial to the era of logging railroads.

The height of land is a nice mix of hemlock, pine, birch, cherry, and

America's first "oil boom" occurred in August 1859 at Titusville, PA, about 50 miles west of the Henry's Mill trailhead, with the development of the first commercially viable oil well. Since then, enough crude oil to fill over a billion and a half barrels has been sucked from the Pennsylvania oil fields. Although that 19th-century boom has long since petered out, the presence of oil- and gas-bearing shale formations and the development of new extraction technology have created a second boom in northwestern Pennsylvania, extending north into New York and west into Ohio, wherever the Marcellus shale layer is found. Drilling activity has impacted NCT users, particularly in areas like the Allegheny National Forest, where the US Forest Service, the NCTA, and a number of drilling companies have worked together to minimize the impact of the drillers. The trail is still intact and weaves through drilling locations. Hikers may occasionally see drilling and pumping equipment and smell the distinctive odor of seeping natural gas; trucks are more frequent. To learn more about the oil industry in the area from a historic perspective, visit the following locations:

Drake Well Museum, 202 Museum
Ln., Titusville, PA 16354; 814-827-2797
Oil Creek State Park, 305 State Park Rd., Oil City, PA 16301; 814-676-5915
Penn-Brad Oil Museum, St. Rte. 219, Bradford, PA 16701; 814-362-1955

beech. The NCT makes a slight descent down to Pell Run and a rusted pump jack, now an active gas well. After the trail transits a stand of hemlock, it reaches a left turn onto another railroad grade. At the top of this grade, active, newer gas wells line both sides of the trail. The next 1.5 miles follow a railroad grade and then the broad tree-lined avenue of a natural gas pipeline. Then the NCT descends a tributary to Upper Sheriff Run, where, next to the wooden bridge, there is a lovely shelter (HM-003), built in 2006 by Keith Klos of the NCTA's Allegheny National Forest Chapter. There are plenty of camping opportunities around this shelter, which is 5.9 miles from Henry's Mills trailhead.

Beyond the shelter, the NCT follows Upper Sheriff Creek upstream on the trail tread and an old woods road. The trail rises gently to a ridgetop and Forest Road 179. At 1.5 miles beyond the shelter, FR 179 (HM-004) provides parking for two or three vehicles.

The trail crosses FR 179 through a stand of small beech trees on a skid road. After a sharp turn to the right (HM-005), it descends gradually to Lower Sheriff Run through ferny woods. After the stockade-shaped bridge, the trail climbs and crosses another Forest Service Road (FR 255) (HM-006).

The NCT next descends past large rocks laced with mountain laurel, to Fool's Run. After Fool's Run Bridge, the NCT climbs gradually to the Minister Road trailhead (HM-007), 2.8 miles from FR 255.

From Minister Road, the NCT continues level through the parklike forest. Where it begins a slight descent, it passes a junction (HM-008) with Minister Creek Trail. (This excellent side trail connects with the developed Minister Creek Campground, which is run by the US Forest Service and open year-round, no reservations required.) The NCT continues down past huge sedimentary rocks, tasty springs, and sylvan glades until it reaches Triple Forks Campground, a flat, cleared, undeveloped area suitable for tent camping, with fire rings and an all-seasons water supply but no amenities. Many fine informal campsites are available in these lovely bottomlands.

Beyond Triple Forks Campground, there is a junction with a side trail on the left that heads off to good views of the Minister Creek valley. Be sure to follow the blue-blazed NCT as it turns sharply right and goes steeply uphill, eventually passing several fine campsites (HM-009, HM-010). The trail rises to follow an old road and soon reaches FR 419.

The trail follows FR 419 for 0.3 miles until veering left onto a level trail, going west 0.3 miles through the woods. It becomes a railroad grade for 0.3 miles through a long avenue of hemlocks.

The trail veers left away from the grade and up over a little knoll. Only 0.1 miles from the end of this hike, the trail crosses an ancient, major railroad grade.

The trailhead at the finish of this hike is at FR 116 (Bob's Creek Road) (HM-011).

Pennsylvania—Henry's Mills

Waypoint ID	Description	Mileage	Latitude	Longitude
HM-001	Henry's Mills Trailhead	0.0	41.63592	−79.04263
HM-002	Locomotive Tender	1.2	41.63264	−79.05725
HM-003	Hunter Station Shelter	5.7	41.65019	−79.10241
HM-004	FR 179	7.4	41.66592	−79.11966
HM-005	Sharp Turn	7.9	41.65982	−79.11825
HM-006	FR 255	9.2	41.6552	−79.13978
HM-007	Minister Road Trailhead	10.1	41.6549	−79.15148
HM-008	Junction—Minister Creek Trail	11.2	41.64544	−79.16587
HM-009	Campsite	12.5	41.65495	−79.18226
HM-010	Campsite	12.7	41.65719	−79.18515
HM-011	FR 116	13.4	41.66363	−79.19343

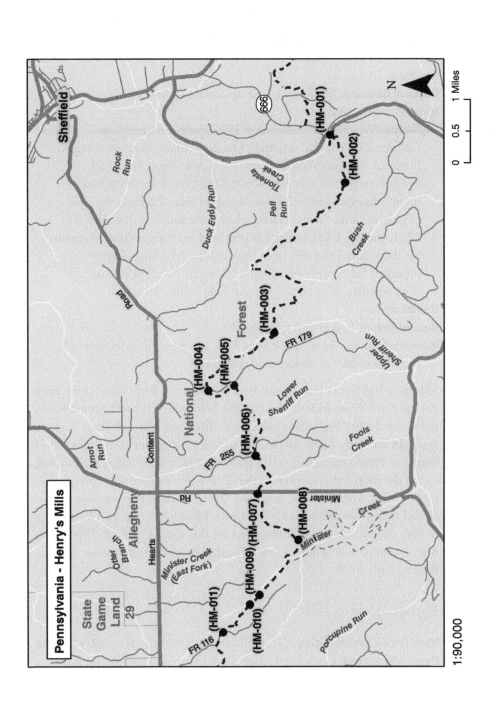

Pennsylvania - Henry's Mills

1:90,000

2. Cook Forest State Park (Cook Forest Fire Tower to Highland Drive trailhead)

Distance: 7.15 miles

Physical difficulty: Moderate (some up and down and three inclines)

Navigation difficulty: Easy

Highlights: Views from Cook Forest Fire Tower and Scurry and Galbreath Overlooks, waterfall, Hemlock Island, and the Clarion National Wild and Scenic River. The Cook Forest State Park Ridge Camp (N41.336700 W079.223318) is located opposite the northern end of Fire Tower Road on State Highway 36. The Highland Drive Shelter is located near the finish of this hike. (In 2011, the NCTA's Clarion Chapter paid for construction materials for the shelter primarily from the proceeds of selling chapter president Ed Scurry's homemade hiking sticks at the annual "Geowoodstock" geocaching event held in July 2011.)

Visitation: Low

Nearest towns: Leeper and Clarion, PA

More information: Cook Forest State Park campground information is available online at cookforest.com/parkinfo/.

This hike highlights both Cook Forest State Park and Clear Creek State Forest. Attractions include the Clarion National Wild and Scenic River, the Cook Forest Fire Tower, and ruins from the Clarion River logging era from the early 1800s to the end of the 19th century. Hillsides full of beautiful Pennsylvania mountain laurel, coupled with serene views along one of the most rustic sections of the Clarion River leave an impression on the soul that won't soon be forgotten. This is that truly rewarding section of trail that drives hikers to scour through hiking guidebooks. Don't forget to grab the camera when heading out on this section of trail. This hike is one to take slow, not because it's difficult, but to savor the magic of these Pennsylvania wilds.

Trip Planner

Map: PA-02 (Pennsylvania 02), available from www.northcountrytrail.org

Beginning access: Cook Forest State Park Fire Tower parking lot (CF-001)

Parking: Fire Tower parking lot. There is room for about 50 cars. The lot is located on Fire Tower Road, off of State Highway 36, across from Ridge Campground.

Ending access: Highland Drive trailhead

Parking: The trailhead parking lot on Highland Drive has room for 8 to 10 cars, with two overflow parking areas. Highland Drive is located off of Miola Road, right beside the Kalyumet Campground's Fore Fun putt-putt golf course.

Contact information:

PA Regional Trail Coordinator: HQ@northcountrytrail.org

Clarion Chapter, NCTA: cla@northcountrytrail.org, www.northcountry.org/cla

Trail Guide

This hike begins at the Cook Forest State Park Fire Tower parking lot (CF-001), 1.2 miles from State Highway 36, at the southern end of Fire Tower Road. Follow the access trail into the woods 0.1 miles to a junction with the blue-blazed NCT. There is a side trail here (0.1 miles) to Seneca Point Overlook, which showcases the next 5 miles of the NCT.

Follow the trail another 0.1 miles southeast to the Cook Forest Fire Tower (CF-002). Note that the trail's customary blue blazes are accompanied here with the yellow blaze of the Baker Trail (a pathway that is maintained by the Rachel Carson Trails Conservancy, a volunteer-based, nonprofit 501(c)(3) organization dedicated to the development, protection, and promotion of hiking, biking, and walking trails throughout western Pennsylvania (www.rachelcarsontrails.org/). The Baker Trail is 132 miles long.

From the Cook Forest Fire Tower, the trail descends across a hillside featuring mountain laurel and rhododendron to the banks of the Clarion

Built in 1929, the 80-foot Cook Forest Fire Tower (CF-002) delivers a 15- to 20-mile panorama. Though the structure was decommissioned in 1966, its lookout cabin is sometimes open for interpretive programs. Climb it for a magnificent view of the Clarion River valley, especially in spring when mountain laurel is in bloom.

National Wild and Scenic River. From here, the trail alternates between Clear Creek State Forest and Cook Forest State Park.

Follow the trail downstream to Henry's Run (CF-003). Beyond Henry's Run, private landowners' opposition to locating the trail on their lands caused the NCTA to relocate the trail high up on the pine and oak hillside above the Clarion River. Along the way to Henry's Run, there are great views not only of Hemlock Island but also of streams that teem with bass and native trout as well as of woods full of wildlife. Henry Run's spillway was built to power a logging-era sawmill. Cross the creek on a stone bridge, once part of the mill.

After crossing Henry's Run, the trail takes a sharp turn to the right. After approximately 200 feet, turn left and go uphill past a spring, which offers the last water until near the end of this hike. The trail goes about a mile across the hillside to Scurry Overlook (named for longtime NCTA Clarion Chapter volunteer Ed Scurry) and its lovely view of a great bend in the forest-bordered river. The trail next descends steeply 0.3 miles to Gravel Lick Road (CF-004), through a canopy of mountain laurel.

At Gravel Lick Road, there is parking for two or three vehicles slightly to the right, beside a guardrail. The trail crosses Gravel Lick Road and parallels the creek downhill through the woods to a junction with a white-blazed trail, which goes to the Baker Trail.

The NCT climbs Thompson Hill steeply 0.4 miles to the parking area at the top (CF-005). For the faint of heart or short of breath, there is a welcoming bench three-quarters of the way up. At the top of Thompson Hill, there is a gravel parking area off the end of Shadetree Lane.

From the parking area, the trail follows an old gas company road down the wooded far side of Thompson Hill and to the banks of a remote section of the Clarion National Wild and Scenic River. The unique nature of the Clarion River is part of what makes this section of the NCT so special. The steeply wooded banks coupled with the narrow, winding river create a sense of remoteness—a delight for urban-weary hikers.

The trail parallels the lovely river downstream. Camping is available at Porter's Landing Canoe Camping Area (CF-006). For reservations, contact Cook Forest State Park (814-744-8407, www.visitpaparks.com).

After leaving these campsites, the trail follows the Clarion River for approximately 1 mile. One of the finest views is located at a bend where there is a convenient wooden bench.

After leaving the Clarion River, the trail follows a long-abandoned lower piece of Kline Drive (CF-007) to a wooded mesa above the river. The trail follows this mesa for approximately 1 mile. Along this section of trail is Galbreath Overlook, which offers another scenic view of the Clarion River. After this section, the trail descends to a little creek valley that angles away from the river. The trail follows an old logging road up this hollow for about 0.5 miles to a junction marked by a cairn (CF-008). The trail diverges left to the heights.

The spring along this stretch is the last water source for 0.3 miles before the NCT reaches Highland Drive shelter and then the Highland Drive trailhead (CF-009). (The distance from Gravel Lick Road to the Highland Drive trailhead totals 4.7 miles.)

Pennsylvania—Cook Forest State Park

Waypoint ID	Description	Mileage	Latitude	Longitude
CF-001	Cook Forest State Park Fire Tower Parking Lot	0.00	41.32198	−79.2119
CF-002	Fire Tower	0.10	41.32065	−79.2096
CF-003	Henry's Run	1.36	41.32143	−79.2268
CF-004	Gravel Lick Road	2.16	41.31676	−79.2418
CF-005	Thompson Hill and Parking Area	2.54	41.31517	−79.2459
CF-006	Porter's Landing Canoe Camping Area	3.57	41.30864	−79.256
CF-007	Road Junction— Kline Drive	4.14	41.30516	−79.264
CF-008	Trail Junction	4.58	41.31055	−79.266
CF-009	Highland Drive Trailhead	7.15	41.30049	−79.2825

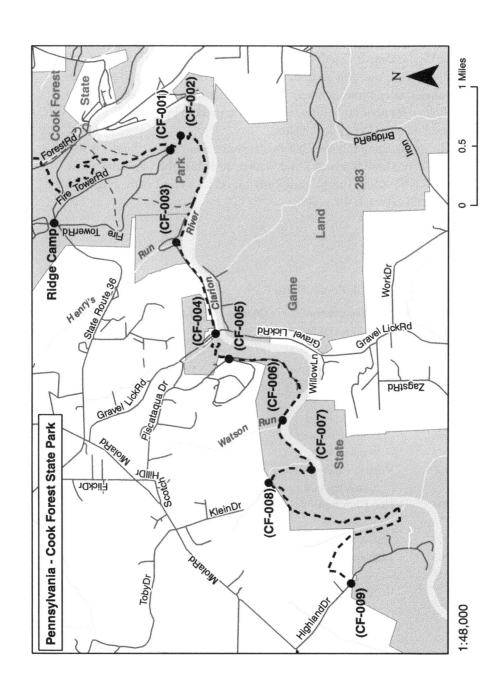

Pennsylvania - Cook Forest State Park

1:48,000

3. Hell's Hollow (Alpha Pass to Hell's Hollow)

Distance: 7.7 miles
Physical Difficulty: Moderate
Navigation difficulty: Easy
Highlights: A gorge, a creek, small waterfalls, and McConnells Mill
State Park. From May through October, the historic gristmill is
open on weekends and holidays for free tours. For information,
visit www.dcnr.state.pa.us/stateparks/findapark/mcconnellsmill/.
Visitation: Moderate (though each end is quite popular)
Nearest town: Portersville, PA
More information: The NCTA-managed, Revolutionary War-era Davis
Hollow Cabin in Moraine State Park is available for overnight rental.
For cabin reservations, contact dhcabin@northcountrytrail.org.

This hike wends its way through cool, shady hemlock forests and delightful, deciduous woods. The NCT follows Slippery Rock Creek's Class III/
IV rapids, staying alongside the streambed and then climbing the ravine
a couple of times for nice views. It then follows Hell's Run upstream to
the trailhead parking lot. There is a covered bridge and a working, water-
driven, 19th-century gristmill. Geologically, this valley was formed by the
outflow from a huge glacial lake at the end of the last ice age.

This hike terminates near a half-mile side trail along Hell's Run, a fascinating sunken creek that descends from a small waterfall named Hell's
Hollow Falls. There's also an old lime kiln.

Trip Planner

Map: PA-03 (Pennsylvania 03), available from www.northcountrytrail.org
Maps are also available at various kiosks within McConnells Mill State
Park and at the South Shore office of nearby Moraine State Park.
Beginning access: Alpha Pass trailhead (HH-001)
Parking: At the Alpha Pass trailhead (HH-001), on McConnells Mill
Road. Or there is a larger parking lot (and a restroom) about an
eighth of a mile down the road, at the corner of McConnells Mill
and Johnson Roads.
Ending access: Hell's Hollow trailhead on Shaffer Road

Parking: Near Hell's Hollow Falls at Shaffer Road
Contact information:
PA Regional Trail Coordinator: HQ@northcountrytrail.org
Wampum Chapter, NCTA: wam@northcountrytrail.org,
     www.northcountrytrail.org/wam

Trail Guide

Start the hike at Alpha Pass (HH-001). This interesting name derives from
being the first (alpha) place where a lake of the last ice age breached its dam
to discharge into what became Slippery Rock Creek. Nearby Lake Arthur
partially re-creates the lake of the ice age.

From the Alpha Pass trailhead, the trail descends on steps past a mossy
sandstone ledge, where a short, unmarked side trail (to the right, partway
down the steps) leads to a delightful waterfall. Watch your footing; Slippery Rock Creek was so named for a reason.

The trail then follows Slippery Rock Creek 0.5 miles through its
hemlock-bordered gorge. No swimming is allowed in this park, because
the water can be very dangerous even in times of placid flow. Hydraulic
currents around deeply submerged boulders annually drown the unwary.

The historic 1869 gristmill in McConnells Mill State Park is open to visitors
daily from Memorial Day through Labor Day and seasonally on weekends and
holidays. A water-driven turbine provides the power once used to operate
roller mills, conveyors, and elevators—machinery remarkably well preserved
and packed into the three fascinating floors of the mill. Millstones still operate, demonstrating the grinding of corn into cornmeal. Admission is free.

The gristmill is nestled in the 400-foot deep Slippery Rock Gorge, which is
a National Natural Landmark, one of fewer than 600 in the nation. (Beware of
the dangerous river currents.) During higher water, kayakers are challenged in
the Class II, III, and IV rapids. Hungry? Be sure to stop to eat your bag lunch
in the courtyard beside the covered bridge.

Interpretive rangers explain how the gristmill made meal from corn, oats,
wheat, and buckwheat with power derived from the old mill dam. Specific
tour and trail information and the mill's seasonal hours are available from the
Moraine State Park office (morainesp@pa.gov).

Nevertheless, this is a popular kayaking stream through the beech, birch, linden, and hemlock forest.

The trail crosses the creek via an honest-to-goodness covered bridge (HH-002). This picturesque structure is still used by vehicles. Hikers should use caution.

The trail skirts the west side of Slippery Rock Creek's rapids and pools for 1 mile to Eckert Bridge (HH-003). Across this large concrete bridge and up the hill, fee camping is available at Breakneck Campground. For reservations, call 724-368-3405 or visit www.breakneckcampground.com.

From a trailside millstone at the Eckert Bridge, the trail follows the creek for another 2 miles, climbing partially to the top of the gorge. The trail then descends to the creek's floodplain at Walnut Flats (HH-004) at the 2-mile mark. (Camping is not permitted within the park.) The trail continues to parallel Slippery Rock Creek for another delightful 2 miles.

Finally, the trail turns west and continues for 2.4 miles up the val-

---

The Davis Hollow Cabin is one of the historic facilities along the NCT. NCTA volunteers manage and maintain the cabin, devoting their time and energy to preserve the cabin's history for future generations to enjoy.

Construction began on the cabin in 1780. The hand-hewn logs and hand-carved stone are superb examples of pioneer construction. Located behind the Davis Hollow Marina at present-day Moraine State Park, the cabin most recently served as a summer home for Mrs. Katherine Davis and her sister, Miss Eleanor Holt, before the park's development. Today, the NCTA leases the cabin from the park.

Davis Hollow is available by reservation for group retreats, events, and overnights, including by hikers, with advance reservations. The cabin has a great room with a large stone fireplace, a fully equipped kitchen, eleven upstairs bunk beds, and two half baths (showers are available at the nearby marina). Tent camping is also available; outdoors, there are picnic tables and a fire ring.

To plan an overnight or rent the cabin, contact dhcabin@northcountrytrail .org.

Davis Hollow cabin is a great place for hikers to stop over, for lunch or overnight. Photo displays on the cabin's walls tell stories spanning back 230 years.

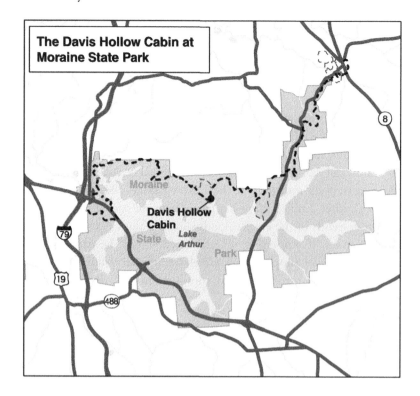

The Davis Hollow Cabin at Moraine State Park

ley of Hell Run (HH-005), past some curious limestone formations, to this featured hike's end at the Hell's Hollow parking area on Shaffer Road (HH-006).

Anyone wishing to extend this hike could add a southerly side walk of 0.5 miles along the Hell's Hollow Trail. Walk in about 300 yards, cross a bridge, reach a Y, and take the right branch, which goes to Hell's Hollow Falls and an old lime kiln.

Pennsylvania—Hell's Hollow

Waypoint ID	Description	Mileage	Latitude	Longitude
HH-001	Alpha Pass Trailhead	0.0	40.95988	−80.16879
HH-002	Covered Bridge	0.6	40.95291	−80.17002
HH-003	Eckert Bridge	1.5	40.94057	−80.17621
HH-004	Walnut Flats Sign	3.6	40.92451	−80.19018
HH-005	Trail Sign—Hell Run	5.3	40.91661	−80.21512
HH-006	Hell's Hollow Parking Area	7.7	40.93135	−80.23996

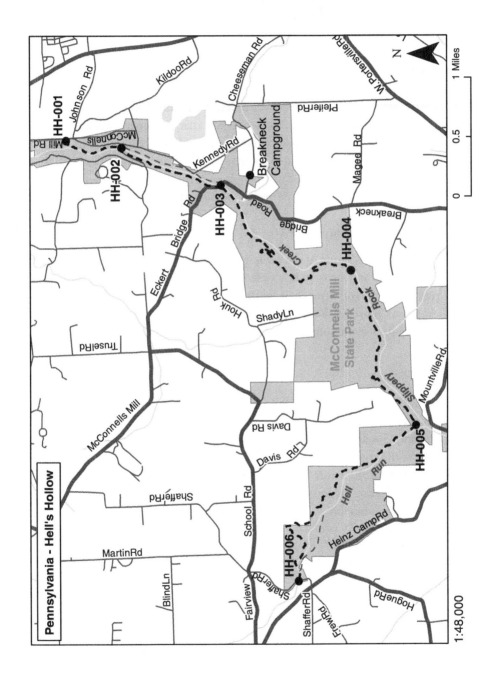

Pennsylvania - Hell's Hollow

1:48,000

4. Wampum (Sankey Hill Road to Edwards Road)

Distance: 10.4 miles
Physical difficulty: Moderate
Navigation difficulty: Easy
Highlights: Located on the Beaver River, Wampum, PA, is designated as an "NCT Trail Town," which means that the town embraces its role in welcoming hikers and providing hiker hospitality. In addition to this hike, there are many miles of pleasant, well-maintained trail, as well as a couple of surprises, such as a hoary lime kiln where a local farmer made his fertilizer in years past.
Visitation: Low
Nearest town: Wampum, PA

Wampum, PA, is one of the earliest communities to adopt the "NCT Trail Town" label and strive to be a welcoming place for hikers to base camp and gather before and after their excursions. The Appalachian Trail may have America's most celebrated trail town in Damascus, VA, but Wampum is hoping to provide some of that same magic for NCT hikers.

Trip Planner

Map: PA-03 (Pennsylvania 03), available from www.northcountrytrail.org
East access: Sankey Hill Road trailhead
Parking: Shoulder parking for three or four vehicles at the trailhead, at the intersection of Sankey Hill Road and Snake Run Road
West access: Edwards Road trailhead
Parking: Room for four or five cars
Contact Information:
PA Regional Trail Coordinator: HQ@northcountrytrail.org
Wampum Chapter, NCTA: wam@northcountrytrail.org, www.northcountrytrail.org/wam

Trail Guide

This Wampum hike starts out at the intersection of Sankey Hill Road and Snake Run Road (W-001). The blue-blazed trail enters the woods and ascends multiple switchbacks, emerging at the top of the ridge beside a field. The trail then traces along several fields until it suddenly veers left onto a jeep trail (W-002). Just after the turn, there is a decrepit-looking house on the left that seems to beg for stories to be told about it. The trail continues via a two-track pathway, past old abandoned coal mines (located up to the right on the hillside), to eventually reach Fletcher Hill Road (W-003).

After crossing Fletcher Hill Road, the trail rises up a short incline and then continues through fields and then an overgrown orchard. After another field, the trail descends back down into the woods, curves around a large rock formation, and passes several small limestone cave entrances. After crossing a small stream, the trail reaches a homemade lime kiln, last used in the 1930s by a farmer who used local coal to bake the lime out of his abundant limestone for use as fertilizer.

Once past the kiln, skirt the end of a cornfield, cross Snake Run on a substantial bridge (W-004), and then ascend a switchback up to Snake Run Road. This trailhead on Snake Run Road has room for two or three cars.

The next 0.6 miles of the trail is a blue-blazed road walk (to the right) down Snake Run Road, bypassing private property. At the 0.6-mile mark (on the right side of the road), the trail enters the property of the CEMEX cement company at the NCT sign (W-005). This trailhead has a bench that was installed by a local Eagle Scout and room to park several vehicles.

The trail continues through a small field, crosses a stream on a bridge, returns back into the woods, and then ascends a hill via a switchback. From here to the next road, the hike is primarily a woods walk, although it does temporarily utilize an old skid road above the switchback. The trail

A trail register is a logbook where hikers can record anything from their names to detailed impressions of their experiences. Maintained by hiking clubs or individuals, they are typically found at shelters, trailheads, resupply points, and trail angels' homes. Initially, they were used to help locate lost hikers, and they still serve that purpose. Today, they also help educate hikers on trail etiquette and conditions, as well as offering hikers a chance to personalize their experience—to "tweet" their hike, so to speak. In western Pennsylvania, near the Ohio-Pennsylvania state line, there is a trail register at State Game Lands Number 285, another at the shelter 4 miles east, and another 2 miles farther along at Indian Rock (also part of State Game Lands Number 285). In Wampum, look for registers at the Possum Hollow Road trailhead, at the Route 18 trailhead, and at the River Road trailhead on the east side of the Beaver River. Don't forget to sign in at Snake Run Road and at Sankey Hill Road to read what others have shared about their hikes.

leaves the skid road after 0.1 miles and heads back into the woods. Watch closely for the blazes to the left. This 0.8-mile section ends at Chewton West Pittsburgh Road (W-006), where there is room to park three or four vehicles.

Soon after crossing Chewton West Pittsburgh Road, the trail uses a substantial bridge to get across a very deep gully. After that, a slight ascent follows. There is a large beaver dam about 50 yards away through the woods on the right. Much of the next half mile is a field walk through an old, reclaimed coal and limestone strip mine. This section totals 0.5 miles from Chewton West Pittsburgh Road to the poorly maintained Tony Dytko Road (W-007).

The trail heads downhill for the next 1.2 miles to River Road (W-008) and the Beaver River. Along the way, the trail passes some interesting large rock formations and scenic views (such as the aptly named Corn Field Vista). Near the bottom of this hill, the trail crosses the Buffalo and Pittsburgh Railroad tracks and then slants southward along the hillside until reaching River Road. Parking is very limited at this trailhead, but there is a boat launch with parking 0.2 miles to the south.

Three-tenths of a mile from the River Road trailhead, the trail bears right onto Canal Street. The trail follows this lesser-used, closer-to-the-river roadway for 0.5 miles. Just before the Beaver River Bridge, there is an informal swimming hole where water issues from two big culverts. After that, the trail goes under the highway bridge and swings left past a white house to begin crossing the bridge. Follow the bridge's sidewalk across the river to Wampum, PA.

The trail does not enter the heart of downtown. Instead, it promptly climbs Darlington Road. After crossing two sets of railroad tracks, it goes left on State Route 18. After continuing 0.3 miles south, the trail passes beneath a bridge bearing an unused CEMEX access road. Soon afterward, it follows a driveway up to the top of that bridge (W-009).

The trail crosses an old concrete bridge over State Route 18 (located approximately 0.3 miles south of the intersection of Darlington Rd. and Rte. 18). Access to the bridge is along a private driveway, so please don't block the drive when parking. The homeowners are aware of and supportive of the trail and are used to vehicles being left parked on the grass alongside the driveway, where there is room to park five or six cars.

After crossing the bridge, the trail goes westward up the grade to the Gateway property. Gateway is in the underground storage business, using old mines. The trail climbs to the bench above this old strip-mined area and wends westward. Along the way, there is a short, white-blazed spur trail leading off to the left to a view of the Beaver River Valley and Chewton, PA. There is also a later view westward of Pennsylvania farm country. At 1 mile, the trail begins its descent from the bench. At the 1.3-mile mark, it crosses a small, unnamed creek on a wooden footbridge. About 0.1 miles farther west, the trail reaches a dirt road built and maintained by the Mines & Meadows ATV Riding Park.

The trail crosses over the Mines & Meadows dirt road and continues through the woodsy ATV park. (Its owners are NCT supporters and do their best to discourage riders from using the trail.) The trail traverses Mines & Meadows for 0.4 miles until reaching State Game Lands Number 148 (W-010).

After crossing into State Game Lands Number 148, the trail ascends an abandoned (often muddy) two-track trail. At the top of this hill, the trail passes Game Commission feed plots as it follows a maintained two-track trail down a large hill and then back up the other side. After climbing out of that valley, the trail follows a slight downward grade. The Game Commission two-track trail leads to the Possum Hollow Road trailhead (W-011), where there is a maintained parking area and room for many vehicles. The distance from State Route 18 to Possum Hollow Road totals 3.2 miles.

After crossing Possum Hollow Road, the trail reenters the woods on Game Commission property along a single-track trail that skirts farm fields for 0.4 miles. When the trail reaches Wampum-New Galilee Road (W-012), it follows the road for about one hundred yards to the right. Then it leaves the Wampum-New Galilee Road and jogs back off to the left into a pine forest on the Edwards family farm.

After a short distance, the trail exits the pines and skirts the edge of a cornfield. It reenters the woods for the final half mile down to the intersection of Edwards Road and State Route 60/Interstate 376 (W-013). The distance from this section's starting point at State Route 18 to the Edwards Road trailhead totals 4.3 miles.

Pennsylvania—Wampum

Waypoint ID	Description	Mileage	Latitude	Longitude
W-001	Sankey Hill Road			
	Trailhead	0.0	40.93357	−80.31278
W-002	Jeep Trail	0.4	40.93275	−80.31782
W-003	Road Junction—			
	Fletcher Hill Road	1.2	40.92795	−80.31931
W-004	Bridge—Snake Run	1.9	40.92191	−80.31656
W-005	Road Junction	2.5	40.91361	−80.32116
W-006	Chewton West			
	Pittsburgh Road	3.3	40.90721	−80.32835
W-007	Tony Dytko Road	3.8	40.90150	−80.32949
W-008	River Road	4.9	40.89809	−80.34174
W-09	State Route 18 Hwy			
	Bride Trailhead	6.3	40.88419	−80.33437
W-010	State Game Lands			
	Number 148	8.1	40.87404	−80.34822
W-011	Possum Hollow Road			
	Trailhead	9.6	40.85977	−80.35666
W-012	Wampum–New Galilee			
	Road	10.0	40.85971	−80.36410
W-013	State Route 18 to the			
	Edwards Road			
	Trailhead	10.4	40.86260	−80.36793

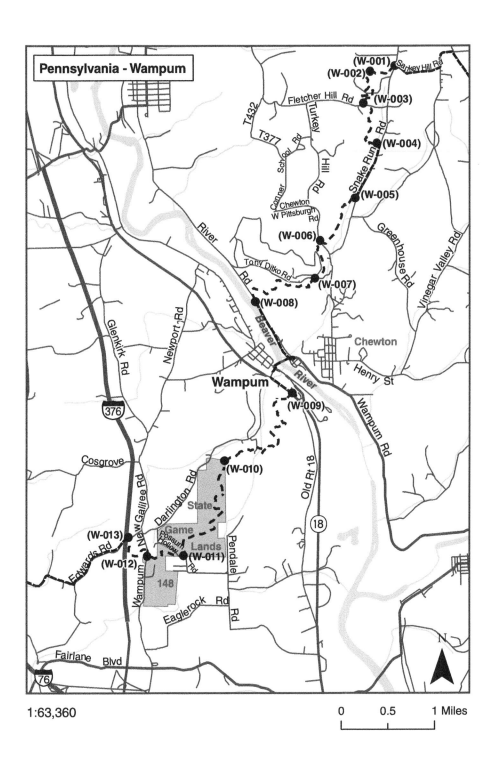

Ohio

In Ohio (as in New York), the NCT follows the path of a preexisting trail for part of its length. Nine hundred ninety-three of the 1,070 miles of the NCT's Ohioan tread are graciously hosted by the Buckeye Trail. Founded in 1959, the Buckeye Trail Association builds and maintains a 1,444-mile route circumnavigating Ohio.

Though the Buckeye Trail is often woodsy, it also passes through so many small towns that it has a distinct "front-porch America" character. That impression is further magnified by the volunteer spirit and midwestern friendliness of the folks you meet on the trail.

Buckeye Trail aficionados are adamant that Ohio is one great place to hike. Motorists who only know Ohio from its uninspiring interstate highway corridors would be surprised by the diversity and riches to be found along the NCT/Buckeye Trail. Rural pleasures on the trail include several

The Buckeye Trail Association promotes "the construction, maintenance, and use of a state-wide trail system, within the State of Ohio, to be supplemented with side trails, campsites, and other facilities, so as to render accessible some of the historical and scenic spots of the Buckeye State. The trail shall be primarily a footpath, but certain portions may be designated for use by horsemen and/or other non-motorized users."

The Buckeye Trail dates back to a 1958 article by Merrill Gilfillan, who proposed creating a trail from Cincinnati to Lake Erie to urge youngsters to appreciate Ohio's many attractions. Several people, including Merrill and legendary hiker Grandma Gatewood (the first woman to solo thru-hike the Appalachian Trail—at age 67), met in Columbus in February 1959 to discuss building such a trail. In June, they formed a nonprofit organization—the Buckeye Trail Association. The Buckeye Trail's first 20 miles were dedicated on September 19, 1959, in Hocking County. In 1980, the final section was finished near Deer Lick Cave in the Cuyahoga Valley National Recreation Area. For information about the Buckeye Trail Association's hikes, outings, meetings, and publications, contact info@buckeyetrail.org.

state parks, two outstanding 19th-century canals, a cave system, and a National Wild and Scenic River. Away-from-the-woods attractions include everything from a historic communal village to a major city with a national aeronautical museum.

Eastern Ohio's lovely hills contrast with western Ohio's more subdued terrain. But everywhere in Ohio, there are plenty of inducements to linger on the NCT. The trail parallels the state's U-shaped borders as they make a huge southward loop between Pennsylvania and Michigan. Along the way, the record of human endeavor illustrates Ohio's rich cultural traditions, as hikers find themselves walking in the footsteps of Native Americans, canal and river boaters, escaping slaves and those who offered them refuge, loggers, miners, and pioneers of the railroad, airplane, and agricultural industries. Ohio's six featured hikes sample this scenic and historic variety. Far from "rusting away," the state of Ohio and its abundant natural resources make the perfect transition for the NCT from the eastern mountains, steep valleys, and laurel-studded plateaus of New York and Pennsylvania to the rich-loamed bottomlands, oak openings, and, later, sandy hills of the lower Midwest.

Beginning at the Pennsylvania border, the NCT parallels an Ohio State Wild and Scenic River called Little Beaver Creek. After passing through the Big Creek State Forest and State Park, the NCT follows the abandoned Sandy and Beaver Canal towpath and passes through Lisbon, OH, meeting the Buckeye Trail just before the village of Zoar, OH. This is one of the most historic featured hikes in this guide.

Following the Buckeye Trail south, the NCT traverses the never-glaciated Allegheny Plateau in Wayne National Forest to Marietta, OH, at the confluence of the Muskingum and Ohio Rivers. The NCT continues south to the hills of Ohio's coal country, then on to the village of Chesterhill (a point on the Underground Railroad), Burr Oak State Park, the Athens Unit of the Wayne National Forest, and the village of Shawnee. The Tar Hollow State Forest and the Hocking Hills region offer hikers hemlock forests, sandstone cliffs, exciting caves, waterfalls—and the most popular section of hiking trail on the NCT.

In south central Ohio, the NCT traverses the Pike and Shawnee State Forests and State Parks as well as private lands and Ohio Historical Society lands. Local attractions include Fort Hill and the Serpent Mound, mysterious serpentine earth formations built by prehistoric cultures. Next, the trail passes only 2 miles from the Ohio River and the Kentucky border, the southernmost point on the entire NCT.

Between the Shawnee State Forest and East Fork State Park, there is a long road walk. Milford, OH, sits at the junction of the American Discovery Trail, the Ohio to Erie Trail, the Underground Railroad, the Sea-to-Sea Route, the Little Miami Scenic Trail, and the Little Miami River Water Trail.

From Milford, the NCT continues north along the Little Miami Scenic Trail to Yellow Springs, OH.

At Dayton, OH, the NCT utilizes the Five Rivers MetroParks trails and bikeways system—including a splendid featured hike routed through downtown Dayton along the Great Miami River Recreation Trail.

In northwest Ohio, the NCT follows the Miami and Erie Canal through historic canal towns into a region of the state formerly known as the Great Black Swamp. Where the towpath reaches Napoleon, OH, the NCT finally splits from the Buckeye Trail and heads northwest to form its own Wabash Cannonball hurtling toward Michigan.

The first half of the 19th century was the golden age of canal building in America. Interconnecting the abundant waterways of the northeast, canals enabled commerce, opened new markets, and facilitated settlement and westward migration. Towing canal boats with oxen or mules required one side of the canal to be maintained as a towpath. Canals were a key element in the race for the young nation to access and exploit the lands of what was called the Northwest Territory, including Ohio. But canals were short-lived in almost every case. By the time of the Civil War, railroads were starting to eclipse canals, and the advent of the steam engine's technology made larger shipping vessels speedier, more reliable, and a better economic choice. Canal ways were abandoned, in some cases leaving remarkably little evidence of their former presence except to the trained eye. Today, the old towpaths make very attractive, level, easy-walking places for hikers and, in some places, bikers. Both the NCT and the Buckeye Trail include many delightful miles along canal ways of the past, including some in these featured hikes of Ohio. It's not hard to saunter along a towpath and feel transported back 175 years to a slower-paced era, as if walking alongside a mule at a canal boat's tempo.

Ohio's Featured Hikes

1. **Beaver Creek State Park** (Leslie Road Campground to Sprucevale Road)

2. **Zoar Village and the Ohio and Erie Canal Towpath Trail** (Canal Lands Park to the Zoar Village)

3. **Hocking Hills State Park/State Forest** (Grandma Gatewood memorial to Ash Cave parking lot on State Route 56)

4. **Shawnee State Forest** (Forest Road 6 to State Route 125)

5. **Dayton** (Huffman Prairie Flying Field Interpretive Center to Deeds Point MetroPark)

6. **Snaketown** (Snaketown to Meyerholtz Park)

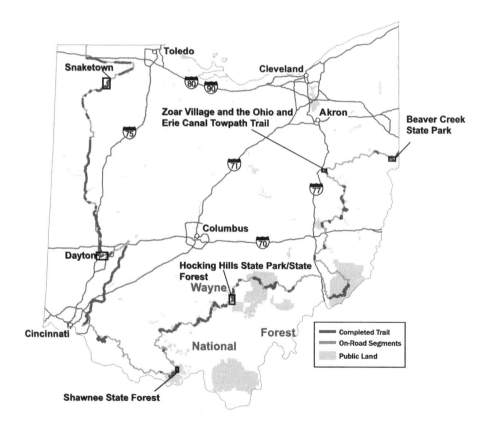

1. Beaver Creek State Park (Leslie Road Campground to Sprucevale Road)

Distance: 6.2 miles
Physical difficulty: Easy to moderate
Navigation difficulty: Easy
Highlights: Delightful riverside walking, remnants of a long-ago canal, and a historic village complete with its own working flour mill
Visitation: Moderate
Nearest town: Lisbon, OH

Little Beaver Creek's deep valleys and dense forests are a rich resource for hikers. Geologically unique, the Little Beaver Creek valley is the only stream valley thus far discovered that holds evidence of all four major glaciations. A walk along the river is an introduction to not only fast-flowing rapids but also how early 19th-century residents lived. Most fascinating are the remnants of a 73-mile-long waterway known as the Sandy and Beaver Canal, which connected the Ohio River to another canal at Bolivar, OH, carrying commerce from 1828 to 1852. The Sandy and Beaver Canal Association celebrates this history today. For more information, visit sandy beaverassoc.org.

Inspiring to the more adventurous imagination may be the evidence of Wyandot or Mingo Native American peoples found along the riverbanks; the stories of notorious rogue Simon Girty, reported to have frequented the area in the early 1800s; or stories of the capture nearby of Confederate cavalry general John Hunt Morgan, at the end of his spectacular and terror-spreading 1863 raid that traversed southern Indiana and Ohio.

Beaver Creek State Park includes an Ohio State Wild and Scenic River, as well as the family-friendly, reconstructed Gaston's Mill and Pioneer Village, located at the entrance to the park. The restored gristmill from the 1830s operated until 1928, and the village re-creates a pioneer village of the 1830s, featuring a one-room schoolhouse, blacksmith shop, chapel, and general store—all constructed from logs. The Malone Covered Bridge is from 1870. There is a lock from the Sandy and Beaver Canal. Be sure to visit the Beaver Creek Wildlife Education Center's live animals, natural history dioramas, and gift shop, where cornmeal and buckwheat flour ground at the mill are available for purchase. The village buildings are open to the public on weekends from May 1 through October 31. For more information, visit www.friendsofbeavercreekstatepark.org.

Trip Planner

Map: OH-101 (Ohio 101), available from www.northcountrytrail.org
Beginning access: Beaver Creek State Park, Leslie Road Campground
dump station (BC-001)
Parking: At the dump station on Leslie Road
Ending access: Sprucevale Road parking lot and trailhead
Parking: Parking lot
Contact information:
OH Regional Trail Coordinator: HQ@northcountrytrail.org
Great Trail–Sandy Beaver Canal Chapter, NCTA: gts@northcountrytrail.org,
www.northcountrytrail.org/gts
Beaver Creek State Park, 12021 Echo Dell Rd., East Liverpool, OH 43920;
330-385-3091

Trail Guide

Arrive by car at Leslie Road Campground on the northwest side of Beaver
Creek State Park. Parking is near the dump station (BC-001) on Leslie
Road. Follow the campground road east 75 yards. Turn right onto the
blue-blazed NCT at the Dogwood Trail sign. The trail will pass an old railroad grade, then descend to Beaver Creek in an ash, hemlock, and maple
forest. Note that the NCT uses the white-blazed Dogwood Trail. Follow
the trail down to the creek.

Turn left on the paved road at creek-side, and walk through the picnic
area. The trail continues downstream to within sight of and just before the
1910 Echo Dell Bridge. At that point, a side trip across the bridge to the
Pioneer Village will be difficult to resist.

Before reaching the bridge, the trail turns left up an old, stony road
known as the Upper Vondergreen Trail. Follow this road upward through
the hemlocks and the sandstone formations. At a culvert at the top of this

The Sandy and Beaver Canal was a spur route from the Ohio and Erie Canal
at Bolivar, OH, to the Ohio River at Glasgow, PA. Containing 30 dams and 90
locks, it was a masterpiece of early 19th-century engineering. For instance,
the double-curved stone staircase at Lusk's Lock still inspires wonder. In
1853, competition from the Cleveland and Pittsburgh Railroad Company put
an end to the Sandy and Beaver Canal.

long rise, turn right. Continue through a pine plantation via a tree-lined corridor atop the river bluff.

At a junction with a horse trail (BC-002), continue straight ahead. Follow the trail through a broad, brush-and-tree-filled bottomland (well out of sight of the creek).

Beginning at an island, the trail will occupy the east bank of Little Beaver Creek for the rest of this hike. At Grey's Lock (BC-003), look carefully for the oak dam timbers at low water. They are part of the lock ruins that enabled navigation of this section of the 73-mile-long Sandy and Beaver Canal that once connected the Ohio River with the Ohio and Erie Canal at Bristol, OH.

From Grey's Lock, follow the trail to cross a small wooden bridge (BC-004) over a minor brook. Look carefully for more remnants of the old canal.

At a junction (BC-005), follow the trail left to Gretchen's Lock. Pass the foundation of an old house and climb steeply north up to an unmarked junction (BC-006). Veer left. After 100 feet, turn right on the signed Vondergreen Trail. Walk northeast along the edge of the bluff. The trail will go ever higher in elevation. On a hot summer day, be thankful for the breeze that rises from the unseen valley far below. Look for peekaboo views to the southwest through the tall maples and oaks across the glacier-gouged, steep slope. Avoid the confusing horse trails by carefully following the NCT's blazes.

After a steep descent, follow the trail where it diverges from horse trails at some abandoned sawmill machinery. Continue along the trail to the end of this segment at the parking lot on Sprucevale Road (BC-007).

Ohio—Beaver Creek State Park

Waypoint ID	Description	Mileage	Latitude	Longitude
BC-001	Beaver Creek State Park, Leslie Road Campground Dump Station	0.0	40.73179	−80.62282
BC-002	Trail Junction—Horse Trail	3.2	40.72342	−80.60549
BC-003	Grey's Lock	3.4	40.72042	−80.60483
BC-004	Small Wooden Bridge	3.9	40.71599	−80.60272
BC-005	Trail Junction	4.2	40.71279	−80.59931
BC-006	Trail Junction	4.3	40.71433	−80.59859
BC-007	Parking—Sprucevale Road	6.2	40.70571	−80.58259

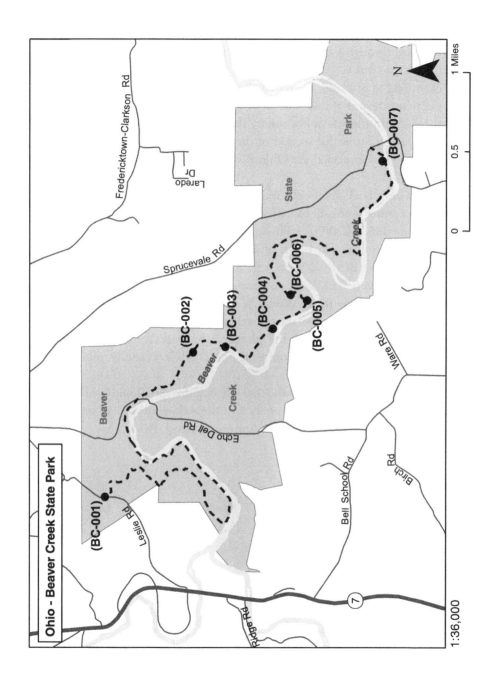

Ohio - Beaver Creek State Park

1:36,000

2. Zoar Village and the Ohio and Erie Canal Towpath Trail (Canal Lands Park to Zoar Village)

Distance: Less than a mile
Physical difficulty: Easy
Navigation difficulty: Easy
Highlights: Tuscarawas River, Ohio and Erie Canal, Ohio and Erie Canal Towpath Trail, and historic Zoar Village
Visitation: Moderate to heavy
Nearest town: Zoar, OH

The NCT joins the Buckeye Trail on this delightfully short walk, which delivers not only bucolic scenery along a charming river but also a history lesson through a village that appears to exist in a 19th-century time warp. Founded in 1817 by German religious dissenters, the Society of Separatists of Zoar flourished for seven decades as a distinct religious entity. Zoarites paid for their land here by digging a stretch of the Ohio and Erie Canal. Remnants of this communal lifestyle are still visible today in the buildings and gardens that the communards left behind. Take a guided walking tour of downtown.

Trip Planner

Map: Buckeye Trail Massillon Section Map, available from www.buckeyetrail.org
Beginning access: Canal Lands Park (Z-001)
Parking: Canal Lands Park parking lot
Ending access: 430 Main Street, Zoar, OH (Z-003)
Parking: There is plenty of on- and off-street parking in the village.
Contact information:
OH Regional Trail Coordinator: HQ@northcountrytrail.org
Buckeye Trail Association: info@buckeyetrail.org
More information:
Historic Zoar Village: www.zca.org/
ohsweb.ohiohistory.org/

Trail Guide

Begin this walk at the Canal Lands Park (Z-001), just off Dover Zoar Road. This is actually the site of Fort Laurens, Ohio's only Revolutionary War fort. Descend the access trail from the Canal Lands Park informational kiosk. After 200 feet, turn left on the Ohio and Erie Canal towpath. Though this part of the canal has not been used for commerce in living memory, it still holds enough water to suggest the era when canal boats plied the waters and mules plodded the towpath. Eagles, raccoons, deer, and other wildlife may appear along the ancient towpath beside the Tuscarawas River.

Continue for 0.2 miles and cross beneath Dover Zoar Road. The route is bordered by basswood, ash, and sycamore trees, many of which are festooned with luxuriant vines of poison ivy.

The trail soon reaches a steel-truss road bridge that is devoted nowadays to nonmotorized users. This spot is significant in that it is the junction where the NCT, arriving from Pennsylvania, begins to share the Buckeye Trail's tread and continues doing so for close to a thousand miles. Climb the wooden stairs (Z-002) to the bridge, and walk across the bucolic river to the other side. Follow the unused, grassed-over, asphalt road to Dover Zoar Road.

Communal living with hundreds of other people is clearly an acquired taste and evidently not terribly popular, given the lack of such communities in America. But there was a time when their popularity was greater than today, and America offered the freedom for groups to practice this lifestyle, which proved to be quite a commitment. Walking through Zoar Village gives some perspective with which to compare lifestyles of the present. Strolling through the small, quaint town of Zoar Village with a local guide is a great way to learn more of the origins of its unusual lifestyle. What might life be like if electricity and modern conveniences were no longer available? What if everything was shared? Could Zoar's clever technology and peaceful ways make up for the loss of automobiles, dishwashers, and computers? (Note: Zoar Village would be washed away if its protective levee were to collapse. To learn how to help the Zoar Community Association, visit www.zca.org/membership.html.)

Walk northeast on Dover Zoar Road, which very soon occupies part of the Corps of Engineers levee protecting historic Zoar Village from floods. Drop down across the grass to the town's parking lot. Walk along its west side to Zoar's post office on First Street.

Turn right and walk 100 feet to Main Street, heading north. As mentioned earlier, this historic thoroughfare is a showcase of one of the early 19th century's finest communal settlements. Walk 0.3 miles uphill through Zoar Village (Z-003). The Zoar Bakery, at 430 Main Street, is, sad to say for hungry hikers, purely ornamental.

Ohio—Zoar

Waypoint ID	Description	Mileage	Latitude	Longitude
Z-001	Canal Lands Park	0.00	40.60714	−81.42667
Z-002	Wooden Stairs	0.11	40.60850	−81.42845
Z-003	Zoar Village	0.38	40.61054	−81.42486

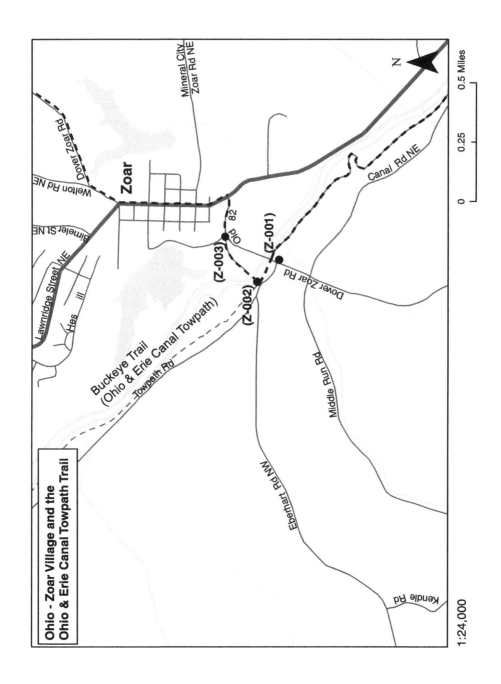

Ohio - Zoar Village and the
Ohio & Erie Canal Towpath Trail

Zoar

Mineral City
Zoar Rd NE

Dover Zoar Rd

Welton Rd NE

Bimeler St NE

Lawnridge Street NE

Hes
ill

Buckeye Trail
(Ohio & Erie Canal Towpath)

Towpath Rd

(Z-002)

(Z-003)

OIO

82

(Z-001)

Dover Zoar Rd

Canal Rd NE

Middle Run Rd

Eberhart Rd NW

Kendle Rd

N

0   0.25   0.5 Miles

1:24,000

3. Hocking Hills State Park/State Forest (Grandma Gatewood memorial to Ash Cave parking lot on State Route 56)

Distance: 5.15 miles
Physical difficulty: Moderate
Navigation difficulty: Easy
Highlights: Old Man's Cave, Cedar Falls, and Ash Cave
Visitation: High (3.3 million people visited the most popular spots
    in 2010)
Nearest town: Logan, OH

The Hocking Hills region is celebrated as the most beautiful landscape of southeast Ohio, and the NCT/Buckeye Trail passes right through the heart of it on the 6-mile Grandma Gatewood Trail. This hike, from Old Man's Cave to Ash Cave, is also the route of the annual Hocking Hills Winter Hike, which draws crowds of 5,000 people in the NCT's largest organized "hike." Annual visitation to the area is pegged at over three million visitors, giving credence to the claim that the Hocking Hills hike is the most popular one on the entire NCT.

The trail's namesake, Grandma Gatewood (1887–1973), was a hiking celebrity—the first woman to solo thru-hike the Appalachian Trail and an early activist for and founding member of the Buckeye Trail Association. Gatewood loved this scenic jewel of the unglaciated Allegheny Plateau for its superb hiking, exciting biodiversity, and exotic sandstone gorges. If she visited the Old Man's Cave area today, she would find the Naturalist Log Cabin, the State Park Visitor Center, a dining lodge, and plenty of lodging, shopping, and dining. Happily, she would also still be able to experience the charm and beauty of the trail, now named in her honor, and places she loved, such as the 700-foot-wide by 90-foot-tall Ash Cave, the largest rock shelter east of the Mississippi.

Trip Planner

Map: Buckeye Trail Old Man's Cave Section Map, available from
    www.buckeyetrail.org
www.dnr.state.oh.us/Portals/2/parkmaps/hockinghillstrailmap.pdf
Beginning access: Grandma Gatewood Plaque (HH-001)

Parking: Parking lot with access to Old Man's Cave
Ending access: Ash Cave parking lot on State Route 56 (HH-008)
Parking: Parking lot at Ash Cave
Contact information:
OH Regional Trail Coordinator: HQ@northcountrytrail.org
BTA Old Man's Cave Section: oldmanscave@buckeyetrail.org,
   info@buckeyetrail.org, www.buckeyetrail.org/sec-oldmanscave.html
Hocking Hills State Park, 19852 St. Rte. 664 S, Logan, OH 43138;
   740-385-6842; www.dnr.state.oh.us/tabid/743/default.aspx

Trail Guide

This hike begins at Old Man's Cave, with the bronze plaque (HH-001) honoring Grandma Gatewood. Cross the bridge, and follow the trail down to the Upper Falls, the most photographed waterfall in Ohio and the site of an early water-powered mill.

After passing the Devil's Bathtub (a natural bowl formed by erosion), descend the rock steps originally built by the Civilian Conservation Corps in the 1930s during the Great Depression. Entering this gorge, look for some of the plants unique to the area. Even though glaciers never reached the park, their influence is evident in the vegetation. Even after the glaciers retreated, the cool, moist climate persisted in deep gorges such as these in the Hocking Hills, leaving behind remnant species such as hemlock, Canada yew, and yellow and black birch. Note how sandstone acts like a giant, moist sponge to create a perfect home for large eastern hemlocks.

At the side steps to the State Park Visitor Center, many people report seeing a light-colored image of a whale on the cliff wall. Ferns, vines, and mosses adorn the walls in a stage set for a hidden world made all the more exotic by the upended roots of hemlocks.

Nearby and worth noting is Conkle's Hollow State Nature Preserve, which holds the deepest gorge in Ohio, at over 200 feet on both sides. Noted for the views from its sandstone bluff top, spring wildflowers, and a 100-foot-wide Lower Gorge, this preserve can accommodate visitors of all abilities (but no pets). Situated off State Route 374 on Big Pine Road, Conkle's Hollow is so deep and narrow that little sunlight reaches its valley floor.

At the spectacular, natural overhang that is Old Man's Cave, imagine the life of pioneer/hermit Richard Roe, the namesake "old man" who lived here for many years (and died here) in the early 1800s. Look for the spiny-stemmed plant known as devil's walkingstick. Useful to the Native Americans as a food source, its fall-ripening berrylike fruit was prized. Women would put the aromatic flowers in their hair because of the lemony smell.

At Lower Falls (HH-002), avoid the temptation to take a prohibited swim.

The trail turns upstream along Queer Creek, heading generally east. After 4,100 feet, the trail passes beneath an inconspicuous rock shelter from which a trickle of water falls during the summer. In winter, this site hosts a stalagmite and stalactite ice formation. Just across a bridge, the trail reaches a sign that says "OMC 2.0 miles" and points also to a trail going to the north end of the Cedar Falls parking lot. Stay on the NCT/Buckeye Trail as it turns southeast up a gorge across two bridges.

The trail climbs westerly on steps through a gorge cut by a tributary to Queer Creek. Soon, a trail diverges east past an overlook of Cedar Falls and continues up to a small parking area off State Route 374 (HH-003).

The trail continues south up stairs to the parking area, heads west beside a drive through an orange pipe gate, and ascends west gradually on a service road. At a three-way junction, the trail continues southwest on a service road across a culvert. As the trail leaves the service road, it climbs steeply and heads south onto a footpath along a creek.

The trail heads south through a parking area, around the gate to a fire tower. The trail then turns southwest downhill on a footpath to a service road, which it crosses and later rejoins. At the end of the service road, the trail descends on a footpath for about one-third of a mile, joining a footpath along an intermittent stream. After another one-third of a mile, the trail goes down a set of wooden steps into Ash Cave (HH-004).

The largest rock shelter in Ohio, Ash Cave's ceiling is 90 feet high. The rim of the cave is horseshoe-shaped, with an intermittent stream falling from above, creating a wonderful sound as well as spectacular ice formations in colder weather. About 100 feet deep, the cave is named for the great piles of ashes European explorers discovered within in the 1830s. Commonly attributed to Native Americans, the possible reason for the ash piles remains obscure.

Picnic facilities are available near Ash Cave. A shelter may be reserved. Call Hocking Hills State Park for information (740-385-6842). Follow the trail 0.39 miles to the Ash Cave parking area (HH-005).

Ohio—Hocking Hills State Park/State Forest

Waypoint ID	Description	Mileage	Latitude	Longitude
HH-001	Grandma Gatewood			
	Plaque	0.00	39.43635	−82.53911
HH-002	Lower Falls	1.06	39.42307	−82.54528
HH-003	Small Parking Area			
	off State Route 374	2.38	39.41833	−82.52475
HH-004	Ash Cave	4.76	39.39958	−82.54424
HH-005	Ash Cave Parking Area	5.15	39.39612	−82.54551

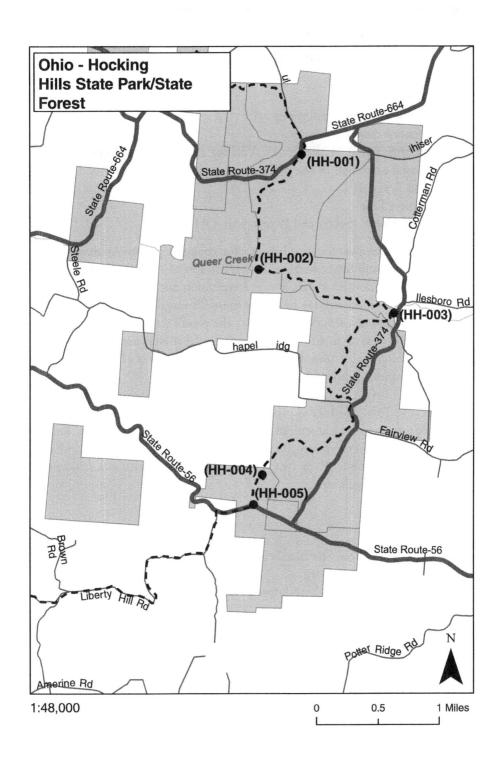

Ohio - Hocking Hills State Park/State Forest

State Route-664

State Route-664

ihiser

State Route-374

(HH-001)

Steele Rd

State Route-664

Cotterman Rd

Queer Creek (HH-002)

Ilesboro Rd

(HH-003)

hapel idg

State Route-374

Fairview Rd

State Route-56

(HH-004)

(HH-005)

State Route-56

Brown Rd

Liberty Hill Rd

Potter Ridge Rd

N

Amerine Rd

1:48,000

0   0.5   1 Miles

4. Shawnee State Forest (Forest Road 6 to State Route 125)

Distance: 2.3 miles
Physical difficulty: Challenging
Navigation difficulty: Moderate
Highlights: Ohio's "Little Smokies" deliver a southern Appalachian forest ecosystem in one of the most southerly areas of the NCT/ Buckeye Trail.
Visitation: Low
Nearest towns: Peebles and Portsmouth, OH

This southernmost featured hike is close enough to Kentucky that there is always a possibility of hearing the faint strains of "Dixie" when the wind is right. There's also a chance to see vegetation not present farther north, perhaps the most striking being the umbrella magnolia, whose individual leaves can reach 30 inches in length. The plant's fragrant, May-blooming flowers can be up to a foot wide. Be sure to visit Shawnee State Park Nature Center for an introduction to the Shawnee Forest's flora and fauna, including many rare and endangered species.

This hike is part of a 14-mile contiguous off-road section of the NCT/ Buckeye Trail. The hike is primarily downhill, and nearby Shawnee State Park provides all the amenities for a comfortable vacation at a rustic lodge, complete with a swimming pool and a restaurant. For information, call the park at 740-858-6621 or visit www.dnr.state.oh.us/parks/parks/shawnee/tabid/788/Default.aspx.

Trip Planner

Map: Buckeye Trail Shawnee Section Map, available from www.buckeyetrail.org
www.ohiodnr.com/Portals/18/forests/pdf/Shawnee%20Backpack%20Broch_2.pdf
Beginning access: From the state park kiosk on State Route 125, drive 0.1 miles to Forest Road 3. Turn right on Forest Road 3 and go 1.9 miles. Turn right and follow Forest Road 6 for 0.1 miles to the trailhead (SSF-001).

Parking: Informal, at trailhead
Ending access: The trailhead opposite the Shawnee State Park kiosk
on State Route 125 (SFF-002)
Contact Information:
OH Regional Trail Coordinator: HQ@northcountrytrail.org
BTA Shawnee Section: info@buckeyetrail.org

Trail Guide

Begin walking south at the NCT/Buckeye Trail trailhead on Forest Road 6
(SFF-001). After a brief rise, follow the trail downhill through the forest.
Look for sassafras, hickory, yellow poplar, American beech, dogwood, and
white and red oak.

Initially steep, the trail then becomes a lovely, gradual, serpentine descent to a seasonal streambed. Many of the tall trees, such as white oak
and yellow poplar, host very healthy poison ivy vines. During the summer,
the air is likely to hum with the buzzing of several kinds of bees and other
insects.

The trail weaves and crosses the bed of an unnamed creek. Look for the
long, oblong leaves of the pawpaw tree and for the impressive, leafy whorls
of the umbrella magnolia. They benchmark this southerly hike. Continue

Shawnee State Park has a fascinating nature center that schedules a variety
of fun activities for amateur naturalists. Its wild edible walks, creek crawls,
and informative wildlife programs are fun for the whole family. Check the cal-
endar of nature programs that is posted at the lodge, park office, nature center, and campground for more details.

The nature center offers visitors the opportunity to gain hands-on experience with local flora and fauna. Open between Memorial Day and Labor
Day, the center is located at the east end of Turkey Creek Lake on State
Route 125. (If the center is closed, the park office is happy to assist with any
questions about natural history.) Contact naturalist Jenny Richards, Shawnee
State Park Region (4404 St. Rte. 125, West Portsmouth, OH 45663; 740-858-
6652).

to follow the trail's gentle grade, now up a different tributary, through its understory of umbrella magnolias. After 0.2 miles, the trail switches to an even smaller tributary and begins a steep ascent—the final on this hike.

The descent will be more gradual. On this side of the ridge, the trail is well constructed. Soon, it wanders into the bottom of another creek valley. Hikers emerge at the parking lot near the state park's informational kiosk on State Route 125 (SFF-002).

Ohio—Shawnee

Waypoint Id	Description	Mileage	Latitude	Longitude
SSF-001	Parking	0.0	38.76786	−83.19726
SSF-002	Trailhead	2.3	38.74231	−83.19730

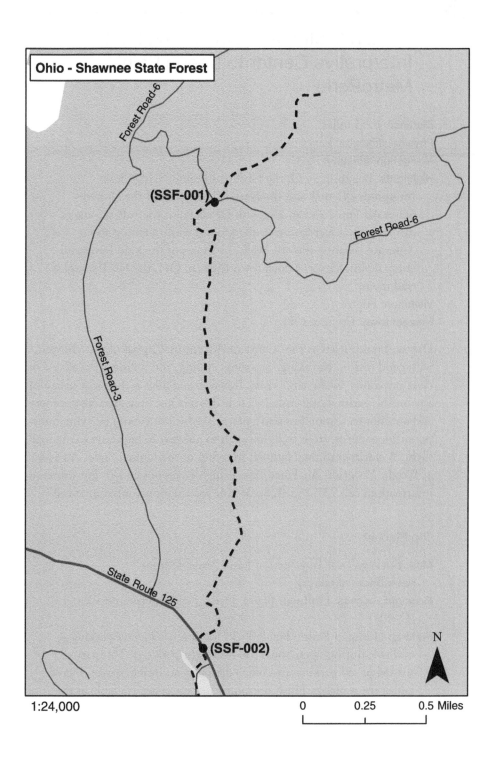

Ohio - Shawnee State Forest

Forest Road-6

(SSF-001)

Forest Road-6

Forest Road-3

State Route 125

(SSF-002)

N

1:24,000

0   0.25   0.5 Miles

5. Dayton (Huffman Prairie Flying Field Interpretive Center to Deeds Point MetroPark)

Distance: 6.33 miles
Physical difficulty: Easy
Navigation difficulty: Easy
Highlights: Beginning with the Huffman Prairie Flying Field Interpretive Center and the National Museum of the United States Air Force and ending with Deeds Point MetroPark, hikers can keep their feet firmly on the ground while learning about America's aviation history. Walk the shores of the Mad River and enjoy skyline views of downtown Dayton, OH, the NCT's largest trail town.
Visitation: High
Nearest town: Dayton, OH

Dayton brands itself as the "Outdoor Adventure Capital of the Midwest," with good reason. Kayaking, canoeing, cycling, and hiking are available in close proximity to the city's core. This featured hike is the most urban of any on the entire 4,600-mile NCT. It delivers not only attractive scenery and outdoor recreation but also a practical education about evolving transportation patterns, from trails to canals to railways to highways to manned flight. A side trip to the National Museum of the United States Air Force at Wright-Patterson Air Force Base is highly recommended. For museum information, call 937-255-3286 or visit www.nationalmuseum.af.mil/.

Trip Planner

Map: Buckeye Trail Troy Section Map, available from www.buckeyetrail.org
Beginning access: Huffman Prairie Flying Field Interpretive Center (D-001)
Parking: Huffman Prairie Flying Field Interpretive Center parking— available during open hours (no overnight parking). This partially shaded paved parking area offers disability accessible spaces. Picnic tables are available. Flush restrooms and water are available in the interpretive center.

Ending access: Deeds Point MetroPark (510 Webster Street, Dayton, OH; 937-275-7275) (D-009)

Parking: Free street parking along Deeds Park Drive, directly adjacent to Deeds Point MetroPark

Contact information:

OH Regional Trail Coordinator: HQ@northcountrytrail.org

Five Rivers MetroParks: email@metroparks.org; 937-275-7275

www.metroparks.org/GetOutside/NorthCountryandBuckeyeTrail.aspx

info@buckeyetrail.org

More information:

www.metroparks.org/recreation

www.metroparks.org/GetOutside/NorthCountryandBuckeyeTrail.aspx

www.mvrpc.org/transportation/bikeways-pedestrians

www.nps.gov/daav/index.htm

Five Rivers MetroParks is a regional agency that promotes a dynamic mix of conservation, education, and recreation in the belief that physically active citizens make Dayton a stronger, more vibrant place to live. Local municipalities and government agencies have collaborated to promote the idea that people will thrive if they have a livable, nature-rich community to call home. Thus, Dayton is a "Bicycle Friendly Community," with the largest connected bikeways network in the country. Dayton is also home to three state-designated water trails and to hundreds of miles of hiking trails (including the Buckeye Trail and the NCT). These and other attractions are showcased each October at the Midwest Outdoor Experience (see www.outdoorx.org) and each February at the Adventure Summit (see www.metroparks.org/adventuresummit/).

MetroParks programs include backpacking, road cycling, mountain biking, fly-fishing, and kayaking (see www.metroparks.org). The goal is to shepherd novices until they gain the confidence to become independent outdoor enthusiasts. Once they have the skills, they can incorporate their experiences into a newly active lifestyle by backpacking the Twin Valley Trail, kayaking the Mad River, or mountain biking local trails, all within 20 minutes of downtown Dayton.

Trail Guide

Begin hiking at the Huffman Prairie Flying Field Interpretive Center's hill-top (D-001) north of downtown Dayton. The spirit of the famous avia-tion inventors, Wilbur and Orville Wright, permeates this city and this featured hike. The National Park Service's interpretive center commemo-rates the years when the two brothers tinkered with their original flying machine at a nondescript farm pasture nearby, until they had worked out the controls that, to this day, enable airplanes to fly in a sustained, directed manner. Contrasting that modern achievement are the center's two large and four small burial mounds, dating back to Dayton's prehistoric mound-building culture.

Cross the spacious grounds, past the picnic tables and prehistoric mounds, and descend through the ash forest. Follow the trail through the woods paralleling the Air Force base's chain-link fence and parking lot; do not cross the railroad tracks. Where the trail emerges (D-002) from the woods at a railroad overpass, walk the grassy shoulder of the four-lane Springfield Pike. From Gate 1B of Wright-Patterson Air Force Base, con-tinue west beside the road on the grass, following the blue blazes.

At Gate 28B visitors can make a side visit to the National Museum of the United States Air Force, Ohio's premier tourist attraction and one of the world's finest aviation museums. For information, visit www.national museum.af.mil/.

At the intersection of Springfield and Bong (Gate 28B) turn right and immediately left on Huberville Avenue. Continue until the Comfort Suites hotel. Turn right beside an antebellum yellow-brick mansion. Follow the grass lane (below Harshman Road) to the railroad tracks. Carefully cross the tracks and continue northwest through the grass. Walk the pavement of an access road to beyond a maintenance facility. Reach a large, sliding gate, enter it, and continue along the same access road. Go straight onto grass toward the river where the access road turns left.

Do not cross Harshman Road at crosswalk. Walk parallel to it down the grass slope to the Mad River (D-003), then turn left under the highway bridge to follow the river downstream. On the left, there is a shady picnic area (D-004) complete with parking, tables, and changing cabanas. This is a popular put-in for kayakers.

Follow the trail along its woodsy corridor of ash, locust, and sycamore beside Mad River. This is Dayton's most popular stretch of river for pad-

dlers of all levels. Hiking this cool and shady trail is made more pleasant still by the sound of the cheery current. Listen for the chatter of kingfishers and the quacking of mallards.

The trail parallels the river for 0.1 miles across the grass to a double blue blaze (D-005). Turn left toward a large sycamore tree, easy to locate by its patchwork of smooth, scaly, gray bark, unusual among the park's stately ash trees. Cross the canal bridge. Turn right at the interpretive signs for the NCT/Buckeye Trail (D-006).

Follow the paved Mad River Recreation Trail along the river past a fire department training facility. Walk the trail under the high-voltage lines. After passing a large factory, go under the Findlay Street Bridge (D-007). An inviting skyline prospect of distant, downtown Dayton will open before you.

As the Mad River courses toward the fabled city of innovation, the path beside the grassy dike recalls the last great flood, in 1913, when the city was almost washed away. That disaster inspired the community to create the Miami Conservancy District's elaborate dam and levee system, under the mantra "Never Again!"

Approaching the city, flocks of geese will be prevalent, as is a shoreline invaded with purple loosestrife, an exotic weed with a beautiful flower competing too successfully with native species such as cattails. Note the old stone aqueduct abutment, which long ago carried a canal over the river. Most spectacular of all is downtown Dayton's magical, sky-high Five Rivers Fountains of Light. Six towers shoot water 200 to 400 feet in the air to create one of the largest fountain displays in the world. The show erupts every hour, on the hour, for about five minutes.

Leave the Mad River Recreation Trail by crossing a pedestrian overpass to Deeds Point MetroPark (D-008) at the confluence of the Great Miami and Mad Rivers. One of America's loveliest urban parks, Deeds Point is a convenient place from which to explore Dayton's scenic, historic, and educational treasures. If time permits, walk back across the bridge and turn east on the recreation trail, traveling 0.2 miles to RiverScape MetroPark. Stroll along its Inventor's River Walk to learn more about why Dayton is known as the innovation capital of the world. This hike concludes in the Deeds Point parking lot (D-009).

In 1796, Israel Ludlow surveyed and platted the town of Dayton along the Great Miami and Mad Rivers. Within a year, more than 40 log cabins and frame houses were built. Within 50 years, Dayton had become one of the largest and wealthiest communities in Ohio, in part due to the completion of the Miami and Erie Canal in 1829, which connected Lake Erie with the Ohio River.

Dayton was heavily involved in Ohio's early industrialization. In the 1880s, John H. Patterson opened the National Cash Register Company in Dayton. Later, two brothers, Orville and Wilbur Wright, firmly cemented Dayton's legacy by making the first successful flight in a powered aircraft.

The devastating Flood of 1913 temporarily halted the city's growth. But the people of Dayton recovered from the disaster and helped create the Miami Conservancy District to limit future flooding. These efforts led to the abundance of green corridors throughout the city, as levees, now often topped with parks and trails, wind along the river corridors.

Dayton was on the world stage in 1995 as the site of the Dayton Peace Accords. With the support of the United States, Serb and Bosnian representatives negotiated a peace settlement at Wright-Patterson Air Force Base that led to a decline in ethnic violence in Bosnia. Visit the peace monument at Deeds Point MetroPark at the end of this hike.

Ohio—Dayton

Waypoint Id	Description	Mileage	Latitude	Longitude
D-001	Huffman Prairie Flying Field Interpretive Center	0.00	39.79529	−84.08879
D-002	Springfield Pike	0.42	39.79392	−84.09581
D-003	Under Harshman Road Bridge	2.16	39.78834	−84.12326
D-004	Picnic Area	3.02	39.78229	−84.13701
D-005	Double Blue Blaze	3.22	39.78097	−84.14039
D-006	Interpretive Sign	3.35	39.77950	−84.13922
D-007	Findlay Street Bridge	4.60	39.77468	−84.15977
D-008	Pedestrian Overpass	6.20	39.76667	−84.18659
D-009	Deeds Point Metropark Parking Lot	6.33	39.76875	−84.18623

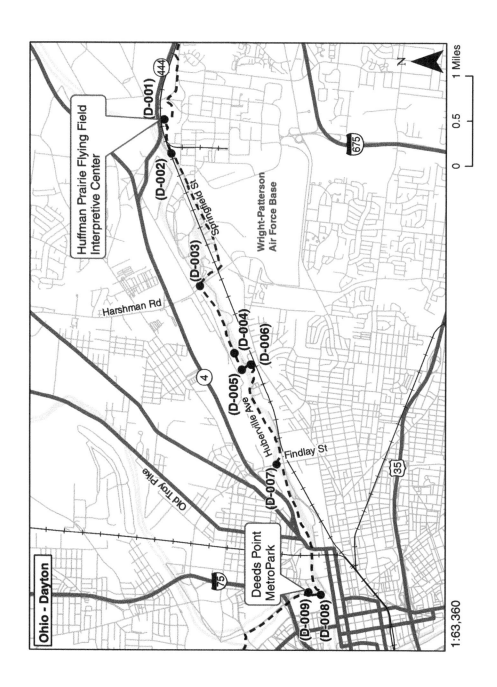

Ohio - Dayton

Huffman Prairie Flying Field
Interpretive Center

(D-001)

(D-002)

(D-003)

(D-004)

(D-005)

(D-006)

(D-007)

(D-008)

(D-009)

Harshman Rd

Old Troy Pike

Springfield St

Huberville Ave

Findlay St

Wright-Patterson
Air Force Base

Deeds Point
MetroPark

444

4

75

675

35

N

0   0.5   1 Miles

1:63,360

6. Snaketown (Snaketown to Meyerholtz Park)

Distance: 6.1 miles
Physical difficulty: Easy
Navigation difficulty: Easy
Highlights: This is a good place to learn about the War of 1812, the Great Black Swamp, the Maumee Valley Heritage Corridor, the Henry County Park District, and the Miami and Erie Canal towpath. Or, forget the history and just go out for a delightful stroll!
Visitation: Low
Nearest town: Napoleon, OH

This hike is perfect for a saunter beside a pretty river, catching the glint of sunlight on the ripples. Nothing could be more relaxing than to explore from Snaketown (Florida, OH) to Meyerholtz Park on the NCT/Buckeye Trail. Begin on a towpath alive with surprises—whether turtles sunning on logs, eagles flying the Maumee River, or the mysterious past of Girty's Island. The hike ends at Meyerholtz Park's primitive camping area, where camping is allowed by the approval of the City of Napolean Parks and Recreation Department (419-592-4010).

Trip Planner

Map: Buckeye Trail Defiance Section Map, available from www.buckeyetrail.org
Beginning access: Independence Dam State Park parking lot (ST-001)
Parking: Independence Dam State Park parking lot
Ending access: Meyerholtz Park (ST-009)
Parking: Meyerholtz Park parking area
Contact information:
OH Regional Trail Coordinator: HQ@northcountrytrail.org
BTA Renegade Section: info@buckeyetrail.org
BTA Defiance Section: info@buckeyetrail.org
henrycountyparks.blogspot.com/2011/02/welcome-to-henry-county-ohio-parks.html
www.blackswamp.org/
www.maumeevalleyheritagecorridor.org/
www.metroparkstoledo.com/metro/parksandplaces/index.asp?page_id=517

Trail Guide

This hike, at the site of the former Native American village Snaketown (subsequently known as Florida, OH), begins at Independence Dam State

Reminiscing on the early days in the development of the Buckeye Trail, Greg Wisniewski, Buckeye Trail Association Renegade Section president, remembers, "This trail was uniquely developed by volunteers from all the surrounding communities. One of the best examples was a 17-year-old Eagle Scout named Josh Cox from Troop 147. He is now an engineering and German student at Ohio Northern University. People like Josh are what make the trail possible for everyone to enjoy."

Josh Cox responds, "Because I love hiking, I chose to help the Buckeye Trail Association to restore and preserve the Buckeye Trail from the Spillman Bridge just east of Snaketown to State Route 109 just west of Napoleon. My project consisted of three parts. In Part One, we built and cleared 1/4 mile of the trail of all roots, shrubs, limbs, etc. In Part Two, I organized a crew to pull out 800 pounds of trash, 23 bags of garbage, 26 tires, 5 truckloads of metal, 11 55-gallon drums, a refrigerator, and a stove. In the Final Part, I led a team that constructed 3 benches and placed them along the trail. I had 20 volunteers who worked 198 1/2 hours. I spent 55 1/2 hours planning and working, which included drawing up blueprints, contacting businesses and organizations for donations to build the benches and other expenses, contacting the landfill, buying materials, finding and supplying the proper tools to be used, etc. I took the metal to a recycling center and used the money I received toward expenses for the benches. I also donated one load of metal to the Scrap Metal for Kids Christmas Program. The volunteers ranged in age from 10 to 60 years old. All debris was removed from the canal by manual labor. The entire project meant a lot to me because the trail is a great place where I can meditate, hike, and enjoy the great outdoors. Planning and executing my project was definitely a learning experience that I will cherish my whole life."

Park's parking lot (ST-001). On the south side of the canal, walk along the private driveway of an abandoned house. Continue on the Miami and Erie Canal towpath between the farm field and the canal's sylvan lining of ash, poplar, sycamore, redbud, locust, maple, hackberry, and walnut. After 200 foot, follow the canopied towpath into the trees, keeping an eye out for poison ivy. Follow the towpath in the same direction as the water flow, on its way north to Lake Erie. The canal-side homes of the village of Florida are soon left behind.

At the canal's dam, cross the narrow bridge to the north side. Continue east along the trail. After passing a part of the canal that was destroyed years ago, a newer section of the trail soon returns to the south side.

After about a half mile on public land, continue east onto the private property of Eberle Farm (ST-002), passing an outhouse and a cabin.

Pass Girty's Island (ST-003), supposedly the scene of "riotous doings" when early 20th-century residents sought refuge from the mores and strictures of the times.

Still on the Eberle Farm, pass a footbridge and a restored cabin. To see this location's old cemetery, in which resides at least one Revolutionary War veteran, veer right at the cabin and follow the path to the headstones. Just before the barn, there is an icehouse on the canal's north side, where big blocks of ice sawn from the frozen canal were stored for summer use. Potable water is available at the hose between the canal and the barn.

Follow the next canopy-free section past cropland to Coon Hollow, named for the preponderance of raccoons. At the farm access road (ST-004), continue along the towpath under its magnificent canopy of trees. Coon Hollow ends at an RV campground (ST-005) located on leased state land.

Follow the towpath through the canal's tall trees to a point where local residents have built an access road atop the towpath (ST-006). Use this gravel road until coming to where the resurrected towpath again enters the towpath canopy. Leaving the houses behind, with farm fields and RV campsites on the right and the canal on the left, the trail eventually returns to the river.

The trail leaves the towpath (ST-007) and enters the dry canal to reach the next trailhead at State Route 424.

Cross State Route 424 (W. Riverside Ave.) and walk along Henry County Road 15C to the nearby Wayne Park. This facility has a privy, potable water, and picnic amenities. Follow the stone-surfaced trail north past the stone-built shelter. Cross State Route 424 again on the bike trail on road shoulder (ST-008), walking north on road shoulder for 0.1 miles into Napoleon at the Meyerholtz Maumee River Access.

Follow the bike path where it soon diverges from State Route 424. Once again, the scenic/historic Maumee River will be on the right. This is Ritter Park in Napoleon. From a picnic pavilion, continue another mile to the primitive camping area at the end of this hike, at Meyerholtz Park (ST-009), beyond the boat launch.

Ohio—Snaketown

Waypoint ID	Description	Mileage	Latitude	Longitude
ST-001	Independence Dam State Park Parking Lot	0.00	41.32161	−84.20044
ST-002	Eberle Farm	2.40	41.33054	−84.16017
ST-003	Girty's Island	2.54	41.33065	−84.15770
ST-004	Farm Access Road	3.00	41.33319	−84.15002
ST-005	RV Campground	3.60	41.34120	−84.14568
ST-006	Access Road	4.08	41.34824	−84.14495
ST-007	Trail Junction—Towpath	5.18	41.36170	−84.15267
ST-008	Road Crossing State Route 424	5.43	41.36592	−84.15323
ST-009	Meyerholtz Park	6.10	41.37407	−84.14950

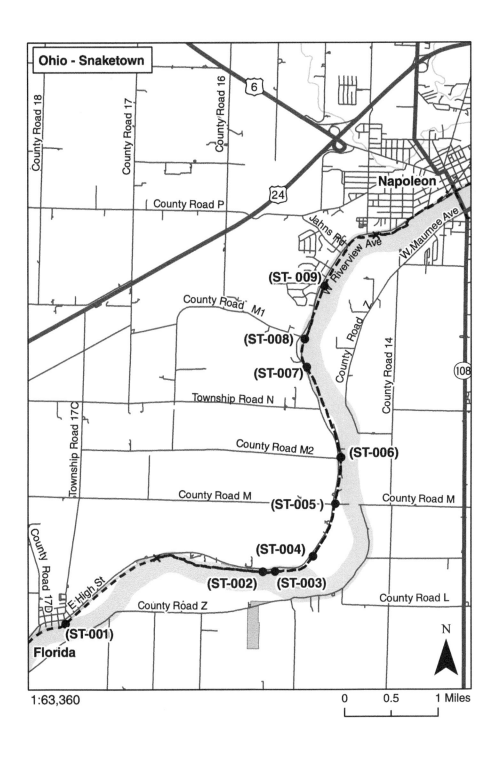

Michigan

Michigan holds a very special place in the NCT's geographical and symbolic landscape. Not only is it the trail's midpoint, but it carries more NCT miles (1,150) than any other state. Michigan is the state with the greatest number of NCTA chapters and volunteers. The NCTA was founded in Michigan, and its main office is located in Lowell, MI, the approximate halfway point on the trail. In addition, the National Park Service, which is the federal administrator of the trail as well as the NCTA's major partner, also has an office in Lowell.

Ohio hands off the NCT to Michigan at its southeast/central border, from which the trail journeys ever northward, leaving canal country behind in favor of lowland farms that give way to rolling forested sand hills. In the southern third of Michigan's Lower Peninsula, there are some truly exceptional sections of the NCT, but many connecting road miles in between await enterprising volunteers to adopt and build new sections of the trail. NCTA volunteers chip away at converting road miles to trail tread every year. Off-road bright spots already exist in Fort Custer National Cemetery, Yankee Springs State Recreation Area (a hike featured in this guide), and Middleville and Barry State Game Areas. A bit farther north are two more sizable off-road hikes at the Lowell State Game Area/Fallasburg County Park (a hike featured here) and the Rogue River State Game Area, before the NCT enters the Manistee National Forest for some truly wild country. Michigan's northern sections of the NCT are rich in magnificent forests and inspiring wildlands and wilderness. This hiking paradise resonates well with anyone who loves wildlife, woods lore, adventure, and walking in the footsteps of history.

The Manistee River Loop hike featured in this guide is the most popular hiking destination in Lower Michigan. Other classic Great North Woods hiking venues in the Lower Peninsula include the Pere Marquette State Forest, the Valley of the Giants, the Jordan River Pathway, the Mackinaw State Forest, the Wilderness State Park Loop, and the Mackinac Bridge.

In 1957, the "Big Mac Bridge" opened, linking the agricultural and industrial Lower Peninsula to the sparsely populated, heavily forested Upper Peninsula, or UP—an event long-lamented by "Yoopers," who preferred to keep their distance from the "trolls" living below the bridge. Of particular interest to hikers is the one morning a year they can actually hike this 5-mile stretch of the NCT—during the Labor Day Bridge Walk.

The UP delivers large lakes, old growth forests, rugged hills, and the shorelines of Lakes Superior and Michigan as the NCT wends its lonely way some 625 miles amid great tracts of remote, uninhabited country. From St. Ignace, just north of the Big Mac, the trail crosses the eastern UP in the Hiawatha National Forest, turning westerly toward Tahquamenon Falls State Park (home to a hike featured in this guide, the third largest waterfall in the eastern United States, and the only brewery located right on the NCT). Heading west, the NCT passes through Muskallonge Lake State Park, Lake Superior State Forest, and Pictured Rocks National Lakeshore.

The 43-mile Lakeshore Trail beside Lake Superior in Pictured Rocks National Lakeshore is widely considered to be one of the NCT's jewels. However, it is not highlighted in this book for several reasons. First, as befits a major unit of the National Park System, the bluffs and beaches of Pictured Rocks National Lakeshore already receive public visitation of over 425,000 annual visitors. Second, noted author Jim DuFresne has done a superb job of describing it in his highly recommended *Backpacking in Michigan* (beautifully published by the University of Michigan Press). Third, the NCTA seeks to introduce hikers to other worthy parts of Lake Superior's shoreline receiving far less notice and impact.

Continuing west in the Upper Peninsula, the NCT traverses the western unit of the Hiawatha National Forest, the city of Marquette, Presque Isle City Park, the McCormick Tract Wilderness Area, Craig Lake State Park, the Copper Country State Forest, the Sturgeon River Gorge Wilderness Area, and Old Victoria's copper mining district. In the Ottawa National Forest, the NCT follows the wild canyon of the Black River and eventually reaches a rugged finale in Porcupine Mountains Wilderness State Park before slipping over the border into Wisconsin.

The Peninsula State has something for everyone. In fact, the problem for Michigan's hikers is deciding where to start—which of the 13 featured hikes to choose first. Will it be the easily accessible Lower and Upper Tahquamenon Falls? Perhaps the greater physical challenge of the 18-mile Manistee River Loop might prove more enticing. Why limit the fun? Check off all of Michigan's highlighted hikes, one by one. Michigan's hikes are well supported by hiking maps available from the NCTA (northcountrytrail.org/shop).

Michigan's Featured Hikes

1. **Yankee Springs State Recreation Area and Barry State Game Area** (Norris Road west trailhead to Chief Noonday Road/State Route 179 trailhead)

2. **Lowell** (Lowell River Walk to Fallasburg Park)

3. **Birch Grove Trail Loop**

4. **Bowman Lake Loop**

5. **Manistee River Loop**

6. **Traverse City** (Guernsey Lake Campground to Dollar Lake parking area trailhead)

7. **Jordan River Pathway Loop**

8. **Wilderness State Park Loop** (West Sturgeon Bay Trail [county road] trailhead to Lakeview Road)

9. **Tahquamenon Falls State Park** (Lower Falls parking area to Upper Falls parking area)

10. **Lake Superior Shoreline** (Muskallonge Lake to Perry's Landing)

11. **Marquette** (Wetmore Landing to Echo Lake Road)

12. **Old Victoria Overlooks** (Norwich Road to the Old Victoria Restoration Site)

13. **Black River Falls** (Great Conglomerate Falls to Black River Harbor)

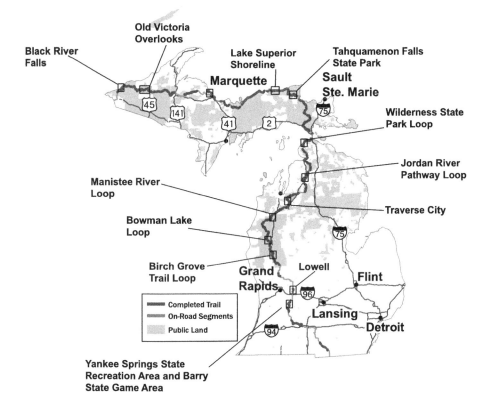

Old Victoria
Overlooks

Black River
Falls

Lake Superior
Shoreline

Tahquamenon Falls
State Park

Marquette

Sault
Ste. Marie

Wilderness State
Park Loop

Jordan River
Pathway Loop

Manistee River
Loop

Traverse City

Bowman Lake
Loop

Birch Grove
Trail Loop

Lowell

Grand
Rapids

Flint

Lansing

Detroit

Completed Trail
On-Road Segments
Public Land

Yankee Springs State
Recreation Area and Barry
State Game Area

1. Yankee Springs State Recreation Area and Barry State Game Area (Norris Road west to State Route 179 trailhead)

Distance: 7.4 miles
Physical difficulty: Moderate
Navigation difficulty: Easy
Highlights: Hall Lake, geological features, and opportunities for loop hikes
Visitation: Low
Nearest town: Middleville, MI

According to local legend, there once was an Indian village located midway between Kalamazoo and Grand Rapids. Its location, now called Middleville, is part of the NCT north of this Yankee Springs hike.

Yankee Springs Recreation Area was once the hunting domain of the Algonquin Indians and their famous leader Chief Noonday. In the mid-19th century, Yankee Springs (named for Yankee Bill Lewis, who owned and operated a hotel) was a stagecoach stop between Kalamazoo and Grand Rapids. Its namesake old spring is no more than 0.1 miles north of the west trailhead at Norris Road. From the trailhead, walk north/downhill along the power line until reaching the creek. Though the historic site is visually unimpressive (there are no dramatic ruins), it continues to serve as a source of water, although the water must be treated for drinking.

Local NCTA volunteers are especially proud of their "Little Mac" bridge, one of their earliest feats of construction. Yankee Springs State Recreation Area is a recreational mecca that provides opportunities for orienteering, geocaching, skiing, mountain biking, horseback riding, and, of course, hiking the NCT.

Trip Planner

Map: MI-02 (Michigan 02), available from www.northcountrytrail.org
Beginning access: Norris Road west trailhead (YSP-001)
Parking: The NCT crosses Norris Road at this location, and there are ample parking areas on both sides of that road.
Seasonal midpoint access: McDonald Lake or Bassett Lake Road crossing. These two locations are generally inaccessible in winter. There is ample parking at McDonald Lake, and there is limited parking at the Bassett Lake Road crossing.
Ending access: State Route 179 trailhead

Parking: There is ample parking at the State Route 179 (also known as Chief Noonday Rd.) trailhead (YSP-005).

Contact information:
Chief Noonday Chapter, NCTA: cnd@northcountrytrail.org, www.northcountrytrail.org/cnd

More information: No "dispersed camping" (i.e., camping along the trail) is permitted in the Yankee Springs State Recreation Area, where camping is restricted year-round to the designated campgrounds: the Deep Lake Unit on Yankee Springs Road and the Gun Lake Unit on Briggs Road. In the Barry State Game Area (between Bassett Lake Rd. and St. Rte.179), dispersed camping is allowed from October 1 through May 15 with a free permit, to be obtained from the Barry State Game Area Headquarters (Barry Field Office, 1805 S. Yankee Springs Rd., Middleville, MI 49333; 269-795-3280).

Trail Guide

This featured hike follows in the footsteps of the Native American trail that ran between Kalamazoo and Grand Rapids, later to become a stagecoach route. The NCTA's trailhead is located on land purchased in 1835 by Yankee Bill Lewis, who built a hotel to service travelers on the stage route. This hike is located mostly in the Yankee Springs Recreation Area, whose many trails are segregated according to use.

The hike begins at the westernmost of the two parking areas on Norris Road (YSP-001). Restricted dispersed camping is permitted just east of here, on the Barry State Game Area (with the seasonal restrictions and

The NCT passes through Michigan State University's W. K. Kellogg Biological Station's Pasture Dairy Center near Hickory Corners a few miles south of this featured hike. This 220-acre research farm houses scientists working on projects related to milk production as well as environmental restoration. Hikers are welcome to stop by the big white barn to learn about the future of efficient dairy farming. Professor Santiago Utsumi of Michigan State University says, "This 'smart farm' is unique. We use hi-tech equipment to demonstrate efficiency and reduced waste in small- to medium-sized dairies. Our cows even milk themselves at their own schedule. Come and see for yourself!"

Kellogg Biological Station is about 17 miles south of the Yankee Springs hike. Note also that the renowned Kellogg Bird Sanctuary is adjacent to the biological station. For information, visit www.kbs.msu.edu.

permit described earlier). The NCT follows a puncheon bridge and then climbs a hill, where the Michigan Department of Natural Resources did a prescribed burn in 2006 to maintain the open habitat required for cerulean warblers and rare butterflies. The trail then crosses a red pine plantation, a remnant of the Great Depression's Civilian Conservation Corps and their tree-planting efforts.

The trail crosses a junction (YSP-002) with a Department of Natural Resources horse trail, which can be followed north to access the Deep Lake Unit campground. For additional information about places to camp in the area managed by the NCTA's Chief Noonday Chapter, go to www .northcountrytrail.org/cnd/camping.htm.

Citizen stewardship is a conservation model in the United States that creates public and private partnerships to accomplish goals that could never otherwise be done. Without the sweat equity of thousands of volunteers over the past 30 years, the NCT would still be a conceptual drawing in a bureaucrat's file, buried somewhere in Washington, DC. Instead, there is a vibrant community of fiercely independent volunteers scattered the length of the trail, devoting their energies and resources to gifting America with this long-distance hiking trail.

Opportunities abound for volunteering on the NCT. Of course, the obvious ones have to do with building trail—using Mackenzies, Pulaskis, and other specialized trail tools to bench, level, and blaze. Maintainers use saws, loppers, mowers, and trimmers to keep the NCT clear and easy to follow. There are specialized needs requiring the talents of engineers, GIS-trained folks, and others.

The NCTA desperately needs folks who enjoy advocacy—building relationships and communicating with legislators and land managers. There's a need for folks skilled in communications, designing and writing newsletters, sending letters to the press, writing grants, and promoting events. There's a need for folks, skilled in outreach, who enjoy meeting people and telling the NCTA story. There are marketing needs as NCTA grows its membership. There are logistics needs in planning weekend work outings. Cooks are needed to provide meals for hungry trail crews. These wide-ranging opportunities are most often needed at the local level.

Although volunteers don't need to be members of the NCTA, the association enables volunteers to be most effective, and offers well-deserved recognition. Visit northcountrytrail.org/get-involved to learn more about how you can volunteer.

After continuing between two swamps, the trail crosses a white pine plantation. Next, the trail crosses the Old Pines Scenic Trail, continuing on a series of glacial moraines for the rest of this hike. Demonstrating the area's many recreational uses, the trail passes a post marked with information about the Southern Michigan Orienteering Club.

Spring-fed Hall Lake is not only very scenic but is also known for its fishing (bluegill, crappie, and bass). There is a public boat launch and parking to the right of where the trail emerges from the south onto Gun Lake Road (YSP-003). Hall Lake is at the beginning of a network of Department of Natural Resources trails and roads, some of which are also used by the NCT. All DNR trails and the NCT portions are clearly signed with labeled Carsonite posts, and the NCT is also blue-blazed.

Going north from Gun Lake Road, the trail is on its own for 0.2 miles and then follows successive segments of the Hall Lake Trail (0.7 mile), the Long Lake Trail (0.3 mile), and the Chief Noonday Trail (0.8 mile), before continuing on its own again for the remaining 2.8 miles to the State Route 179 trailhead. At Bassett Lake Road, 1 mile east of McDonald Lake, the trail crosses from the Yankee Springs Recreation Area into the Barry State Game Area (YSP-004), for the remainder of this hike.

The most significant landscape feature north of Hall Lake is the Devil's Soup Bowl, a wooded, glacially carved kettle formation surrounded by a moraine. There is a signed side trail to it.

A short distance past where the Chief Noonday Trail takes off from the Long Lake Trail, pass a small pond. Continue across parklike hills. Just before the side trail to McDonald Lake, there is a potentially confusing mix of NCT, snowmobile, and lake trails. Just follow the blue blazes past the trail kiosk. The NCT's Yankee Springs hike ends at the State Route 179 trailhead (YSP-005), also known as Chief Noonday Road.

To extend the hike, follow the NCT from that point northeasterly toward Middleville. See NCTA Map MI-02.

Michigan—Yankee Springs State Recreation Area and Barry State Game Area

Waypoint ID	Description	Mileage	Latitude	Longitude
YSP-001	Norris Road West Trailhead	0.0	42.60532	−85.46302
YSP-002	Trail Junction	0.5	42.60624	−85.46875
YSP-003	Gun Lake Road	2.6	42.61239	−85.48371
YSP-004	Barry State Game Area	5.5	42.63415	−85.48112
YSP-005	State Route 179 Trailhead aka Chief Noonday Road	7.4	42.63862	−85.45461

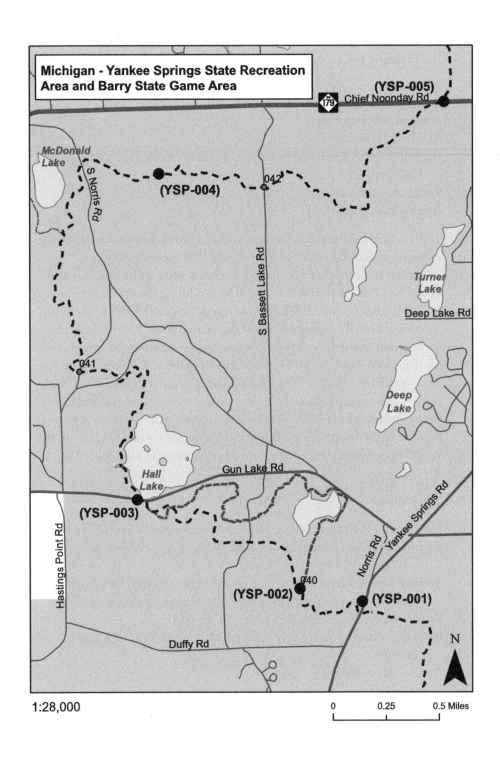

Michigan - Yankee Springs State Recreation Area and Barry State Game Area

(YSP-005)
Chief Noonday Rd

McDonald Lake

S Norris Rd

(YSP-004)

042

S Bassett Lake Rd

Turner Lake

Deep Lake Rd

041

Deep Lake

Hall Lake

Gun Lake Rd

(YSP-003)

Hastings Point Rd

Norris Rd

Yankee Springs Rd

(YSP-002)

040

(YSP-001)

Duffy Rd

N

1:28,000

0   0.25   0.5 Miles

2. Lowell (Lowell River Walk to Fallasburg Park Drive NE)

Distance: 7.8 miles
Physical difficulty: Easy
Navigation difficulty: Easy
Highlights: NCTA national headquarters, plus a scenic hike along the Flat River
Visitation: Moderate
Nearest town: Lowell, MI

This featured hike parallels the beautiful Flat River, famous for its history, plentiful smallmouth bass, waterfowl, and bald eagle sightings.

Lowell is a historic flour-milling town. Located at the junction of the Grand and Flat Rivers, the tall silos of King Milling Company have been a Lowell landmark since 1890. A more recent landmark from a hiker's perspective is Lowell's status as home of the National NCTA Headquarters.

The trail enters Lowell from the south, after crossing the Grand River on the Alden Nash/South Hudson Street Bridge and following the Flat River north into the city. The Kent County Fairgrounds offer NCT backpackers their first public camping opportunity since the Middleville State Game Area. Call 616-897-6050 to make a reservation. Camping may be possible farther north, at the Boy Scout Cabin, and is also available in the Lowell State Game Area except from May 15 through September 10.

Trip Planner

Map: MI-03 (Michigan 03), available from www.northcountrytrail.org
Beginning access: Start of Lowell River Walk at M-21 (Main St.) (L-001)
Parking: Lowell Municipal parking lot off Monroe Street. Park in the row closest to the library to avoid the two-hour parking section.
Ending access: Fallasburg Park Drive NE (L-013)
Parking: Fallasburg Park Drive north of McPherson Road. Parking is roadside.
Contact information:
Western Michigan Chapter, NCTA: wmi@northcountrytrail.org, www.northcountrytrail.org/wmi

Trail Guide

The Lowell featured hike begins at the River Walk on Main Street (L-001), just upstream from the Flat River's confluence with the Grand River.

The nerve center of the NCT (though not the heart and soul, as staff are quick to point out) is located at 229 East Main Street in Lowell, MI. The NCTA Headquarters houses all the NCTA staff except the three regional trail coordinators located in Minnesota, Wisconsin, and Ohio. The headquarters is on the corner of Monroe and Main Streets, just across from Lowell City Hall, one block east of the NCT as it crosses and then parallels the Flat River.

Lowell hosts both the NCTA Headquarters and the office of the National Park Service's NCT superintendent and trail manager, currently located in the Lowell Chamber of Commerce office building. The NCTA Headquarters was originally located in the Birch Grove Schoolhouse near White Cloud, now run as a hostelry by the NCTA's Western Michigan Chapter. It moved to Grand Rapids and then, in 2001, to its current location. The headquarters is roughly equidistant from the eastern and western termini of the NCT. Conveniently located for hikers, the headquarters has office and TrailShop hours from 9:00 to 4:30 on Monday through Friday. Call ahead (616-897-5987) or drop in. For directions and a map, visit northcountrytrail.org/contact-us/.

Look for Lowell's statue of a fishing troll, unique on the NCT. Follow the Riverwalk one block upstream to the faux sternwheeler *Robert E. Lee,* also known as the Lowell Showboat, source of summer entertainment for Lowell's residents since 1932.

Follow the Riverwalk past the library. Turn right at the boat launch (L-002). Go one block and turn left to walk north on North Monroe Street to the Oakwood Cemetery (L-003). Turn right on Fremont Street and follow it east along the cemetery's south boundary.

Turn left on North Washington Street. Follow it north to the NCT trailhead (L-004) on the right just before the Boy Scout Cabin. Parking is also available at the cabin for those preferring to start their hike at the Scout Cabin trailhead.

Follow the trail east as it begins to gradually swing north through a mature woods of red pine around the Boy Scout property. Cross the utility corridor, a cleared east-west swath known locally as "the sliding hill." Follow the trail into the woods. Soon it parallels the lazy, broad Flat River heading upstream.

At Devil's Peak (L-005) at the top of the riverside ridge, there is a blue-blazed arrow post directing hikers to make a sharp right away from the river and private property and into the Lowell State Game Area. Aside from seasonal hunters, the primary users of this trail are joggers.

Follow the trail south and briefly west through the pretty maple forest. On a cool, foggy morning, eastern box turtles will probably cheer your progress. Watch for the blue blazes to avoid straying onto unmarked hunters' trails. At 0.58 miles from Devil's Peak, the trail veers left at a directional post at the uphill edge of an oak savanna. The trail then emerges onto Grindle Drive (L-006). The distance from Washington Street to Grindle Drive is 1.2 miles.

Go west 0.25 miles on Grindle Drive. At a beige house where the road makes a 90-degree turn north, go straight and reenter the woods on the trail (L-007).

There is a parking spot where the trail crosses Grindle Drive (L-008) for the second time. The trail continues northerly through the woods, passing a pile of stones, a reminder of early settlers' attempts to clear the land for farming. Look for other signs of people's early uses of the landscape. Traverse a pine plantation, walk a small creek valley's puncheon bridge, and go over a stream crossing. Follow the trail across a wooded hill and descend to an unmarked junction on the edge of an opening. Turn left and cross the opening, reaching the paved Flat River Drive (L-009).

The trail crosses Flat River Drive, turns right, and parallels the road for about 100 yards. At a parking area, the trail angles to the left up a pine hill, to then descend a broad ridge to a rivulet. It switchbacks up again to a scenic overlook over the Flat River, with views reminiscent of those found in the UP. The trail follows a two-track hunting trail but turns left (watch for it!) before it reaches an ossuary of deer bones at a parking area on Montcalm Avenue.

A few hundred yards farther, the trail emerges onto the gravel Montcalm Avenue (L-010), where the road walk to the left (north) descends steeply through dense woods before leveling out along the river bottom. Follow Montcalm Avenue for almost a mile beside the scenic Flat River to Covered Bridge Road NE, where it makes a leftward diagonal crossing to get back onto the trail heading north.

This crossing is near the Fallasburg School Museum, which can be seen to the right (east). The 42-acre Fallasburg Historical Village's 19th-century buildings are a project of the Fallasburg Historical Society (see www.fallasburg.org) and include a historic and picturesque covered bridge 0.3 miles west.

The trail crosses the road (L-011) and passes behind the restored Tower Farm barn, then entering Fallasburg Park and skirting a disc golf course. Follow the banks of the Flat River through a picnic area to the large, concrete McPherson Street Bridge (L-012). The total distance from Covered Bridge Road to McPherson Bridge is 0.8 miles. The lower section of the bridge is pedestrian only.

Cross the Flat River on the pedestrian bridge, and look for the NCT's blue blazes to the right (north) immediately after crossing.

Follow the trail 0.9 miles along the thickly forested hillsides and west bank of the Flat River on some beautifully constructed hiking trail. The trail ends on climbing to Fallasburg Park Road. The distance from Main Street's Flat River Dam to the end point at Fallasburg Park Drive (L-013) totals 7.8 miles.

Michigan—Lowell

Waypoint ID	Description	Mileage	Latitude	Longitude
L-001	Main Street at Lowell River Walk at M-21 (Main Street)	0.0	42.93456	−85.33801
L-002	Boat Launch	0.2	42.93654	−85.33774
L-003	Oakwood Cemetery	0.6	42.94307	−85.33910
L-004	NCT Trailhead	1.2	42.94961	−85.33665
L-005	Devil's Peak	1.7	42.95198	−85.33079
L-006	Grindle Drive	2.3	42.94752	−85.32698
L-007	Trail Junction	2.6	42.94779	−85.32192
L-008	Grindle Drive	2.9	42.95129	−85.31961
L-009	Flat River Drive	4.2	42.96602	−85.32001
L-010	Montcalm Avenue	5.4	42.97331	−85.31264
L-011	Covered Bridge Road	6.4	42.98201	−85.32269
L-012	McPherson Street Bridge	7.1	42.98658	−85.33214
L-013	Fallasburg Park Drive	7.8	42.99169	−85.32732

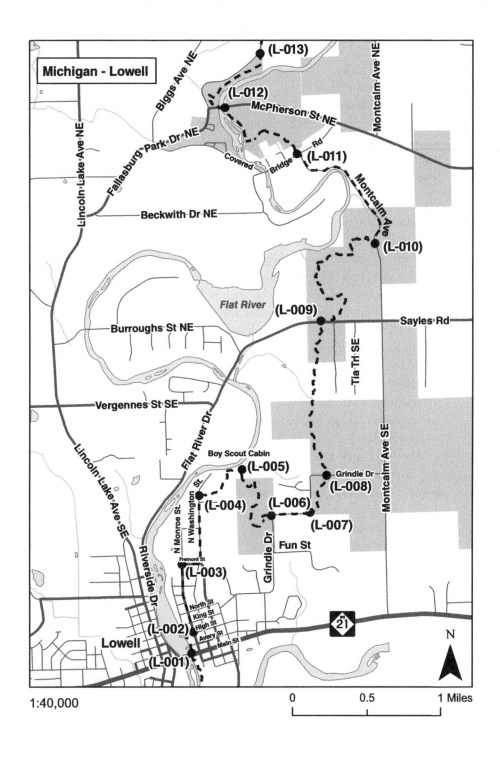

Michigan - Lowell

1:40,000

0   0.5   1 Miles

N

3. Birch Grove Trail Loop

Distance: 7.9 miles
Physical difficulty: Easy
Navigation difficulty: Easy
Highlights: Birch Grove Schoolhouse and Loda Lake Wildflower Sanctuary
Visitation: Low
Nearest town: White Cloud, MI

The Birch Grove hike celebrates the interconnected cultural and natural histories of central Michigan as well as the evolution of the NCTA. In the mid- to late 19th century, central Michigan's virgin white pine thundered away on an extensive network of logging railroads, downriver logging drives, and Lake Michigan lumber schooners to build the city of Chicago. Near the location of this hike, the town of Park City flourished while forests were stripped. After the timber was gone, farming settlers tried their luck with the mostly subpar sandy soils but were soon discouraged and abandoned their efforts. The Dust Bowl drought of the 1930s finished off those who remained, and both people and soil vanished from the area. The Manistee National Forest was formed in 1938, when the federal government acquired the abandoned logging lands and homesteads. The Civilian Conservation Corps planted untold numbers of pine trees in efforts to reclaim the land.

The NCT arrived four decades later, when the NCTA's first president and original promoter, Lance Feild, acquired Park City's abandoned one-room school. Fittingly located just off the midpoint of the NCT's entire 4,600 miles, it became the NCTA's first headquarters. Today, after decades of restoration by volunteers, the Birch Grove Schoolhouse serves the NCTA's Western Michigan Chapter as a meeting place, hiker shelter, and occasional hostelry. For more information or to reserve a spot, contact Birch

Grove Schoolhouse (3980 N. Felch Ave., White Cloud, MI 49399; 231-245-8455; northcountrytrail.org/wmi/schoolhouse.php).

Trip Planner

Map: See guidebook map.
Beginning access: Birch Grove Schoolhouse (BG-001)
Parking: There is plenty of parking at the schoolhouse.
Ending access: Birch Grove Schoolhouse
Contact information:
Western Michigan Chapter, NCTA: wmi@northcountrytrail.org,
    www.northcountrytrail.org/wmi
Huron-Manistee National Forest, 650 N. Michigan Ave., PO Box D,
    Baldwin, MI, 49304; 231-745-4631

Trail Guide

This hike is a loop, beginning and ending at the historic Birch Grove Schoolhouse (BG-001). Interpretive signs on the side of the schoolhouse give a rich history about the building, the surrounding area, and the NCT. There's a map there with an overview of the trail's path within the Manistee National Forest.

From the schoolhouse, start with a road walk heading north about 250

The **Huron-Manistee National Forest** is doing a major habitat restoration project around the NCT, just a half mile beyond the northernmost point of this featured hike. The goal is to re-create the savannah/barrens habitat that Europeans found when they arrived here in the mid-1800s. A side trip north is worthwhile to watch attempts at revival of this rare habitat of prairie grasses, including little and big bluestem, and forbs, such as butterfly weed and lupine.

The NCT showcases these types of northern ecosystems and habitats. This Loda Lake restoration project will be ongoing for several years and will involve the removal of nonnative trees and other vegetation. The cutting will be obvious to hikers, many of whom may wonder about the many stumps. At least one of the beneficiaries will be the endangered Karner blue butterfly.

feet on Felch Avenue. Turn left onto Five Mile Road, hiking west on this lightly traveled gravel road. After about a mile, Five Mile Road narrows. Continue a few hundred feet to intersect with Forest Road 5771.

Turn right (north-northwest) on Forest Road 5771. Continue along this road, which turns west. Here, the Forest Service uses blue paint to mark trees for cutting or to denote boundaries—be careful not to confuse these with the dollar bill–sized rectangles of the NCT blue blazes. A quarter mile past the intersection, the road becomes noticeably softer. Carefully looking along this roadbed may reveal the tracks of the various animals that make this area their home. Commonly sighted tracks include deer, raccoon, turkey, and snake. After another quarter mile, the road finally meets the NCT proper at the signed and marked trailhead (BG-002). At a little turnaround in the sandy oak forest, begin to walk north on the trail. Follow the trail through the beech-oak forest, crossing remnants of pine plantations planted by the Civilian Conservation Corps during the Great Depression. Grassy openings are dominated here by sedges, intermixed with ferns and wildflowers, such as Saint-John's-wort, bergamot, daisies, and black-eyed Susans.

After 1.2 miles cross a small wooden bridge over Mena Creek (BG-003). (Sam Mena was a logger/railroader in the late 19th century). Surmount a parklike, beech-covered hill and then travel along the woods south of West Six Mile Road.

Cross a heavy-duty gravel road (which connects to White Cloud) just south of its junction with Six Mile Road. Continue northeast through the woods, following the trail's blue blazes, to a junction (BG-004) with West Six Mile Road.

Turn right on Six Mile Road and walk 230 feet. Reenter the woods. Sign in at a register box at a grassed-in pond. Continue past several more eutrophic ponds. At the junction with the Birch Grove Trail (BG-005), a sign points north to Seven Mile Road (0.8 miles away) and south to Five Mile Road (3 miles away).

Go south on the white-blazed Birch Grove Trail. Note that the NCT continues north. Pass through a pine plantation and turn right on an old railroad grade. Continue through the woods for a total of 1 mile on the Birch Grove Trail.

In 1949, the US Forest Service, in conjunction with the Federated Garden Clubs, began to manage this spring-fed lake, wetland, and reverted-to-nature farm site as the Loda Lake Wildflower Sanctuary. Overnight camping is prohibited. A fascinating self-guiding nature walk begins at the picnic area.

After hiking on the Birch Grove Trail about a mile, views of Loda Lake will appear. Then the trail intersects with the Loda Wildflower Trail near a small pond with an outlet, over which a bridge carries both trails. Paralleling the north side of the stream, the trails come to another bridge back over it. The wetlands will be to the east or left of the trail, and careful observation reveals the birch grove giving rise to the trail's name.

The trails reach another intersection where the Loda Wildflower Trail heads to the southwest. Look for the kiosk at this intersection, with its interpretation of the history of the area. Stay on the white-blazed Birch Grove Trail, heading south to Five Mile Road (BG-006).

Tired hikers have the option to turn right and walk west 0.7 miles on the asphalt Five Mile Road to the Birch Grove Schoolhouse and the beginning of this loop. The more adventurous can travel about a half mile farther by crossing Five Mile Road to continue south on the Birch Grove Trail. These hikers will be rewarded with views of bogs in various stages of maturity. Sign in at the next registry box, at an intersection, then turn right (north), passing more bogs on your way back to again reach Five Mile Road, closer to the Schoolhouse. Turn left and hike the remaining half mile back.

Michigan—Birch Grove Trail Loop

Waypoint ID	Description	Mileage	Latitude	Longitude
BG-001	Birch Grove Schoolhouse	0.0	43.62571	−85.83106
BG-002	Trail Junction	1.6	43.62841	−85.86230
BG-003	Mena Creek	2.8	43.63428	−85.85057
BG-004	6 Mile Road	3.2	43.64042	−8584492
BG-005	Trail Junction—Birch Grove Trail	4.9	43.64951	−85.82825
BG-006	5 Mile Road	7.3	43.62625	−85.81699
BG-001	Birch Grove Schoolhouse	7.9	43.62571	−85.83106

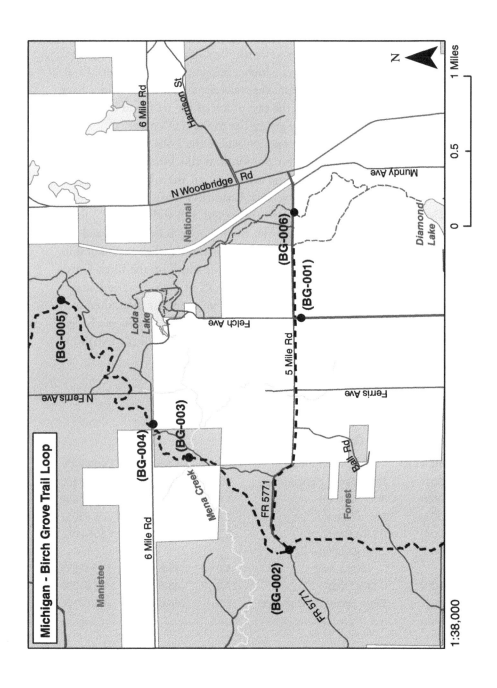

Michigan - Birch Grove Trail Loop

1:38,000

4. Bowman Lake Loop

Distance: 5.4 miles
Physical difficulty: Moderate
Navigation difficulty: Moderate
Highlights: Delightful oak-maple forest hike and Bowman Lake
Visitation: Moderate
Nearest town: Baldwin, MI

Unscrupulous land speculators lured unwary Europeans to worthless Michigan clear-cuts with advertisements promoting the region as an agricultural paradise; many took the bait and immigrated to America. They failed in farming these unproductive soils, and many farms were abandoned long before the Great Depression spiked the final nail in the coffin of those few remaining. Reverting to federal ownership, these abandoned farms eventually became part of the Manistee National Forest, which encompasses great tracts of woodlands in the west-central part of Michigan's Lower Peninsula. Bowman Lake and its surrounding area are managed for forest recreation and resource use, for the benefit of NCT hikers and others.

Trip Planner

Map: MI-04 (Michigan 04), available from www.northcountrytrail.org
Beginning access: 40th Street trailhead (BW-001)
Parking: Unimproved 40th Street parking area
Ending access: 40th Street trailhead
Parking: Unimproved 40th Street parking area

Volunteers are the key to the growing success of the NCT. Ed Chappel is a perfect example, illustrating the remarkable dedication and persistence of many NCT fans. Despite having Parkinson's disease, Ed physically led a three-year effort of the NCTA's Spirit of the Woods Chapter to transform a swamp slog into an attractive, wheelchair-accessible part of the NCT. South of the Bowman Lake Loop, at a bird-watching mecca known as Sterling Marsh, Ed worked ceaselessly to lead a variety of helpers (including many over age 70) to build more than a half mile of wooden tread, spread out across 1.5 miles of trail. Ed, who retired from the automobile industry, modestly downplays his own role. He says, "What our volunteers accomplished was unbelievable. Without our Senior Team's tremendous effort we would have nothing. As the trail coordinator, I was blessed with a great bunch of people."

Contact information:
Spirit of the Woods Chapter, NCTA: spw@northcountrytrail.org,
    www.northcountrytrail.org/spw
Huron-Manistee National Forest, 650 N. Michigan Ave., PO Box D,
    Baldwin, MI, 49304; 231-745-4631

Trail Guide

This hike parallels the Pere Marquette River, which flows several miles to the east. From the unimproved 40th Street parking area (BW-001), walk south on the Bowman Lake Trail. Note that this is not yet the blue-blazed NCT. In 0.2 miles (BW-002), cross the NCT (on which this hike returns from the lake to complete the loop).

Continue south on the Bowman Lake Trail through the open hardwood forest and its understory of bracken fern and oak seedlings. This is prime habitat for crow-sized, pileated woodpeckers (the largest woodpeckers in the North Country), because they like the many bugs found in mature and dying aspen trees. This area was logged over at least once to provide lumber for cities, especially after the Great Chicago Fire of 1871. After the hardwoods were logged, seedlings generated from the stumps, eventually becoming clusters of tall trees.

The Bowman Lake Trail crosses a long height of land and eventually reaches a trail junction (BW-003) in a grassy meadow. Continue east on the Bowman Lake Trail, traveling through the forest to Bowman Lake (BW-004).

Walk a very short side trail from Bowman Lake's campsites to a junction (BW-004) with the NCT. Turn left (north) on the NCT to start your return to the 40th Street parking area. This pleasant walk through the woods begins along the lake's high eastern rim. Walk the trail 2.7 miles back through the open-forest, gently rolling terrain to the flats at the beginning of the hike and the junction with the Bowman Lake Trail. Return to the Bowman Lake Trail and walk its final 0.2 miles to the 40th Street parking area.

Michigan—Bowman Lake Loop

Waypoint ID	Description	Mileage	Latitude	Longitude
BW-001	40th Street Parking Area	0.00	43.91646	−85.98745
BW-002	North Trail Junction w/NCT	0.2	43.915542	−85.986737
BW-003	NCT Junction/Bowman Lk Loop	2.14	43.89414	−85.97661
BW-004	South Trail Junction w/NCT	2.66	43.89307	−85.96701
BW-001	Return to Start	5.4	43.91646	−85.98745

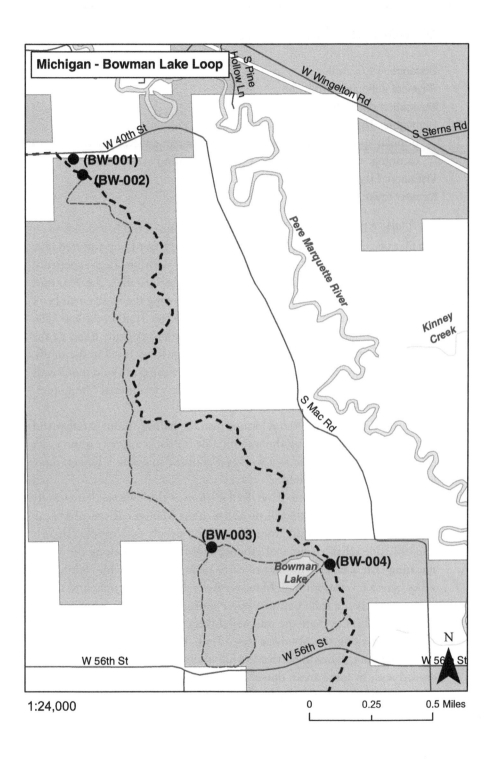

Michigan - Bowman Lake Loop

W 40th St
(BW-001)
(BW-002)
S Pine Hollow Ln
W Wingelton Rd
S Sterns Rd
Pere Marquette River
Kinney Creek
S Mac Rd
(BW-003)
Bowman Lake
(BW-004)
W 56th St
W 56th St
W 56th St

N

1:24,000

0   0.25   0.5 Miles

5. Manistee River Loop

Distance: 19.67 miles
Physical difficulty: Moderate
Navigation difficulty: Easy
Highlights: The lovely Manistee River Valley is one of the most popular spots on the entire NCT. There are long views, good camping, splendid hiking, and surprises around every corner.
Visitation: High
Nearest town: Mesick, MI

The lovely Manistee River Valley is justifiably one of the half dozen most popular places on the entire NCT. The Manistee River Loop featured hike provides day hikers and weekend backpackers with an ideal experience in an outstanding natural environment. The loop parallels the Manistee River on either side, with the NCT proper following the west/north bank of the river high above, and with the Manistee River Trail on the east side. Natural starting places at either end are at Hodenpyl Dam Road to the north (upstream end) or at Red Bridge off Upper River Road to the south.

This is a popular hiking destination. Hikers wishing to avoid the crowds can choose to hike during the week or during less traditional hiking periods in spring, fall, or winter.

With a formal campground located near the halfway point at either end and with many spots along the way suitable for backcountry camping, it's easy to complete the hike as a weekend jaunt or to create a longer, more leisurely excursion if desired.

The NCT and Manistee River Trail sections of this hike are dramatically different. On the NCT, there is no access to the Manistee River, which can be a half mile or more away from the trail and steeply inaccessible. There is also only one reliable source of groundwater to be found along the NCT, meaning that a hiker will have to carry plenty of water while hiking 8.5 miles between water sources. Manistee River Trail hikers rarely find themselves more than a mile between water sources. The Forest Service allows mountain bikers to share the trail with hikers on the NCT, while bikes are not allowed along the Manistee River Trail. The NCT has a more stable, developed, and maintained tread, while the Manistee River Trail is more eroded and, in some areas, downright slippery. The NCT side of the trail is characterized by long stretches of uphill walking, followed immediately by long descents, only to start climbing again after the trail has bottomed out. The Manistee River Trail side also has uphills and downhills, but in following along the river bottom, the elevation changes tend to be shorter, with long stretches of trail in between that are relatively flat. The NCT is blazed in a consistent manner, using the familiar two-by-six-inch blue blazes. The Manistee River Trail, in contrast, is blazed inconsistently, with a mix of plastic triangles nailed to trees and blue, white, and gray blazes painted onto trees. Thankfully, there really is only one well-defined trail in the area, which, after all, is following the nearby river, making the Manistee River Trail as easy to follow as the NCT. The Manistee River is not close to the NCT, but nice vistas offer great views, particularly in leafless seasons. The Manistee River Trail, in contrast, hugs the river in many areas, and views are limited, although the scenery is always refreshing. Both sides can be exposed to strong winds that can blow a hikers hat off; a nice breeze is welcome during hot weather or bug season.

This featured hike description starts at the north end, at Hodenpyl Dam. The first day's hike travels south along the Manistee River Trail. On the second day, the hike swaps directions and hops on the NCT to travel back north to the starting point. Hikers can spot or shuttle cars between parking areas if desired.

Trip Planner

Map: SE-MRL (Manistee River Loop), available from
    www.northcountrytrail.org
Beginning access: North Hodenpyl Dam Road trailhead (MRL-001)
Ending access: North Hodenpyl Dam Road trailhead
Contact information:
Spirit of the Woods Chapter, NCTA: spw@northcountrytrail.org,
    www.northcountrytrail.org/spw

Trail Guide

To reach the Hodenpyl Dam Road trailhead, follow State Route 115 west out of Mesick for about 2 miles, turning left (southwest) on North Hodenpyl Dam Road. In about 5 miles, the paved North Hodenpyl Dam Road will merge into westbound Beers Road, with North Hodenpyl Dam Road continuing to the left (south) as a dirt road. Turn left down this dirt road.

"Thursday was supposed to be the last day of Wilderness Survival Week for Brethern, Michigan's SEEDS of Adventure Day Camp," explains Chelsea Hummon, the program's director. "But when an 11-year-old named Porsha suggested we all go camping together, everyone felt that it would be a fun chance to employ what the girls had been learning about wildlife, orienteering, water treatment, and Leave No Trace ethics."

Hummon continues, "Our backpacking trip on the Manistee River Trail was a first for all eight campers. Stepping into the woods together (after I had fitted their backpacks to each of them), each girl had a look of wonder on her face. As we ventured farther away from the familiar sounds of the road, the girls took the initiative to look for a campsite on high ground an appropriate distance from water. They enjoyed swimming in the river, pumping water, cooking over their own fire, playing flashlight tag, telling stories, and sleeping out in tents that they themselves had packed in."

"When it came time to make sure that we packed out everything that we had packed in, the girls learned a lot about minimizing their food's packaging."

"On the way out, as we hiked among majestic cedar trees, the girls all looked more comfortable in their surroundings and carried themselves differently. Everyone felt stronger about carrying a pack and happy about seeing the sun rise across the oxbow section of the river. Some remembered how beautiful the geese had been as they flew along the river's corridor of trees."

"One girl said, 'I want to go backpacking again. I didn't think I could do it, but I did, and that feels really good.' That led to our making a pact to try it again last autumn. And so, the last Friday in October, four of the girls, myself, and Kasha hiked in and set up camp on the other side of the Manistee River. That was quite the frosty night, and it instilled in the girls even more of a sense of accomplishment, stewardship, and belief in their endless abilities. For me personally the whole experience was an amazing gift just to be outside among ten- and eleven-year-old girls while they discovered the wonders of the natural world."

In a few hundred feet, the parking area for the North Hodenpyl Dam Road trailhead (MRL-001) appears to the right (west), complete with a kiosk and signboard.

The hike begins by following an old railroad grade in a southwest direction and, in 0.7 miles, passing a signed junction with directions to the Manistee River Trail (MRL-002). This side trail is a north-end connector between the Manistee River Trail and the NCT and is used as part of the loop for hikers who have started at either the Upper River Road (south) or Marilla (Beers Road) trailheads. For the hike described here, continue hiking down the railroad grade for another 0.6 miles, at which point there will be another junction (MRL-003), with the trail to the right (north), returning hikers to the Marilla trailhead.

Continue straight (west) along the trail, which descends for a quarter mile to Eddington Creek (MRL-004), the last source of water before finishing up the day 9 miles later at Red Bridge. Eddington Creek is a scenic spot to rest before the first climb of the day. Filter or treat water if needed, and make sure packs are fitted for a comfortable carry.

Continue past Eddington Creek, as the trail begins a scenic climb along a ridge paralleling its south side. After one-third of a mile, the trail abruptly turns to the southwest, away from the creek. Late-starting hikers might consider setting up a backcountry camp in a first-rate spot in the stand of red pines below by descending to the creek. Campfires are discouraged along this trail, except at the campsites at Red Bridge and the five marked campsites equipped with fire rings along the hike's Manistee River Trail side. Remember to leave no trace and to pack out more trash than you packed in.

The trail continues its steady climb out of the river valley, with the total climb up from Eddington Creek being over a half mile. Hikers pausing along the climb can look east for outstanding views that only intensify with the climb.

The trail here is characterized by its many ups and downs. At the end of the first section of ups and downs, the trail crosses Forest Road (FR) 8020 (MRL-005). For the next 5 miles, the terrain is similar. Take time with the uphills, slow and steady, and look for those views to the east. The trail crosses Forest Road 8060 (MRL-006) in a little over 2 miles and then Pole Road (MRL-007) in another 3 miles.

About a half mile past Pole Road, the trail follows the edge of a very steep ridge, with the seemingly bottomless slope falling away into a dark, swampy area shaded in thick hemlocks. These steep drops will be com-

monplace for the next half mile or so, until the junction with the connector trail to the Manistee River Trail/Red Bridge. Leave the blue-blazed
NCT at this junction (MRL-008), turning left (southeast) on the connector to Red Bridge.

The Red Bridge connector trail heads downhill to the left (southeast),
with the most severe descent occurring in the first one-third of a mile.
Hemlock, beech, birch, hickory, sassafras, oak, and maple make up the
forest in this area—a nice transformation from the relatively unchanged
woods since Eddington Creek.

At the bottom of the descent, the trail passes a junction with a side trail
to the right (south), which goes to the Upper River Road (south) trailhead
(MRL-009) and a backpackers' parking area. The trail now flattens out and
begins its final stretch to the Red Bridge Campground and the official start
of the Manistee River Trail. The Manistee River soon comes into view, and
the trail exits onto Coates Highway shortly thereafter, with Red Bridge
Campground (MRL-010) across the street.

Red Bridge gets its name from the old red-painted wooden and steel
bridge that used to be located here. Today, a modern paved bridge spans the
Manistee, but the campground's name evokes memories of a simpler time.
The campground area has dual purpose, overnight camping, complete
with vaulted toilets, fire rings, a water spigot (available seasonally), and
designated parking and river access for vehicles with boat trailers. Backpackers and overnight guests should park at the Upper River Road (south)
trailhead, located up the road about a mile west of the campground. There
are only five tent sites at Red Bridge, so backpackers should be prepared
to camp elsewhere. Fortunately, there is plenty of flat terrain for dispersed
backcountry camping within a mile of Red Bridge.

From the Red Bridge crossing, the hike continues east along Coates
Highway for about 0.3 miles, before branching off the highway, north-
bound and to the left (MRL-011). Once off the road, the trail quickly
descends through a beautiful stand of mature birch trees. After yesterday's
hike, there should be no surprise that what goes down must go up, and it's
not long before the trail starts its first climb of the day through a scenic
stretch of cedar, hemlock, and red pine. At the top of this first climb, the
hiker is rewarded with a scenic view of the river below.

The hike along the Manistee River Trail is a winding path primarily along the river, except for stretches navigating wetlands, steep slopes,
and eroded river banks where the trail moves away from the Manistee for

stretches of a half mile or more. These areas tend to be very scenic, crossing many small creeks that feed into the Manistee. The trail here is also more diverse and interesting in terms of the variety of flora and fauna, especially when compared to the previous day's hike on the NCT. Hikers will notice, however, that the trail is steeper and more eroded than the NCT, with roots exposed at the surface in many areas, in addition to sections that may be slick with mud. Poor footing is occasionally an issue, and hikers should take extra care to proceed down the trail at a safe pace.

About 1.2 miles from Red Bridge, the trail crosses Arquilla Creek (MRL-012) on a wooden bridge—the first of many, each varying in style of construction, length, and condition. The bridges provide dry crossings and a stable platform from which to spy wildflowers growing along creek banks. For the backpacker prepared to treat water, frequent creek crossings mean there's no reason to carry more than a liter or two of water at any time. It's best to draw water from the bridges, in order to avoid contributing to erosion of the stream banks.

In about one-third of a mile, the trail returns to the high banks of the Manistee, passing the remnants of an old riverside cottage's foundation. The trail spends the next half mile winding down to the river, crossing a wetlands area along the way. This area makes for a nice spot to rest and watch the current go by.

The trail now makes another steep climb out of the river valley and, for a short time, follows an old road through a red pine plantation. As easy as it is to just take a relaxing stroll down an old forest road, be on the lookout for where the trail leaves the road to the left. The trail soon forks off and heads north, while the road continues straight ahead (northeast).

The trail soon crosses Cottage Road (MRL-013), and skirts the edge of a steep depression. Hiking the trail in this area is like walking along the edge of a great bowl. The river here is just out of view, obscured by the surrounding trees. Notice the contrast between the stark white color of the birch trees that grow along the slope of the bowl and the bright green of the pines growing at the top. The trail turns right (north), leaving the edge of the bowl. Hikers can take a short detour here and continue along the ridge for another hundred feet to be rewarded with a great overlook lunch spot and a fantastic view of the river below.

The trail soon crosses an old forest road and begins yet another steep descent, ending at Cedar Creek (MRL-014). The good news is that the uphill climb, while steep, is short and over before the legs have a chance to complain. Looking back down on the creek, one will be amazed that so much elevation was gained in such a short distance.

In 0.35 miles, the trail crosses South Slagle Creek Road and then Slagle Creek (MRL-015), with its impressive bridge. On the north side of the creek are numerous side trails leading to unofficial campsites. Hikers choosing to camp in this area should select a spot where someone has clearly camped in the past, rather than setting up on a virgin site. Though there are many short intersecting trails in this area, the main trail remains distinct and easy to follow.

The trail follows Slagle Creek upstream along a high ridge before heading due north, eventually leading to an official campsite on the Manistee River Trail, Camp #7 (MRL-016), which affords what can only be described as a commanding view of the river. The trail leaves Camp #7 and heads down to the river. For hikers willing to pack in a fishing rod, now's the time to use it.

No sooner does the trail meet the river than it begins yet another climb. There's a fork here. The path to the left continues to Camp #6 (MRL-017) at the top of the climb, and the path to the right ends at a more secluded campsite in the area. The distance between the two camps is only a few hundred feet, and there's a short trail linking the two, making for a small triangle in the trail.

Moving north from Camp #6, the trail leads inland for a mile and then begins a period of frequent creek crossings. After three-quarters of a mile, the trail comes to Camp #5 (MRL-018). The trail's descent after Camp #5 is characterized by poor drainage and, as a result, can be muddy and slick. After another 0.4 miles, the trail crosses a creek. Up until this point, most creek beds have been a mix of sand and gravel. However, this creek's bottom resembles potters' clay, with stones turned smooth in small bowls carved out by the water's current. After climbing a short distance, the trail reaches Camp #4 (MRL-019), followed almost immediately by another creek and Camp #3 (MRL-020). During wet periods, this creek's flow creates a waterfall, a rarity in Lower Michigan. As with the previous creek, this streambed also resembles potters' clay.

Within 0.6 miles, cross the first of three power line corridors. The end of the hike is now less than 2 miles away. For those low on water, the last reliably flowing water before the trail's end will be found here. The last grand view of the Manistee is also found along this segment. In a little more than a mile after crossing the first power line corridor, the "Little Mac" bridge (MRL-021) comes into view. This 250-foot suspension bridge spanning across the Manistee River was built by Consumer's Energy. Cross the bridge and head straight (northwest) into a marshy area surrounded by cedar trees.

The trail quickly climbs out of the wetland, topping out at the Woodpecker Creek day-use parking area. A trail junction can be found at the west end of the lot, just before the creek. Follow the trail north for about three-quarters of a mile, where it intersects with North Hodenpyl Dam Road. Continue north along the road, returning to the start of this hike at the Hodenpyl Dam Road trailhead.

Michigan—Manistee River Loop

Waypoint Id	Description	Mileage	Latitude	Longitude
MRL-001	N. Hodenpyl Dam Trailhead	0.00	44.37270	−85.82527
MRL-002	Trail Junction—MRT	0.65	44.36750	−85.83573
MRL-003	Marilla Junction	1.24	44.36139	−85.84427
MRL-004	Eddington Creek	1.55	44.36046	−85.84793
MRL-005	FR 8020	2.68	44.34776	−85.85178
MRL-006	FR 8060	5.05	44.32842	−85.86678
MRL-007	Pole Rd	7.86	44.30313	−85.87398
MRL-008	Trail Junction	8.69	44.29337	−85.87506
MRL-009	Upper River Road Junction	8.95	44.29083	−85.87147
MRL-010	Red Bridge Campground	9.83	44.28391	−85.86164
MRL-011	Trail Junction Coates Hwy	10.17	44.28431	−85.85508
MRL-012	Arquilla Creek	10.97	44.29229	−85.85598
MRL-013	Cottage Rd	12.98	44.30565	−85.84438
MRL-014	Cedar Creek	13.32	44.30920	−85.84168
MRL-015	Slagle Creek Bridge	14.01	44.31714	−85.84697
MRL-016	Camp #7	14.53	44.32348	−85.84721
MRL-017	Camp #6	15.09	44.33032	−85.84946
MRL-018	Camp #5	16.83	44.34699	−85.84132
MRL-019	Camp #4	17.33	44.35102	−85.83449
MRL-020	Camp #3	17.39	44.35138	−85.83402
MRL-021	"Little Mac" Bridge	19.07	44.36552	−85.82637
MRL-001	N. Hodenpyl Dam Trailhead	19.67	44.37270	−85.82527

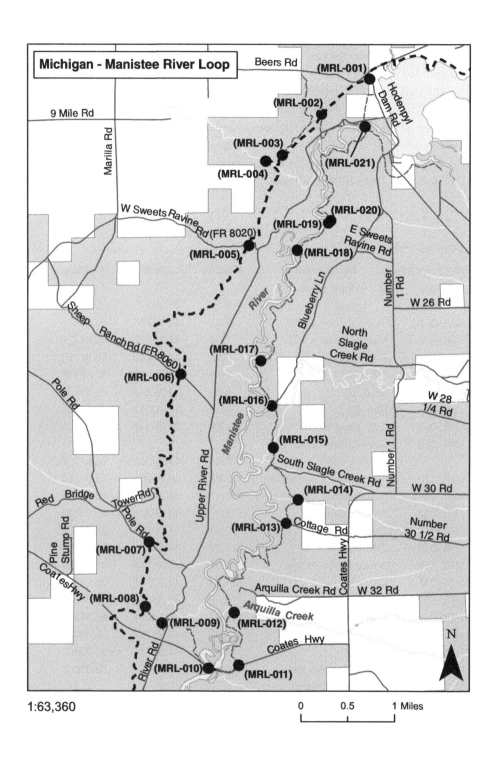

Michigan - Manistee River Loop

6. Traverse City (Guernsey Lake Campground to Dollar Lake parking area trailhead)

Distance: 8.44 miles
Physical Difficulty: Easy to moderate
Navigation Difficulty: Easy to moderate
Highlights: Gorgeous cedar-shaded stretches along the north branch of the Boardman River, mixed northern forests and meadows, and birdlife
Visitation: Low to moderate
Nearest towns: Mayfield, Kingsley, Kalkaska, and Traverse City, MI

This featured hike takes place in the Pere Marquette State Forest between Traverse City and Kalkaska, MI. It includes many illustrations of the diversity found in northern Michigan forests: tall pines; mixed oak and maple forests; open, fern-carpeted woods and meadows; and cedar-shadowed riverbanks interspersed with delightfully clear marl-bottomed lakes. The trail follows the north branch of the Boardman River, a noted trout stream. It traverses Sand Lakes Quiet Area, a 2,800-acre specially regulated area within the state forest where no motorized vehicles are permitted, with some lakes managed for trout. Trails intersperse the Sand Lakes area, with convenient maps found at most trail junctions.

The trail begins at the Guernsey Lake State Forest Campground (where a permit is required for camping) and meanders in a northwesterly direction through the Sand Lakes before heading south to hit the north branch of the Boardman. The trail follows the Boardman westerly for a way, both on its banks and higher up on its overlooks, before leaving the more southbound river bottoms to head west to the trailhead at Dollar Lake. Along the way, it crosses the famed Shore-to-Shore Equestrian Trail, a 220-mile trail across the northern part of the Lower Peninsula, from Empire on Lake Michigan to Oscoda on Lake Huron's shore.

In winter, the area is a mecca for snow travelers, and the NCT is a favorite of cross-country skiers and snowshoers. The Traverse City VASA trail is nearby, with many connecting loops and opportunities for shorter or longer trips. Of note on the section of the NCT immediately to the west is the Valley of the Giants, so noted for the beautiful old-growth forest through which it passes.

The abundance of overnight camping opportunities and side trails make this a great section of the NCT for trying out backpacking. Local

NCT enthusiasts often recommend it to families or small scout groups as a way to work out the kinks and give backpacking a try, in any season of the year.

Trip Planner

Map: MI-06 (Michigan 06), available from www.northcountrytrail.org
Beginning access: Guernsey Lake trailhead (TC-001)
Parking: Guernsey Lake Road to Guernsey Lake State Forest
Campground (permit required). Park in the lot on the left before the split in road at the kiosk and the campground and lake. The trailhead is across the road from the kiosk.
Ending access: Dollar Lake parking area
Parking: There is ample parking on the south side of Supply Road, just west of the junction with Williamsburg Road (TC-018).
Contact information:
NCTA Headquarters: HQ@northcountrytrail.org
Grand Traverse Hiking Club Chapter, NCTA: gtr@northcountrytrail.org, www.northcountrytrail.org/gtr

Trail Guide

This featured hike begins on a white-blazed spur trail leading to the NCT. From the kiosk (TC-001), look northeast across the access road for the

Hikers following the Boardman River often tread on "fisherman's trails," pathways along the river used to get from one fishing hole to the next. Contemplating their first view of the Boardman from the bench conveniently located there, hikers might imagine walking in the footsteps of Ernest Hemingway, who was known to fish the Boardman in his teens. In 1922, the Boardman's hallowed waters gave birth to one of the most effective and enduring fishing flies ever invented, the well-known Adams pattern. Developed by Len Halladay, who ran the nearby Mayfield Hotel, the fly is named after Judge Charles F. Adams, a regular guest at Halladay's hotel. The nearby village of Kingsley held its first annual Adams Fly Festival in 2012, on the first Saturday of June, as a benefit for the local library.

trailhead signs. Follow the spur trail 0.3 miles through a mature red pine forest to the junction with the NCT (TC-002). Turn left (west) on the blue-blazed NCT, noting the Sand Lakes Quiet Area sign and map, which appear regularly at trail junctions within the Quiet Area.

Continue enjoying the tall red pine forest interspersed with hardwoods, and listen for the many different birdcalls, particularly in spring and early summer. About 0.1 miles west, another white-blazed spur trail enters from the left, marked with a Carsonite post. A lake appears on the left, along with the sounds of red-winged blackbirds and shoreline frogs. The trail soon meanders to the right and up a hill, away from the lake.

The trails in this area are well marked and used, although chances are not high of meeting a lot of other hikers. By paying attention and frequently checking for the characteristic NCT's blue blazes, hikers will find it easy enough to stay on the NCT.

Continue along the sandy trail, now with more white pines mixed in with the red. In summer, the forest floor is carpeted with ferns and lowbush blueberry. Listen for the liquid call of the wood thrush.

Where the NCT comes to a junction with an old logging road (TC-003), turn right, following the blue blazes. About 100 yards farther, a spur carrying an underground cable goes right, but NCT hikers stay left. The trail is now clearly on an old railroad bed, elevated by digging on either side to form the railbed and likely used to haul logs out of the woods during Michigan's lumbering heyday. Make a left off the railbed (TC-004) and follow the NCT's blue blazes in a northwesterly direction. Signs marking Sand Lakes Quiet Area make navigation relatively easy on the maze of trails in the area.

The NCT makes a slight ascent and side-hills up a benched section of trail. Birdsong abounds. As line of sight decreases, the meanders create an intimate feel, and hikers get immersed in the natural rhythm of the northern woods. Glacial potholes dot the terrain, and the first large hemlock trees begin to appear. Observant hikers can see the evidence of a long-ago burn in the few charred stumps that remain standing. Large white pines also appear.

The NCT then crosses an old railroad bed (TC-005), continuing straight and slightly downhill through mixed red and white pines toward a small lake. Use care, as there are exposed roots in this section waiting to trip the unwary. The trail then flattens out along a small lake on the right, where evidence of the forest fire is more visible. At the lake level, the trail passes through aspen and some white birch. There is a nice bench (high enough for ski-clad feet to clear). An old two-track woods trail ascends westerly away from the lake, through more large hemlocks.

The NCT is wide enough here for two-abreast hiking or skiing, enabling quiet conversation and camaraderie. The trail starts to descend through open woods of oak with taller red pines interspersed.

At a junction (TC-006), continue straight along the NCT, noting the predominance of larger red pines on the left. The trail starts to ascend, and lowbush blueberries abound amid a more open mixed oak and fern-carpeted woods. Soon, the first of the Sand Lakes appears on the left, and primitive campsites are plentiful. The NCT continues around the lakes on a wide trail.

Latrines (pit privies) and a series of attractive and well-used primitive campsites appear (TC-007). This is the heart of the Sand Lakes Quiet Area, with its series of lakes and primitive campsites among the pines.

At another trailhead (TC-008), the NCT heads left, following the shoreline. Continue left, following the familiar blue blazes and the shoreline. The helpful posted maps are reassuring and continue to be visible at trail junctions until the NCT leaves the Quiet Area.

At a junction (TC-009) a short distance later, a spur trail turns off the NCT to the right. Stay straight on the NCT, following the main blue-blazed trail.

Shortly the NCT arrives at a five-way junction (TC-010). Stay straight on the NCT, passing a trail that turns right to access a lake. Pause to hear the frogs chortle and to watch the dragonflies dimple the placid lake's surface. The sandy beach is very inviting on a hot summer's day.

Continue hiking around the lake. The NCT soon angles right, away from the lake, up an incline and into a sandy oak barrens. This section of the NCT is nothing short of delightful. Glacial hollows dot the landscape, which is characterized by an oak canopy with an understory of lowbush blueberry and sweet fern giving way to taller bracken fern. The trail passes old bogs now overgrown with vegetation.

The trail curves right around a bog on the right and ascends into a younger hardwood stand of maple and aspen. Topping out with an open meadow on the left, the trail again curves right and comes to a junction (TC-011). Cross over the well-worn trail and continue on the NCT (look for the Carsonite post and trail symbol).

The trail leaves the Sand Lakes Quiet Area at this point, entering an open meadow that quickly veers left into a woods. Hikers will immediately note that the NCT is now a single-track footpath surrounded by sweet fern and lowbush blueberry. Beginning an ascent, the NCT enters a delightful open maple woods carpeted with ferns and grasses, transitioning into more oaks as the trail continues. An opening appears on the left, level with the trail, which soon narrows into a corridor of white pine. Summer hikers can only imagine the joy this section of trail must bring when skiing or snowshoeing through its snow-covered branches.

Crossing an unmarked trail, the NCT continues slightly downhill, passing through a ridge and pothole area on the left before entering an open woods with a fern understory. Teaberry and wintergreen are abundant on the forest floor.

Where the Michigan Shore-to-Shore Equestrian Trail crosses the NCT (TC-012), the NCT continues slightly downhill through an open fern meadow, lush and redolent with the scent of the thigh-high ferns in the hot sun.

Crossing a hilltop, the NCT enters and crosses a valley opening with jack pine and pin cherry dotting the blueberry-covered ground. The NCT crosses Guernsey Lake Road (TC-013) and continues downhill through an area of treetop blowdowns from red and jack pines. Traveling a short distance through a mature jack pine forest, the trail emerges onto the north branch of the Boardman River, with a strategically placed bench perfectly situated for a lunch break.

Hikers will enjoy the cooler breeze of the river bottom on a hot summer day and the chance to soak feet in the delightfully cool waters while they munch trail mix (be sure to include dried cherries—a Traverse City specialty—in the mix). The chuckle of the water running through fallen cedars and the smell of the river may send a powerful message about strategic napping at this point on the hike.

The NCT turns right, following the riverbank downstream, and soon passes through the first of many white cedar hollows. Hikers should avoid being lulled by the river at this point, since there are a number of places in the next mile along the river where the NCT diverges from the sometimes more obvious fisherman's trails along the riverbank. Stick with the blue blazes, and use care in avoiding the poison ivy found more frequently in the river-bottom habitat.

At a cable crossing, stay right on the NCT, which departs briefly from the river. The NCT then crosses Broomhead Road (TC-014) near the bridge and cable crossing over the river, offering parking and a car-spotting alternative for a shorter hike.

After crossing Broomhead Road, the NCT is found to the left of the cable crossing, toward the river. There is a primitive campsite here. From here, the trail continues downstream along the higher bank (north side), where the elevation occasionally offers overlook possibilities. The NCT angles right up a hillside via switchbacks on a fairly steep climb, emerging on a two-track woods trail coming from the right, which shows the tracks of the ORV now permitted in the state forest. There is an overlook on the left, one of many in this area of high banks.

The NCT follows this two-track trail for some distance. Where a road enters from the right (TC-015), there are a number of side trails. The NCT follows the blue blazes along the woods road, soon heading left. Another road enters from the right. The trail ascends on a sandy two-track, emerging at the top of the hill with a clear-cut on the right.

After hiking three-quarters of a mile on this two-track on the high banks, hikers should be alert to the NCT turning left off the two-track (TC-016). Here, the trail follows the high banks more closely, and the split is easy to miss. The NCT then meanders steeply downhill to join the river once again, at a lovely campsite among cedars.

Again, the maze of fisherman's trails call for hiker concern in making sure a blue blaze is evident. The NCT follows the river, and it would be tough to get lost, but the NCT can be easy to stray from at times.

Continuing to follow the north bank of the Boardman, the NCT makes a sharp right away from the river at another campsite among cedars, starting another ascent to leave the river for good. Heading northwest at the top of the hill, the NCT enters an open, bowl-like meadow area; look for the blue-blazed trees on the other side. After a short distance, the trail veers right and emerges into another meadow. At a two-track path, go directly across and into an open woods of oak and maple.

Cross another open meadow and go up the opposite hill into the woods. Soon, the NCT again meets the Shore-to-Shore Equestrian Trail (TC-017). Cross the horse trail and watch for the blue blazes of the NCT. Continue up a hill and across another two-track path, remaining on the NCT. The trail levels out into an open woods of mature oak. Next, the trail heads slightly downhill, leading to a red pine opening and then traversing another open meadow and woods.

The NCT continues through an interspersed area of open red pine woods and lowbush blueberry meadows, eventually moving into a more intimate set of meanders, where the efforts of the trail adopters and maintainers of the Grand Traverse Hiking Club are very evident (and greatly appreciated by hikers using this trail).

Soon, the trail passes along the edge of a recent clear-cut, now growing up in aspen thickets dearly loved by the iconic grouse and woodcock of the Great North Woods. Crossing Williamsburg Road and continuing on the NCT on the other side, hikers are only a few hundred years from the Dollar Lake parking lot and trailhead (TC-018). Emerge from the woods to see the trailhead sign and parking lot immediately across Supply Road.

Michigan—Traverse City

Waypoint ID	Description	Mileage	Latitude	Longitude
TC-001	Guernsey Lake Trailhead	0.00	44.71603	−85.32327
TC-002	NCT Junction	0.30	44.71874	−85.32757
TC-003	Old Logging Road	0.74	44.72004	−85.33273
TC-004	Left on NCT	1.13	44.72467	−85.33522
TC-005	Old Railroad Bed	1.67	44.72582	−85.34383
TC-006	Junction	2.26	44.72169	−85.35347
TC-007	Campsites	2.70	44.71876	−85.35949
TC-008	Trailhead	2.74	44.71865	−85.35994
TC-009	Junction with Spur	2.92	44.71689	−85.36095
TC-010	Five-Way Junction	3.11	44.71442	−85.36050
TC-011	Junction	3.83	44.70616	−85.36457
TC-012	Shore-to-Shore Equestrian Trail Junction	4.50	44.69773	−85.36907
TC-013	Guernsey Lake Road Crossing	4.86	44.69375	−85.36562
TC-014	Broomhead Road Crossing	5.27	44.69065	−85.36726
TC-015	Two-Track and Road Junction	5.82	44.68864	−85.37335
TC-016	Two-Track—Left on NCT	6.36	44.68716	−85.38318
TC-017	Shore-to-Shore Trail (Second Crossing)	7.14	44.68731	−85.39318
TC-018	Dollar Lake Parking Lot and Trailhead	8.44	44.69217	−85.41174

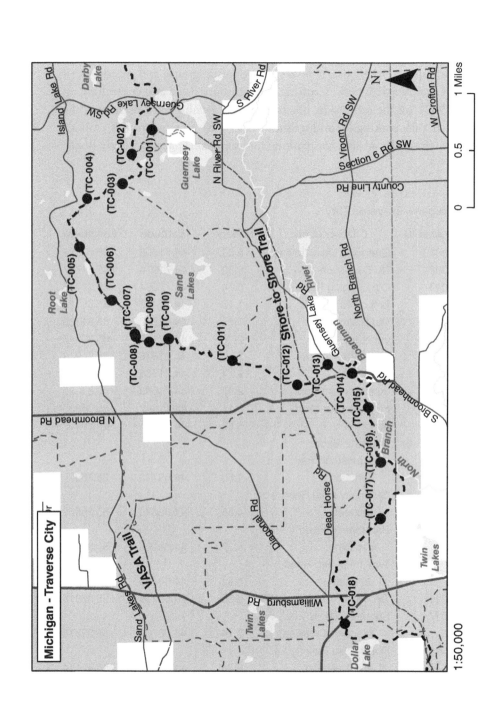

Michigan - Traverse City

1:50,000

7. Jordan River Pathway Loop

Distance: 17.8 miles
Physical difficulty: Moderate
Navigation difficulty: Moderate
Highlights: Scenic riparian wildness and weekend backpack loop
Visitation: Moderate
Nearest town: Alba, MI

The NCT passes through the valley of the Jordan River, a designated Michigan Wild and Scenic River, where it shares portions of the Jordan River Pathway on the Landslide, Pinney Bridge, Three Culverts, and Deadmans Hill sections. This featured hike is a loop trail on the Jordan River Pathway.

There is a walk-in Mackinaw State Forest campground (fees apply) at Pinney Bridge, which makes this a popular weekend backpack trip. Be sure to allow time for a side visit and tour of the Jordan River National Fish Hatchery. This hatchery supplies most of the federally produced lake trout fingerlings for stocking the Great Lakes. There is an interpretive facility, and the US Fish and Wildlife Service staff are very supportive of NCT hikers.

Trip Planner

Map: See guidebook map.
Beginning access: Deadmans Hill parking area (JRP-001)
Parking: Parking lot
Ending access: Deadmans Hill parking area
Contact information:
Jordan Valley 45° Chapter, NCTA: j45@northcountrytrail.org,
www.northcountrytrail.org/j45

Trail Guide

This featured loop begins at the scenic overlook at the Deadmans Hill parking area (JRP-001), the site of a 19th-century logging accident. At the north side of the parking lot, follow the Jordan Valley Loop Trail (blazed with blue circles) down the steep slope 0.2 miles, to a junction (JRP-002) with the NCT.

Turn left (south) on the NCT. Its blazes here resemble an exclamation point (!) because they combine the standard blue rectangle with the

Department of Natural Resources circle. Passing a side trail that leads to an informal bridge across the Jordan River, continue to a beaver marsh (JRP-003). The approach to the marsh is guarded by dense masses of invasive phragmites, reedlike fronds that almost obscure the trail. Cross the long boardwalk between two beaver ponds.

Follow the trail 4 miles to the Jordan River Road (JRP-004). The trail contours around the hillside until reaching a series of Jordan River tributary ponds and their boardwalk bridges. (Water levels in this area are in constant flux thanks to the resident beavers.) Beyond the ponds, the trail passes an open area of former pioneer homesites. Eventually, the trail drops to river level and emerges on the Jordan River Road. (If you wish to visit the Jordan River National Fish Hatchery or need potable water, take the Jordan River Road to the left in about 0.3 miles.)

The trail briefly follows the Jordan River Road. Turn right for a road walk of 0.1 miles to where the highway crosses the river, at a place known locally as Three Culverts. The trail then leaves the road and plunges to the left into the woods along the riverbank. Seasonal seeps may sometimes muddy the trail. But the good news is that there are plenty of water sources, including an excellent spring whose water pressure seems to make the sand boil. Note that camping is only allowed at the Pinney Bridge Campground.

The trail continues down a long-abandoned logging railroad grade and eventually climbs to an overlook with a wooden bench (JRP-005), from

---

The Jordan River National Fish Hatchery (6623 Turner Road, Elmira, MI 49730) is a 116-acre site devoted to raising lake trout and stocking them into Lakes Michigan and Huron. There is a 24-7 display at the hatchery, along with restrooms, a picnic pavilion, and several short hiking trails (including one that climbs the bluff for an excellent view of the valley).

The most extraordinary thing about this hatchery is that its water comes from a set of springs supplying 5,300 gallons per minute. With that incredible resource, the US Fish and Wildlife Service produces two million trout a year for Lakes Michigan and Huron. The goal of this mission is Great Lakes ecosystem restoration—attempting to return lake trout populations to the levels seen before the introduction of exotic and invasive species like the sea lamprey. For more information, call 231-584-2461, or see an online brochure for the hatchery at www.fws.gov/midwest/Fisheries/library/jordan-friends-group.pdf.

which the heavily wooded Jordan River Valley is visible. After that, the trail descends rapidly to the Pinney Bridge Campground (JRP-006). The distance from the Jordan River Road to the campground totals 5 miles.

Pinney Bridge Campground charges $15 for rustic camping with pit toilets and hand-pumped well water. Parking is nearby, just across the Pin-

You'd never know from reading Ernest Hemingway's writings that the author was born in Chicago's Oak Park. Hemingway's prolific writings about northern Michigan might lead you to believe he grew up there—in reality, he merely spent his summers during the early 1900s at Windemere, the family cottage on Walloon Lake near Petoskey.

The NCT passes just east of Boyne City, Horton Bay, and Walloon Lake, heading north into Petoskey and Bay View. Overlooking Little Traverse Bay on Lake Michigan, the trail next heads north toward the east side of Harbor Springs. This is Hemingway country, home to the places that nurtured him, appealed to his prolific imagination, and featured prominently—often by name—in many of his earlier writings. This is the birthplace of Nick Adams, Hemingway's fictitious and most consistent alter ego.

Arguably the most famous of Hemingway's Nick Adams stories is "Big Two-Hearted River," published in 1925. In it, a young man takes a railroad into the Upper Peninsula's wilderness, seeking solace from soul-scarring experiences (presumably from World War I) with the help of camping and fishing. Though Nick travels to the Two-Hearted River in the story, the experience is modeled after Hemingway's visit to Seney's Fox River in 1919. The NCT passes to the north of Seney and the south-flowing Fox system, now the site of a National Wildlife Refuge, and also crosses and follows the Little Two-Hearted River for about 12 miles in Luce County, just west of the Tahquamenon watershed.

After the Little Two-Hearted River empties into Lake Superior, the NCT heads west along the Superior shoreline, soon crossing the main Two-Hearted River as it flows into the big lake known as Gitche Gumee. The river and the trail both parallel the lakeshore for about 7 miles heading west, before the Two-Hearted River veers south. Even if not the actual inspiration for Hemingway's story, the Two-Hearted River clearly fired his imagination, as did the landscape through which both the river and trail pass. In traversing the interior portions of the Upper Peninsula on the NCT, it's not hard to visualize Nick Adams's campsite just ahead, at the bend of the river.

ney Bridge, and the campground often fills quickly with drive-in campers. In peak season, be sure to arrive early. There is no advance registration.

The trail crosses Pinney Bridge, enters the woods, and proceeds up the hill. Landslide Lookout is next, 3.6 miles to the southeast. Along the way, watch for Cascade Creek, Cascade Road, and Landslide Creek. Invisibly, the trail passes over the 45th Parallel (JRP-007). Hikers straddling it stand equidistant from the North Pole and the equator. This is the only such spot on the entire NCT.

Sitting on the Boy Scout–erected bench at Landslide Creek, note the creek's source in the silted-in pond uphill to the left. During the logging era, lumberjacks used this water in winter to spray and ice their skid roads and water their horses.

Landslide Lookout (JRP-008) at Harvey Road offers another excellent prospect out over the valley. From its beautiful vista, leave the southbound NCT for the Jordan Valley Loop Trail heading northeast. The Jordan Valley Loop Trail is blazed with painted blue circles. Follow the contours of the ridges and hills flanking the south valley wall. Cross Section Thirteen Creek and then a nameless additional stream.

Again cross Jordan River Road (JRP-009). After about a mile, cross Turner Road (JRP-010). Another trail for a possible side trip to the fish hatchery is 0.5 miles downhill to the left.

Beyond Turner Road, the trail traverses the forested plateau above the Jordan River Valley. Follow it as it winds its way back to the starting point at the scenic overlook at Deadmans Hill parking area (JRP-001).

Michigan—Jordan River Pathway Loop

Waypoint Id	Description	Mileage	Latitude	Longitude
JRP-001	Deadmans Hill Parking Area	0.00	45.04637	−84.93845
JRP-002	Trail Junction with NCT	0.57	45.04959	−84.94273
JRP-003	Beaver Marsh	1.47	45.04313	−84.95073
JRP-004	Jordan River Rd Crossing	3.53	45.03639	−84.96872
JRP-005	Wooden Bench Overlook	5.57	45.02142	−84.98714
JRP-006	Pinney Bridge Campground	8.05	45.01792	−85.02672
JRP-007	45th Parallel	9.87	45.00000	−85.01568
JRP-008	Landslide Lookout	11.84	44.99493	−84.98656
JRP-009	Jordan River Rd Crossing	14.66	45.01779	−84.96636
JRP-010	Turner Rd Crossing	15.58	45.02370	−84.95380
JRP-001	Deadmans Hill Parking Area	17.80	45.04637	−84.93845

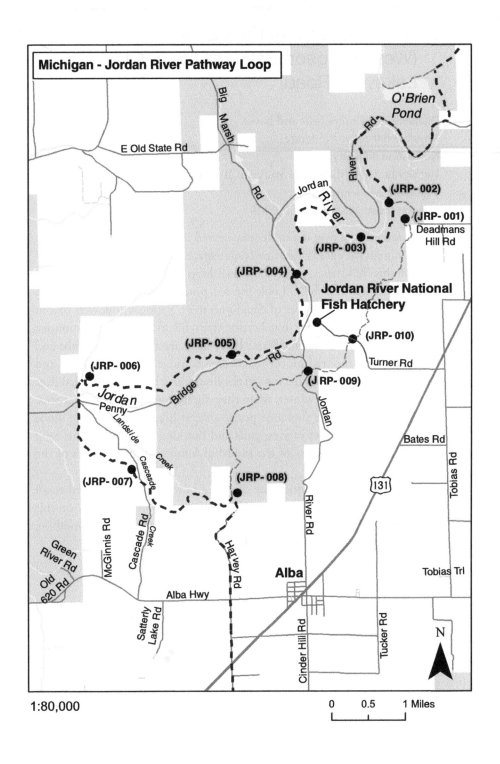

Michigan - Jordan River Pathway Loop

O'Brien Pond

Big Marsh Rd

E Old State Rd

Jordan River

River Rd

(JRP- 002)

(JRP- 001)

Deadmans Hill Rd

(JRP- 003)

(JRP- 004)

Jordan River National Fish Hatchery

(JRP- 010)

(JRP- 005)

Bridge Rd

Turner Rd

(JRP- 006)

Jordan

(J RP- 009)

Jordan

Penny

Landslide

Cascade Creek

Bates Rd

Tobias Rd

(JRP- 007)

(JRP- 008)

McGinnis Rd

Cascade Rd

Creek

River Rd

131

Green River Rd

Old 620 Rd

Satterly Lake Rd

Alba Hwy

Alba

Harvey Rd

Tobias Trl

Cinder Hill Rd

Tucker Rd

N

1:80,000

0   0.5   1 Miles

8. Wilderness State Park Loop (West Sturgeon Bay Trail trailhead to Lakeview Road)

Distance: 5.14 miles (out and back)
Physical difficulty: Moderate
Navigation difficulty: Easy
Highlights: Lake Michigan's Sturgeon Bay and nearby sand hills
Visitation: Moderate
Nearest town: Mackinaw City, MI

Wind and erosion over the millennia created a series of 23 sand-hill ridges so prominent they are visible from outer space. Nowadays, the inland portion of this Wilderness State Park trail loop threads its way across and along many of these hills. Look for red pine, white pine, fir, hemlock, white cedar, and many types of deciduous trees. Spring wildflowers bloom abundantly, and summer blueberries stain hikers' hands and mouths. Though this is an easy to moderate hike, there are a few sharp climbs and descents where the trail moves from ridge to ridge. Lovely corridors and agreeable gradients mark the tops of the linear sand hills. White-tailed deer are especially visible in winter, when they dig through the snow for acorns.

This featured hike's shoreline portion treats hikers to fine white sands as well as the sounds of cawing gulls and breaking waves. Hike this loop to enjoy both the delights of the sand-hill forest and the wonders of the northern Great Lakes.

Very few hints are evident of the once-bustling, now-vanished town of Sturgeon Bay, which grew around a railroad, sawmill, and dock on this segment's coast. This proof of the restorative power of nature is something to take away from any hike in Wilderness State Park.

Trip Planner

Map: MI-07 (Michigan 07), available from www.northcountrytrail.org
Beginning access: West Sturgeon Bay Trail trailhead (WSP-001)
Ending access: Same
Contact information:
Harbor Springs Chapter, NCTA: hrb@northcountrytrail.org, www.northcountrytrail.org/hrb

Trail Guide

From the West Sturgeon Bay Trail (county road) trailhead (WSP-001), follow the NCT north into a pine and oak forest. Within 100 feet, the trail reaches an old railroad bed, now a right-of-way for electric power lines. Turn left, go less than 50 feet along the right-of-way, and then turn right to reenter the forest.

Approximately 0.3 miles from the trailhead, cross over an old logging trail and follow the blue blazes on the other side. At approximately 0.7 miles from the trailhead, the trail begins to follow ridges that mark the eastern boundary of the sand hills. A year-round pond (WSP-002) is visible to the east at the bottom of the ridge. This spot marks the easternmost extent of the sand-blown dunes.

On its way to mile marker 1, the trail descends and traverses a valley. Just past the marker, follow the trail to left (WSP-003) up a steep sand hill to a scenic overlook. At the eastward-looking bench, the trail reaches its highest elevation: 626 feet above sea level. The buildings and farms visible in the distance are about 3 miles away.

There are 5 miles of the NCT that can only be hiked on one morning a year—Labor Day morning. Affectionately known as "Big Mac," the Mackinac Bridge connects Michigan's Upper and Lower Peninsulas. Each Labor Day, hikers get the opportunity to walk the bridge, north to south. At all other times, hikers must arrange transport services from the Mackinac Bridge Authority for a fee of $3.50. Hours when the transport service is available are 8 a.m. to 8 p.m., seven days a week. Visit www.mackinacbridge.org for current bridge conditions and updates.

The Big Mac is the third-largest suspension bridge in the world and the longest in the Western Hemisphere. At its highest point, hikers are 200 feet above the water. Opened in 1957, Big Mac enabled much faster travel between downstate industrial Michigan and the pristine and isolated UP. Some Yoopers (as UP residents take pride in calling themselves) regard the opening of the Big Mac as a black day indeed, since all the "trolls" (Michiganders and others living "below the bridge") could now easily access their unspoiled UP.

NCTA chapters often sponsor Bridge Walk events over Labor Day weekend to encourage awareness among the more than 30,000 bridge walkers that they are also hiking the NCT.

The trail continues another 0.5 miles along ridges that separate the eastern edge of the sand hills from the swamps and flats beyond. The trail now turns left and zigzags along several high ridges. Pass two large stumps, reminders of the lumbering that took place here a century ago.

The trail contours around the side of a steep hill. The trail's next ridge is covered in ironwood, beech, maple, striped maple, and yellow and white birch. From there, follow the trail down through hemlocks past mile marker 2, to a pine, white birch, and aspen forest. Continue over many small hills and past a couple of stagnant ponds. Follow the trail as it parallels a small creek (WSP-004).

Cross the creek, then traverse an oak forest and emerge from the forest onto Lakeview Road. On the other side of Lakeview Road is a Wilderness State Park parking lot (WSP-005), complete with a hand pump and a privy, but no camping is permitted. To park here, vehicles must have the Michigan Recreation Passport endorsement on their license plate. Out-of-state visitors are required to purchase nonresident stickers for $29 annually or $8 daily.

Walk the short distance to the shore of Lake Michigan. To complete the Wilderness State Park Loop, hike south along the sandy shore of Lake Michigan to a prominent willow tree.

Hike North Lakeshore Drive inland (mostly southeast) 0.3 miles to a junction with the county road West Sturgeon Bay Trail (WSP-006). Follow it 0.2 miles east to return to the beginning of this hike (WSP-001).

Michigan—Wilderness State Park Loop

Waypoint Id	Description	Mileage	Latitude	Longitude
WSP-001	West Sturgeon Bay Trail Trailhead	0.00	45.67948	−84.96727
WSP-002	Pond	0.72	45.68632	−84.96040
WSP-003	Junction with trail to scenic overlook	1.75	45.69221	−84.95696
WSP-004	Creek	2.58	45.70018	−84.95265
WSP-005	Wilderrness State Park Parking Lot	2.79	45.70285	−84.95241
WSP-006	Junction W Sturgeon Bay Trail	4.64	45.68303	−84.97389
WSP-001	West Sturgeon Bay Trail Trailhead	5.14	45.67948	−84.96727

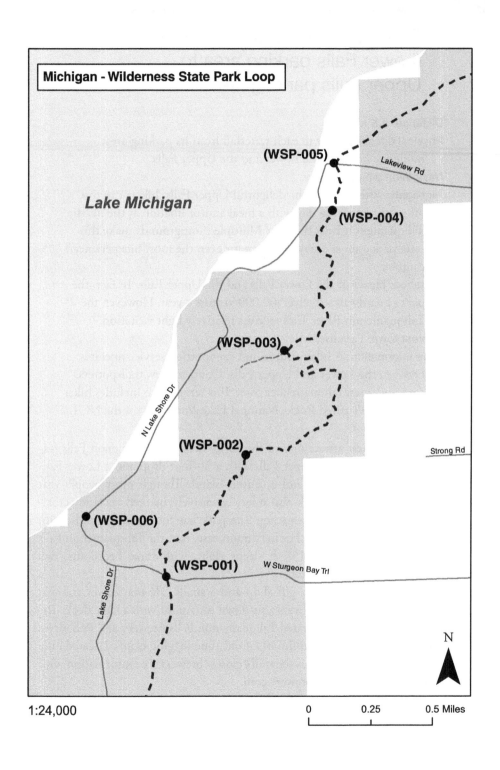

Michigan - Wilderness State Park Loop

Lake Michigan

(WSP-005)

Lakeview Rd

(WSP-004)

(WSP-003)

N Lake Shore Dr

(WSP-002)

Strong Rd

(WSP-006)

Lake Shore Dr

(WSP-001)

W Sturgeon Bay Trl

N

1:24,000

0   0.25   0.5 Miles

9. Tahquamenon Falls State Park (Lower Falls parking area to Upper Falls parking area)

Distance: 4.8 miles

Physical difficulty: Easy to each waterfall from its parking area; moderate between the Lower and the Upper Falls

Navigation difficulty: Easy

Highlights: After visiting the delightful Upper Falls, hikers can top off a very satisfying day with a meal and/or libation at the nearby Tahquamenon Falls Brewery. Multiple campgrounds make this state park a most enjoyable place for even the most inexperienced camper.

Visitation: Heavy at the Lower Falls and the Upper Falls. In fact, the park's boardwalks receive 500,000 visitors a year. However, the Tahquamenon River Trail receives relatively light visitation.

Nearest town: Paradise, MI

More information: A hiker shuttle and car-spotting service operates between the Lower and Upper Falls. Contact www.trailspotters. com and www.tahquatrekker.com. This service also includes hiker shuttles at Pictured Rocks National Lakeshore, also on the NCT.

One of the finest attractions on the entire NCT, Tahquamenon Falls features a 200-foot-wide Upper Falls with a 50-foot drop and a Lower Falls consisting of five ledges and a central island. Though most people visit in summer, the state park also offers extensively marked trails for cross-country skiing and snowshoeing. The park has four campgrounds, with varying levels of comfort. For maximum ease, rent the Tahquamenon Falls Lodge (call 906-492-3415). It sleeps eight, with three bedrooms, two baths, and a furnished kitchen.

The Lower Falls has a gift shop and a small café that serves comfort food. The Upper Falls delivers a sit-down restaurant with a large deck. The privately owned and operated Tahquamenon Falls Brewery and Pub serves its meals and suds in a replica of an old-time logging camp. Located only 0.4 miles off the NCT, it is the trail's closest brewery. For information, visit www.tahquamenonfallsbrewery.com.

Trip Planner

Map: MI-09 (Michigan 09), available from www.northcountrytrail.org
Beginning access: Lower Falls parking area (TAQ-001)
Ending access: Upper Falls parking area (TAQ-002)
Contact information:
Hiawatha Shore-to-Shore Chapter, NCTA: hss@northcountrytrail.org,
  www.northcountrytrail.org/hss
Tahquamenon Falls State Park Headquarters, 41382 West St. Rte. 123,
  Paradise, MI 49768; www.michigan.gov/tahquamenonfalls

Note that Michigan residents must purchase a $11 Recreation Passport for admission to Michigan State Parks. Call 517-241-PARKS. Passports

Theresa Neal is the Department of Natural Resources park interpreter at Tahquamenon Falls State Park. Her enthusiasm and engaging personality continue to bring love of nature to many lucky families. She says, "I can spend hours connecting a first grader with vernal ponds, the magic of pine cones, and the beauty of birdwatching, but if her mom isn't interested in allowing her to be outside other than the playground or the backyard, that first grader isn't going to have the opportunity to expand on her newfound interests. I work to design programs that attract all ages, particularly families, to outdoor recreational activities that are free or inexpensive. Arming families with the tools and introducing them to the activity is how to encourage future stewards of our parks."

"Many adults were raised in situations where being outside was not part of their upbringing," Neal explains, "so they aren't real sure how to even explore or get out there, let alone be comfortable in the outdoors. Some of these adults come to Tahquamenon, or other popular destinations as a first step to exploring with their families. We try to take them the rest of the way through interpretive programs, giving them tools on how to explore a rotten log or how to catch macroinvertebrates in a stream. I hope that families take those tools and use them to explore other areas, including their local parks and backyards." For more information and a schedule of programs, contact Tahquamenon Falls State Park (41382 West St. Rte. 123, Paradise, MI 49768; 906-492-3415; www.michigan.gov/tfallseducation).

are also available at all Michigan State Parks. The fee for nonresidents is $8.40 daily or $30.50 annually. Permits are available for purchase at the park entrance and prices are subject to change.

Trail Guide

Tahquamenon Falls (in the state park of the same name) consists of two parts connected by a section of the NCT that parallels the Tahquamenon River. Most of the many visitors take in one or perhaps two of the principle attractions: the Lower Falls and the Upper Falls. Parking lots for each are easily accessible by vehicle off State Route 123.

In the interest of making this featured hike as inviting as possible, here are three fun options. First, there's a three-quarter-mile walk from the Lower Falls parking area to the Lower Falls viewing area. Second, there's a 0.25-mile walk from the Upper Falls parking area to the Upper Falls lookout. Third, combine the first two options with a 5-mile walk from the Lower Falls to the Upper Falls. Most of the park's annual half-million visitors opt for a day hike to either of the two waterfalls. Far fewer do the hike between the two.

Arriving at the Lower Falls after the easy three-quarter-mile walk from the parking lot (TAQ-001), look for a complex of waterfalls that demarcate a small island. Part of the scene often includes people who can be seen rowing to the island in rental boats and then exploring the rocks. Depending on the time of year and the water flow, there's a good chance to enjoy the broad spectacle of this mini-Niagara and its dark, tannin-colored waters. The Tahquamenon River only drops 22 feet at the Lower Falls, but the panorama is well worth the easy walk from your vehicle.

The Upper Falls requires only a minimal walk from its parking lot. Regionally third only to Niagara Falls in size and beauty, this is one of the greatest highlights of the entire 4,600-mile NCT. Those with more adventurous souls should consider hiking the 5-mile Tahquamenon River Trail from the Lower Falls to the Upper Falls. (A shuttle returns hikers to their vehicle for a small fee.) Watch for giant pines and delightful streamside scenes.

Follow the NCT/Tahquamenon River Trail, stepping over its many roots. After 0.3 miles, climb a pretty bluff. Most of the trail hugs the river, but this little section provides an overview of the woods and river.

Soon back at the stream, follow it for a mile. Halfway from the Lower

Falls, a bench invites contemplation of the scenery or perhaps of the food and cold beer awaiting 2 miles ahead.

Follow the trail up more sets of stairs to gain another bluff-top view. After a steep stairway descent, there is a delightful, flat, half-mile walk beside the water. Then climb more stairs to the next and final bluff. Here's where your pulse begins to race, not so much from the exertion as from the excitement of first hearing the Upper Falls. This swelling sound thrills with the eternal mystery of the Great North Woods.

At another stairway, look for the option to descend to the river for an up-close view of the Upper Falls.

Turn right on the Old Growth Forest Nature Trail and walk 0.4 miles to the Upper Falls parking lot and the Tahquamenon Falls Brewery and Pub.

Michigan—Tahquamenon

Waypoint Id	Description	Latitude	Longitude
TAQ-001	Lower Falls Parking	46.60459	−85.20129
TAQ-002	Tahquamenon Brewery and Parking	46.57918	−85.25291

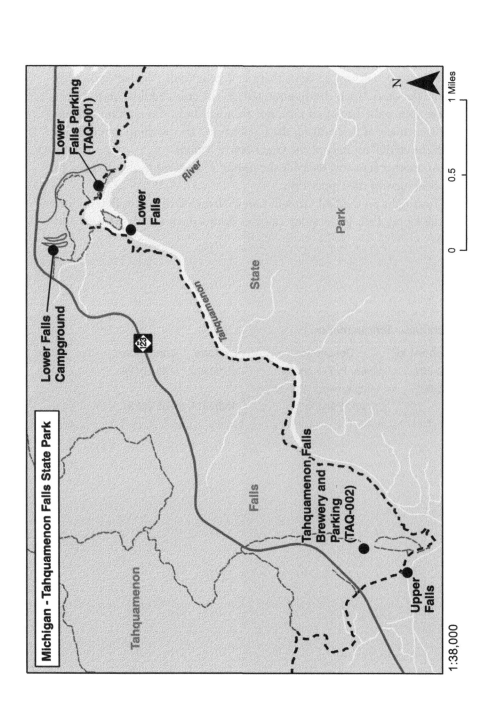

Michigan - Tahquamenon Falls State Park

Lower Falls Parking (TAQ-001)

Lower Falls

Lower Falls Campground

River

Tahquamenon

State

Park

Falls

Tahquamenon

Tahquamenon Falls Brewery and Parking (TAQ-002)

Upper Falls

N

0   0.5   1 Miles

1:38,000

10. Lake Superior Shoreline (Muskallonge Lake to Perry's Landing)

Distance: 5.58 miles
Physical difficulty: Easy
Navigation difficulty: Easy
Highlights: Splendid scenery, get-away-from-it-all remoteness, exciting bird-watching, collectible agates, abundant wild blueberries in season, and plenty of leave-no-trace, flop-down-anywhere camping
Visitation: Low
Nearest town: Grand Marais, MI

The NCTA's Superior Shoreline Chapter maintains this spectacularly beautiful trail located on Michigan state forest land. Though a paved road exists not far inland, this coastal hike delivers a very satisfying feeling of remoteness. Relax and enjoy the views and wildlife. Perry's Landing, the terminus of this featured hike, was named for Robert D. Perry, a foreman with the lumber company of George Dawson and one of the first to log this area in the 1870s.

Trip Planner

Maps: MI-09 and MI-10 (Michigan 09 and Michigan 10), available from www.northcountrytrail.org
Beginning access: County Road 407 trailhead (LSS-001). 1.1 miles west of the Muskallonge Lake State Park entrance
Parking: On the south side of the road, opposite the trailhead, is a level area of dirt and gravel sufficient in size to allow parking up to a dozen vehicles.
Ending access: Perry's Landing Lake Superior State Forest Campground (LSS-004)
Parking: A sand parking area at an extension of a curve in the road is sufficient to safely park six vehicles side by side next to a guardrail.
Contact information:
Superior Shoreline Chapter, NCTA: ssc@northcountrytrail.org, www.northcountrytrail.org/ssc

Trail Guide

This featured hike begins at the trailhead (LSS-001) where the clearly marked NCT crosses County Road 407, 1.1 miles west of the Muskallonge Lake State Park entrance. Walk north toward Lake Superior into the coastal woods of jack, red, and white pines plus striped maples, tag alders, white birch, and black spruce.

Gordon Lightfoot's poignant and powerful song "Wreck of the Edmund Fitzgerald" memorializes the events of November 10, 1975, centering on the disappearance of a 729-foot Great Lakes ore carrier in Lake Superior, with loss of all hands. The largest ship ever to be lost on the Great Lakes, the Edmund Fitzgerald went down about 15 miles north of Whitefish Point. Twenty-nine mariners perished.

Lightfoot's lyrics attribute the lake's name "Gitche Gumee" to a Chippewa legend about Lake Superior. Henry Wadsworth Longfellow referred to Gitche Gumee in his epic poem "The Song of Hiawatha." The Ojibwe name "Gichigami" purportedly means "big water." The anglicized name "Lake Superior" is attributed to the French description of the big lake, "le lac superieur," referring to Superior's map position as "above" Lake Huron, into which the Superior flows via the St. Marys River at Sault Ste. Marie.

Lake Superior is the largest freshwater lake in the world (based on surface area). At its widest, it stretches 160 miles between Canada and Michigan. It has a maximum depth of 1,330 feet and an average depth of 483 feet and contains about 10 percent of all the earth's freshwater. Lake Superior's shoreline is 2,726 miles long. Its average annual surface water temperature is only 40 degrees Fahrenheit.

Such statistics seem insignificant in trying to illustrate the massive impact of Lake Superior on the North Country, something that NCT hikers become intimately familiar with while walking almost the entire southern shoreline as well as almost 300 miles of the Superior Hiking Trail along the north shore.

Hikers will find the Great Lakes Shipwreck Museum in Whitefish Point an interesting side trip. Located about 15 miles off the trail, the museum illustrates the power of the lake and the stories of those who made and still make their living from it—and too often find their fate in its depths. Along the wild shores, the NCT occasionally wanders past the bones of sunken vessels. For more information on the museum, visit www.shipwreckmuseum .com/whitefish-point-4/.

To reach the coast, the trail crosses a large, wooded ridge. Follow the zigs and zags of the blue blazes through trees and across dune topography formed by winds coming off Lake Superior.

At first, the lake is invisible. But glimpses appear, and waves and wind grow louder with each step. In quieter areas, listen for the tap-tap of downy woodpeckers contrasted with the machine-gun hammering of pileated woodpeckers. The raucous cries of sandhill cranes may also be heard.

The trail is well blazed, but navigation isn't an issue, since the route simply parallels the lakeshore— mostly a bit inland, but sometimes on the sand. Avoid trampling beach plants. As hardy as they are to eke out an existence in these harsh conditions, their grip is tenuous enough as it is.

Agates are a fascinating collectible, easily found on this attractive coast. Agate is a form of hard, fine-grained, banded rock that is prized by collectors for jewelry and other decorative uses. More information about Lake Superior agates can be found online at www.dnr.state.mn.us/education/geology/digging/agate.html.

Please note that Lake Superior's reputation for unpredictability is well deserved. Its weather can change alarmingly fast. Hikers should be prepared for sudden, harsh conditions that might include wind, rain or snow, and significant temperature drops. This hike's exposure to the lake emphasizes the need to be prepared.

Though relatively uncommon, hikers should be aware of unexpected water-level changes known as seiches. These are caused by strong and persistent winds forcing water levels higher on one side of the lake, in a manner similar to ocean tides (though caused by wind and atmospheric pressures rather than the moon's gravitational forces). Seiches occur much faster than tides and are not predictable. Though seiches are a regular—even daily— occurrence on large lakes, they go unnoticed in most cases. However, they can occasionally cause a significant rise in water levels.

What does this mean for hikers? Tim Hass, president of the NCTA's Superior Shoreline Chapter, says, "If you cross the Blind Sucker River during a seiche, the river depth may increase by three feet or more. Beware that in these conditions the current will go up river, not down river, and can be quite swift. If you're searching for agates in the water, the rapidly rising lake level may catch you unawares. Your gear may not only get wet but also carried away when the water recedes."

There are numerous beach access points from the nearby, recently paved County Road 407. However, the fishing, bathing, and partying visitors tend not to stray far. The overall NCT gets little use.

After 2.5 miles, the trail emerges out of the woods and brush at the Blind Sucker River (LSS-002). A late July or early August arrival will provide plenty of blueberries. Fording the 50-foot-wide stream at the usual shallow summer depths is easy—the bottom is a firm mix of sand and pebbles. Take off your boots and wade across.

Follow the coast westward, across the sand and toward the trees. The trail is regained along a sand berm above the stream. Aptly named saw grass lines the banks, a favorite stop for Canada geese during their migrations.

From here onward, the trail stays inland off the beach. You will pass a few huge white pines that somehow escaped the country's logging boom. The beach sand, sometimes fine, makes for slow walking. But usually the trail is set back in the trees far enough from the beach to create a combination of solid tread and views of broad watery horizons. Note that at this point, Canada is 90 miles due north.

Pass a grove of large red pines. At a hemlock woods, you will find an understory of wintergreen, ferns, and pieces of fallen, rotting birch. Look for bunchberry (Canadian dogwood) and Labrador tea.

After crossing a road for off-road vehicle access (LSS-003), continue along the trail to Perry's Landing Lake Superior State Forest Campground (LSS-004) and the end of this hike.

Michigan—Lake Superior Shoreline

Waypoint ID	Description	Mileage	Latitude	Longitude
LSS-001	County Road 407 Trailhead	0.00	46.67542	−85.6519
LSS-002	Blind Sucker River Mouth	1.80	46.67938	−85.6835
LSS-003	Off-Road Vehicle Road	4.29	46.67624	−85.7354
LSS-004	Perry's Landing/Lake Superior State Forest Campground	5.58	46.67721	−85.7587

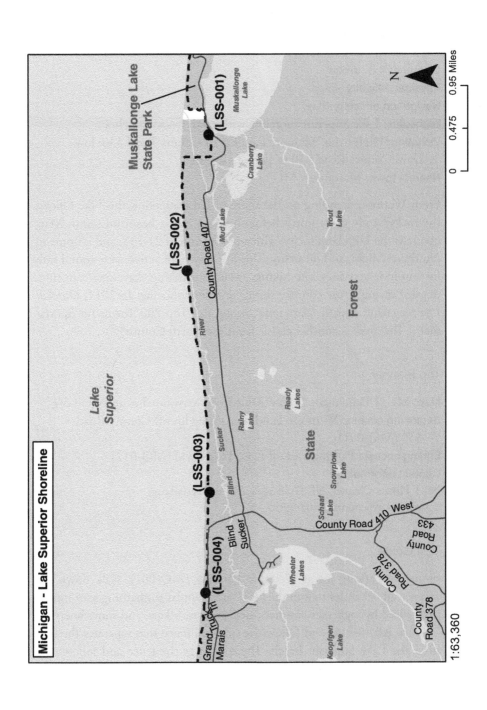

Michigan - Lake Superior Shoreline

Muskallonge Lake State Park

(LSS-001)

Muskallonge Lake

Cranberry Lake

Mud Lake

Trout Lake

(LSS-002)

County Road 407

River

Lake Superior

Forest

Rainy Lake

Ready Lakes

Sucker

Blind

(LSS-003)

State

Snowplow Lake

Schaaf Lake

County Road 410 West

County Road 378

County Road 433

County Road 378

Blind Sucker

Wheeler Lakes

Keopigen Lake

Grand Marais

Tuck Tr

(LSS-004)

N

0   0.475   0.95 Miles

1:63,360

11. Marquette (Wetmore Landing to Echo Lake Road)

Distance: 4.87 miles
Physical difficulty: Easy
Navigation difficulty: Easy
Highlights: Lake Superior shoreline with sandy/rocky beaches
Visitation: High from Wetmore Landing to County Road 550; low from County Road 550 to Echo Lake Road
Nearest town: Marquette, MI

From Wetmore Landing on the shore of Lake Superior, this hike follows the rocky/sandy coast north before heading into a beautiful forest. Marquette is the UP's largest city, with a population of 21,335, and is home to Northern Michigan University. This fine city is an active, year-round hub for outdoor activities like hiking, mountain biking, kayaking/canoeing, dogsled racing, cross-country skiing, and snowshoeing. In 2011, *Outdoor Life* magazine ranked Marquette among its "Top 200 Towns for Sportsmen." This hike is another classic from the North Country.

Trip Planner

Map: MI-11 (Michigan 11), available from www.northcountrytrail.org
Beginning access: Wetmore Landing parking lot off County Road 550 (MQ-001)
Ending access: Parking area off Echo Lake Road (MQ-012)
Contact information:
NCT Hikers Chapter, NCTA: nct@northcountrytrail.org;
www.northcountrytrail.org/nct

Trail Guide

From the parking lot at Wetmore Landing (MQ-001), walk down the access trail 0.1 miles to join the NCT at a popular sunbathing spot much-frequented by joggers, swimmers, dog walkers, bikers, and snowshoers.

Turn left (north) and follow the split-rail fence that separates the trail from the Lake Superior beach. The trail hugs the fence and follows the shoreline north beside brush-free woods of mostly red pine, with some oak, maple, and birch mixed in. Because this section is relatively close to Marquette and Northern Michigan University, it tends to be heavily used.

About 0.1 miles up the trail, pass a third set of beach stairs and reach the end of the split-rail fence. The view includes Sugarloaf Mountain and the power plant by Presque Isle. To the left will be Little Presque Isle. At this point, the trail is sandy underfoot, approaching some rock outcrops on the left and boulders in the water on the right.

There is a beautiful rock feature where the trail becomes rocky and decorated with wild roses. The mixed oak, maple, and balsam forest includes an understory of fern, beach pea, blueberry, and thimbleberry. The rocky trail passes a homemade rock shelter and fire ring.

After 0.35 miles, the trail makes a sharp turn left and climbs a series of 92 steps (MQ-002) to skirt ravines and cliffs. Turn right at the top and follow the trail along a forested ridge high above Lake Superior. County Road 550 is on the left; the trail is between the nearby road and the lakeshore, in mixed woods of pines, balsams, spruce, birch, and striped maple. The

Hikers heading for the first time either north in Michigan or east from Wisconsin toward Michigan's Upper Peninsula may find the proliferation of "pasty" signs puzzling. The pasty (rhymes with "nasty") is basically a pot pie without the pot—a pastry circle laid flat; filled with cubed beef, potatoes, onions, and sometimes rutabaga; seasoned with pepper; folded in half and crimped to form a D shape; and baked. The alternate spelling "pastie" can lead to confusion among the uninitiated, who sometimes pronounce the word as rhyming with "hasty"—which then refers to something else entirely.

A national dish of Cornwall, Great Britain, the pasty accompanied Cornish miners recruited to apply their skills to the UP's mining industry in the mid-1800s. Cornish miners and the Finns who followed and adopted the dish as their own prepared pasties to bring to the mine, where they were often heated on shovels over a coal fire.

Today in the UP, pasty shops proliferate, with fairly stiff competition for gaining a reputation as the best. Each summer in Calumet, there is an annual Pasty Fest to celebrate the culture and tradition. NCT hikers partaking of these carb-loaded delights may find a new favorite.

red rock on the cliffs below and in the lake is marked with bands of white sandstone.

About 0.6 miles from the beginning of the trail, pass a split-rail fence, several varieties of hawkweed, lots of ferns, blue-bead lilies, and numerous dead trees. After a sandy cove, cross a bridge over a deep gully. Broken-off chunks of sandstone litter the shore.

From a nice scenic view, follow the trail as it wanders among the shoreline's trees, negotiates steps, passes a bench, and generally shows off the Superior coast's beauty. Getting down to the water again, walk on the sand beach past rocks and driftwood.

Pass the side trails (MQ-003) that access the Little Presque Isle Point State Recreation Area parking lot. (There is a restroom at the parking area.) Follow the blue-blazed trail to the heavily used Little Presque Isle Point. (There is a wheelchair-accessible path from the parking lot to a cement platform.) This area's pretty pine forest, expansive lakeshore views, and sand dunes are an NCT must-see.

After more side trails, the trail's tread assumes the character of an old railroad grade among blueberries, ferns, maples, balsams, pines, and spruces. Hikers will be thankful that the narrow trail forms a protective barrier from the winds blowing in off the lake.

Pretty green moss lines the trail as it passes a swamp and views of Harlow Creek, a shallow, woodsy trout stream. Off to the right, 2.35 miles from the beginning of the hike, is an access point to the creek.

At 150 feet from a parking access road (MQ-004), turn right and go along the creek on the narrow path. Pass a junction (MQ-005) with the trail that turns left toward the Little Songbird Trail parking area. Continue over a bridge across Harlow Creek.

Beyond the bridge, turn left and then right. Approach County Road 550, but make a sharp right and then a sharp left. The Harlow Creek bridge just crossed is visible on the right as the trail turns left. Curve around and follow the blue blazes past another trail leading off to the left.

Climb old sand dunes through beautiful red pines, oaks, and maples. Pass the marshy area around Harlow Creek and another trail to the left. Descend, then veer to the right. Go uphill through an understory of small brush. A trail coming in from the right meets the NCT as it winds around the marsh on a piney ridge. Follow this trail across gentle, rolling, piney hills—remnants of old dunes.

Eventually turn inland (MQ-006) from the shore on the narrow tread.

At a split (MQ-007) in the trail, go right—the left fork leads to nearby County Road 550 (Big Bay Road). Head toward the lake, up a little rise that holds plentiful ferns and a beautiful carpet of green under the trees. Continue up and down the little hills and through the forest. At a corner where the lake is directly in front of you, turn slightly left to follow the NCT. Beach grass separates the trail from the lake. Off to the right are the cliffs where the shore curves to the right toward Big Bay.

Walk through more red pines in a pretty, less-traveled section complete with a tree tunnel. At a fork, take a sharp right heading back to the shore again (at mile 3.2). Pass a trail on the left. Climb a little knoll to the right for a nice view of the point at Big Bay.

Make a sharp left (MQ-008) away from the lake toward County Road 550 into a mixed forest, meandering up and down a little knoll and then turning left again. The trail is very well-defined here. The blazes do help at cross trails, of which there are quite a few in this heavily used area. There is a little boardwalk through a wet spot at mile 3.75. Turn a little to the left and snake in and out around trees and up and down the little hills. Traffic on County Road 550 may occasionally be heard. These woods and the understory are a lot denser than those experienced earlier. Make a sharp right turn at mile 3.8, then pass a road access trail and a small marsh and boardwalk.

At County Road 550 (MQ-009), cross the road and continue on through ferns, balsams, maples, and birch. After a little hill, reach an intersection with a sign that points left to the Harlow Lake Trail and back to Little Presque Isle Point. Follow the NCT rightward and down a little hill and up a little knoll, where moss and ferns line the route. On this gentle section farther from the lake, the trail passes beautiful mounds of light and dark green moss.

Pass a trail heading left (MQ-010) and veer rightward at mile 4.3 into a nice grove of hemlocks. Cross a rail trail and reenter the woods on its far side.

Pass multiple trails, staying on the blue-blazed NCT. Veer right and then turn sharp right on an old two-track path (MQ-011) at mile 4.42. Although sandy, this tread is relatively easy walking. Thick woods and underbrush line both sides, including tasty thimbleberries in summer. At mile 4.87, there is a deep ditch, easily crossed in summer, but springtime's running snowmelt may necessitate careful fording.

The parking area off Echo Lake Road (MQ-012), 4.9 miles from Wetmore Landing, marks the end of this featured hike.

Michigan — Marquette

Waypoint ID	Description	Mileage	Latitude	Longitude
MQ-001	Wetmore Landing			
	Parking Lot	0.00	46.61501	−87.46817
MQ-002	Steps	0.53	46.61898	−87.46516
MQ-003	Junction Side Trails/			
	Wheelchair Access	1.80	46.63481	−87.46437
MQ-004	Parking Access Road	2.20	46.63383	−87.47259
MQ-005	Trail Junction	2.32	46.63319	−87.47465
MQ-006	Turn Inland	3.13	46.63920	−87.48266
MQ-007	Split	3.19	46.63907	−87.48381
MQ-008	Sharp Left	3.61	46.64185	−87.49128
MQ-009	County Road 550	3.90	46.63916	−87.49286
MQ-010	Trail Junction	4.30	46.63812	−87.49809
MQ-011	Old Two-Track	4.43	46.63909	−87.50155
MQ-012	Parking Area off Echo			
	Lake Road	4.87	46.64308	−87.50724

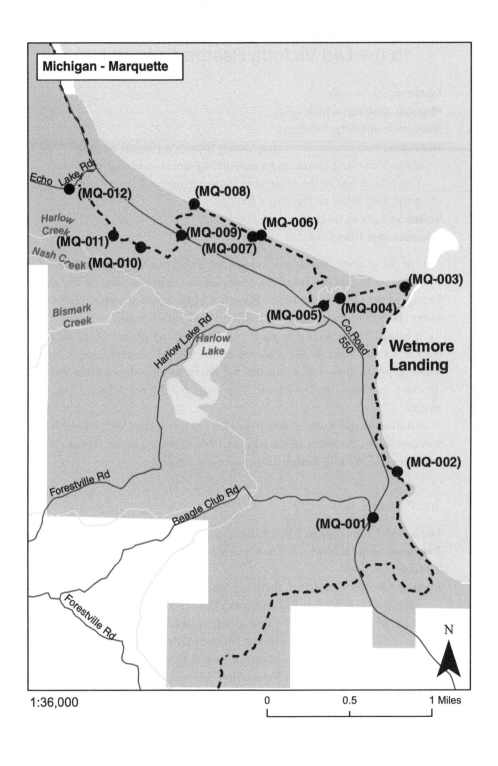

Michigan - Marquette

Echo Lake Rd

(MQ-012)

(MQ-008)

Harlow Creek

(MQ-011)

(MQ-009)

(MQ-006)

(MQ-007)

Nash Creek (MQ-010)

Bismark Creek

(MQ-003)

(MQ-004)

(MQ-005)

Harlow Lake Rd

Harlow Lake

Co. Road 550

Wetmore Landing

(MQ-002)

Forestville Rd

Beagle Club Rd

(MQ-001)

Forestville Rd

N

1:36,000

0   0.5   1 Miles

12. Old Victoria Overlooks (Norwich Road to the Old Victoria Restoration Site)

Distance: 13.83 miles

Physical difficulty: Challenging

Navigation difficulty: Moderate

Highlights: Spectacular views, fascinating history, a historic mining town, a working sauna, and a welcoming screened-in shelter. This hike is one of the most varied, spectacular, and historically interesting hikes on the entire NCT.

Visitation: Low to moderate

Nearest town: Rockland, MI

One of the greatest charms of this segment is that the NCT skirts the long, intermittent line of the Trap Hills bluffs above the broad valley of the west branch of the Ontonagon River. There is a whole series of scenic, bluff-top views about 3 miles in from the trailhead at Norwich Road.

Informal, dispersed camping is possible at many places. Maps on the website of the Peter Wolfe Chapter of the NCTA (www.northcountry-trail.org/pwf/) show which streams are likely to have dependable water. To camp at a high bluff overlook, haul water for the night from a nearby stream.

Another of this featured hike's greatest charms is the Old Victoria Restoration Site, a showcase of the region's 19th-century Copper Range communities and their 12 nationalities and eight languages.

Trip Planner

Maps: MI-13 (Michigan 13), available from www.northcountrytrail.org

Beginning access: Norwich Road (just north of its junction with FR 630) (OV-001)

Parking: On Norwich Road, there is a lot on the west side (poorly signed) that holds a half-dozen cars. The entrance is 250 feet north of Forest Road 630. Though the road is plowed in winter, the trailhead parking area is not. Winter roadside parking is not recommended—snowbanks can be several feet high.

Ending access: Old Victoria Restoration Site and Old Victoria Shelter (OV-012)

Parking: Parking is more secure at Old Victoria than at Norwich

Road. Use a grassy gravel lot just west of Old Victoria on the
northwest side of Victoria Dam Road. The entrance is 130 feet
southwest of the southwest end of the parking area in front of the
restored cabins.

Contact information:
Peter Wolfe Chapter, NCTA: pwf@northcountrytrail.org,
www.northcountrytrail.org/pwf

More information: To arrange a shuttle, contact Superior Shores Resort
(906-884-2653 or info@superior-shores-resort.com). With enough
advance notice, they will run a shuttle for hikers not wishing to
spot a car at Norwich Road.

Trail Guide

From the parking lot on Norwich Road (OV-001) turn right (south) on
Norwich Road, go 100 feet, and look for the trailhead sign on the east
(left) side of the road. For the next mile and a half, the trail ascends the
west side of a ridge, sometimes gently and sometimes steeply, through a
forest of sugar and red maple, yellow birch, eastern hemlock, basswood,
white ash, balsam fir, and white spruce, with occasional northern white
cedar, red pine, and white pine. On open ridges, you'll find bare rock ar-

---

Commercial copper mining operations began in the Norwich area in 1849
and continued sporadically under numerous ownerships until 1921. Victoria
Mine was the final and grandest mine to be operated locally. Though the
industry has disappeared and its ruins are fading into the brush, the Old Victoria Restoration Site is a testament to life during the heyday of the region's
1899 to 1921 copper boom. (To put this history in perspective, it is helpful to
know that, on average, 1 in every 118 miners died in work-related accidents
in the Copper Range each year.)

Some of the miners' log cabins have been restored for visitors who tour
the Keweenaw National Historical Park's Heritage Sites (Victoria Dam Road,
Rockland, MI; 906-886-2617). Guides at the Society for the Restoration of
Old Victoria will be glad to give a tour of the lovingly preserved log buildings.
For information, visit www.ontonagonmi.org/oldvictoria.html.

Also, check out the hikers' shelter at the northeast corner of the site—a
great place to spend the night before or after the hike.

eas with lichens, serviceberry, northern red oak, cherry, ferns, and flowers characteristic of such sites.

Eventually, the trail reaches heights above Norwich Road. After a series of ups and downs, the trail reaches at least four spectacular overlooks. Southwest is the valley of the west branch of the Ontonagon River. To the west are the highest summits of the Trap Hills, and on a clear day, there are views of a 350-foot sheer rock bluff, the highest in Michigan. Far in the distance, to the southwest and south, are hills south of State Route 28, visible most of the way to the Wisconsin line. To the northwest is the stack of the abandoned White Pine Copper Smelter, and beyond that are the hills of Porcupine Mountains Wilderness State Park, Michigan's largest state park. To the north-northwest, the blue horizon of Lake Superior is faintly visible.

The streams, mostly seasonal, offer no guaranteed access to drinking water. However, there is a permanent creek (OV-002).

Follow the trail into a narrow valley marked by high rock bluffs. Then swing west onto high, east-west piney ridges for more nice, short-range views. This area has many 19th-century copper mines, known collectively as Norwich Mine. Mining began on Norwich Bluff in 1852 and continued sporadically until 1916. The ridges traversed by the trail for the next 2 miles are riddled with abandoned mine tunnels and adits (horizontal mine entrances). The Ottawa National Forest sealed up the vertical shafts, except where they installed grates for easy access by bats. Wander these ridges using care not to enter any pits or dangerous, disguised cavities.

Pass a side trail that heads downhill to the west, this is the Ottawa National Forest's Norwich Mine Interpretive Trail (OV-003). Continue ahead on the NCT to a sign on the left indicating a side trail to gated Forest Road 642. The former site of Norwich Fire Tower as well as a fenced-off mine shaft stand about 500 feet north on this side trail.

Descend the NCT into a deep valley, turn right, and encounter the remains of an old road. Stay on the blue-blazed trail, following the valley southward. The trail shortly reencounters another section of the Norwich Mine Interpretive Trail (OV-004)and then turns sharply left. A seasonal stream parallels the old road on the left. Ahead is a trail that leads steeply down to the base of Norwich Bluff and then right to the former site of the community of Norwich. A side trail to the left along the base of the bluff leads to the still-active Norwich Cemetery. The side trip to the mine and cemetery is well worth a visit; the round-trip is about 1.4 miles.

Leaving the valley, the trail climbs onto a ridge to begin a series of ups and downs, past several great views to the south. Camping is possible in red pines near these views, but water is limited to a seasonal stream about 500 feet to the north. If no water is present where the trail crosses the streambed, there are likely pools downstream to the east.

Where the trail turns north, bushwhack east along the ridge for a side trip offering a great view. Cross a hill, descend 100 feet or so, cross a flatter area, and ascend to the summit of a very exposed, rocky knob surrounded mostly by sheer cliffs. Return to the trail by retracing the route in; or, after descending the rocky knob, head northwest on the contour to reconnect with the trail near the seasonal stream.

After the seasonal stream, the trail heads northwest, then north up a steep slope, and then east across a couple of low summits. At the final summit, there is a great view toward some high hills to the south and down the valley of the west branch of the Ontonagon River to the southeast.

Follow the trail north over another hill and then east toward Whisky Hollow Creek (known as Front Run in the 19th century). There is a 1-mile, white-blazed trail (OV-005) that provides access to a parking lot on Victoria Road.

Whisky Hollow Creek is a permanent stream, though a bit cloudy due to clay soils upstream; prefiltering the water before drinking is recommended. Listen for the sounds of rocky rapids ahead and to the right; this is a great place for a break to cool off feet and perhaps even take a shallow dip. Camping is possible across and just upstream from the rapids.

Continue upstream and ford Whiskey Hollow Creek (OV-006). The trail then crosses a gully, a flat area, a low rock hill, and then a minor gravel road. This road also provides access to Victoria Road to the north.

Continue east as the trail climbs a narrow basalt ridge, encountering excellent views all along the way. Extensive open areas on the ridge eventually end, and the trail begins following gentler ridges eastward, still with occasional southward views.

In about half a mile, drop northward off the ridge. The trail then turns east toward Gleason Creek (OV-007), the most spectacular of several streams that flow southward off the ridge, forming gorges and waterfalls during the next few miles. Camping is possible across this permanent stream, a short distance to the northeast in a hemlock grove.

For a side trip, make an excursion down the wild, V-shaped gorge of Gleason Creek, following the primitive Gleason Falls Trail downstream as it hugs the east side of the creek, well above the stream. In a hundred feet or so, pass an adit on the left. Nineteenth-century miners probably found a small vein of copper here; they drilled their way into the hillside for about 20 feet before it appears that the vein petered out. This cool spot on a hot summer day is also potentially a place to escape a sudden thunderstorm. However, spending the night would require removing much loose rock from the adit floor to create a sufficiently level spot. Continue the side trip to reach nearby Gleason Falls. This 100-foot-deep sanctuary of sheer rock walls houses a 20-foot waterfall where the creek issues from a narrow notch into a pool.

Returning to the trail, head east up a valley and southeast onto a high ridge. This ridge is fairly level and provides several more panoramic views to the south. A short connector trail to the north leads to a marked parking spot on an old logging road that can be used as a trailhead to divide this hike into two convenient day hikes. The logging road must be driven with care, because it is blocked by fallen trees sometimes and has some low-clearance areas.

East of that connector trail, the trail is flat for a while then passes another great overlook and breaks out of the woods at the top of a descending rocky ridge with a long eastward view. Note the rocky knob about a mile and a half to the northeast. On reaching it, there will be another opportunity for a scenic side trip.

The trail descends the ridge to first one and then a second small stream crossing. The second crossing, where hikers step across the stream at the top of a narrow canyon, is particularly lovely. A small waterfall dropping over a conglomerate ledge can be seen about 100 feet upstream. Campsites and water are easily found in this area.

Follow the trail's gradual descent to the northeast, dropping from one flat "bench" to the next, and cross a seasonal stream above a rocky gully. The next, obviously permanent stream appears after a long descent. Water is available near the stream, but for camping, continue along the trail to an older hardwood forest on the uppermost flat, below steep rock slopes.

Head east on the level and flat trail. Cross a small seasonal stream, followed by two talus slopes beneath the isolated rock knob mentioned earlier. Soon, reach the end of a smooth rock ridge.

To ascend the knob for a scenic side trip, circle north and northwest around the end of the ridge and head uphill, keeping the ascending rock ridge on the left. There are several notches in the ridge. Climb to the farthest one, which is considerably deeper than the others. Enter the notch and scramble up a very steep slope to the right, grabbing trees at times to facilitate the climbing. Climb to the very top, where there is a stupendous

360-degree view. This is a "don't miss" side trip if the weather is good. Reverse direction to return back to the trail.

Back on the trail, continue east across a flat. Parallel a rock bluff on the left. Leaving the bluff, watch for evidence of past mining activity. A short distance north of the trail is an excavation from the 1840s United States Mine. The mine was short-lived (like most), and little copper was produced there.

Beyond the mine, follow the trail for about a mile across flat country dominated by aspen. Where the flat country ends, cross a minor road. The trail begins a steep ascent of the next hill to the east. The first 300 vertical feet are crammed into about 1,000 feet of trail. It's worth the climb, though, because yet another panoramic view soon appears on the right. Camping would be possible here, but the nearest water source is at least a half mile away.

Follow the trail down a rocky ridge and through the lovely valley of a branch of Cushman Creek, where there are plenty of spots for informal, dispersed camping.

The trail crosses the creek and ascends yet another ridge. Follow the trail down the ridge, steeply at the end, and then down a rocky road. For a so-so scenic view, go left off the road across a flat area and out to the bluff again. A better view lays a couple hundred feed ahead at Lookout Mountain (OV-008).

Enjoy the spectacular panorama of Victoria Dam and its reservoir, looking for the clay cliffs downstream along the west branch of the Ontonagon River. These were deposited in a lake by a glacier at the end of the last ice age. Also note the trench atop Lookout Mountain where a prospector probably searched for copper ore.

Follow the trail east for 0.4 miles off Lookout Mountain along a route frequented by all-terrain vehicles and sometimes snowmobiles. After reaching and crossing Victoria Dam Road (OV-009), a possible parking spot in summer, the trail angles left, recrosses the road back to the west, and follows an old "tram road" for almost 1,000 feet. In the past, cars filled with copper ore were carried down the tram road to a rock crusher near the west branch of the river. Empty cars returned to the mine via the same route, pulled along by the weight of the full descending cars.

Turn left in young aspen and head toward an east-west power line. Eventually turn right, cross the power line, and head northwest into the parklike woods.

Follow the trail downhill to the right and then up and down, passing

a signed, white-blazed trail (OV-010) that heads to the left. Continue on the blue-blazed trail as it descends, turns left and then right, and intersects Victoria Road in the town of Victoria. Note that Old Victoria is still ahead. Follow the road to the left for 200 feet. A fascinating map of this section, including buildings and a 1937 aerial photo with mining structures identified, can be accessed online at www.coppercountryexplorer.com/2011/06/an-old-look-at-old-victoria/.

The large house on the right was formerly the home of the mine "captain," or boss. Just past this house, turn right and continue following the blue blazes, which will skirt many mining ruins. Follow the trail left and right before intersecting a narrow gravel road. Turn right on this road. A mine's sealed entrance to the left is followed by an obvious path to the top of a huge pile of mine waste. This "poor rock pile" provides a grand view north to Lake Superior and east to the hills at the town of Rockland.

Continue east on the gravel road, then veer right and enter a roofless, stone-walled ruin. Cables from this building were used to hoist copper ore out of the mine. Cross the hoist house's cement floor and exit out the back door.

Follow the trail down a circuitous route that soon passes the opening of a short, exploratory mine. Turn left and follow on an old road until it reaches another rocky road. Then go left 75 feet and turn right onto another old road, continuing past the remains of log buildings in the area known as the Sawmill Location. Veer right where that old road peters out. There will soon be another sign for the former interpretive trail (OV-011). Stay right to soon enter Old Victoria.

Pass the sauna (open to anyone who joins the Society for the Restoration of Old Victoria) and then a new outhouse. Ahead is the Arvola house, and to its left is the Usimaki house, which serves as a visitor center. Be sure to drop in for a guided tour.

Continue along the trail on the grass behind the cabins. Then drop down a small hill to the Old Victoria Shelter (OV-012) and the end of this segment of the NCT.

Michigan — Old Victoria Overlooks

Waypoint ID	Description	Mileage	Latitude	Longitude
OV-001	Norwich Road	0.00	46.68118	−89.38954
OV-002	Permanent Creek	0.47	46.67651	−89.38477
OV-003	Norwich Mine Interpretive Trail	1.91	46.66376	−89.38258
OV-004	Norwich Mine Interpretive Trail (Second Junction)	2.26	46.66379	−89.37739
OV-005	White-Blazed Trail to Parking Lot on Victoria Road	3.85	46.66826	−89.36083
OV-006	Whisky Hollow Creek	4.08	46.66887	−89.35628
OV-007	Gleason Creek	5.21	46.67053	−89.33554
OV-008	Lookout Mountain	11.68	46.69199	−89.23598
OV-009	Victoria Dam Road	12.20	46.69464	−89.23041
OV-010	White-Blazed Trail Junction	12.59	46.69757	−89.23474
OV-011	Former Interpretive Trail Junction	13.26	46.70200	−89.23259
OV-012	Old Victoria Shelter	13.83	46.70660	−89.22710

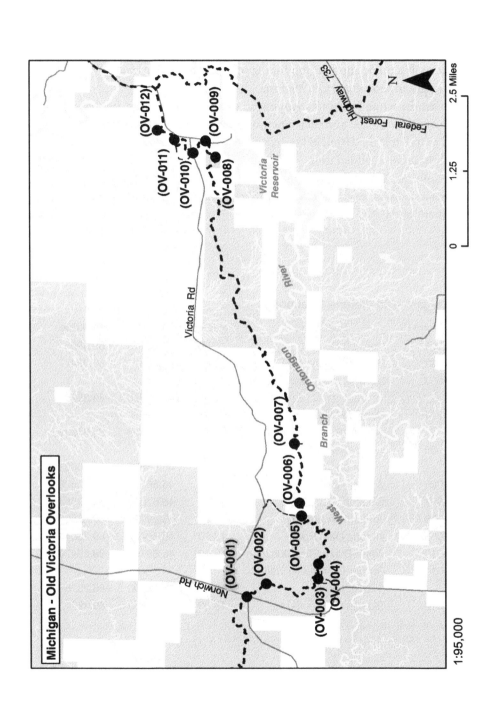

Michigan - Old Victoria Overlooks

1:95,000

0   1.25   2.5 Miles

N

13. Black River Falls (Great Conglomerate Falls to Black River Harbor)

Distance: 3.25 miles
Physical difficulty: Moderate
Navigation difficulty: Easy
Highlights: Five highly varied waterfalls and the US Forest Service's
only deepwater harbor
Visitation: Moderate
Nearest towns: Bessemer and Ironwood, MI

This featured hike is a gateway to the portion of the Great North Woods in the Ottawa National Forest. Adjoining the national forest at the Bessemer Ranger District is nearby Porcupine Mountains Wilderness State Park, a 59,000-acre wilderness area and the largest state park in Michigan. The "Porkies" contain range after range of gnarly mountains, lovely shoreline, old growth giants, and plentiful wildlife. The NCT traverses both the national forest and the state park within one day's hike. While roads access both Black River Harbor (via Black River Road, a 30-minute drive from Bessemer) and the mouth of the Presque Isle River (via Presque Isle Road, a 45-minute drive from Bessemer), no road directly links the two—only the NCT does that.

To combine the interior's scenery with the coast's delights, be sure to hike this route from Great Conglomerate Falls to Black River Harbor. It

Certainly one of the most appealing aspects of the NCT is the never-ending diversity, whether natural, cultural, historic, or simply in the people you meet. That diversity extends to working landscapes as well. As the NCT hiker traverses America's northern heartlands, there are opportunities to experience everything from pristine wilderness, where the touch of human hands can be difficult to discern, to intensely managed landscapes, where the human interface is not only apparent but may also be offensive. Hiking downwind of a chicken farm or following in the footsteps of a manure spreader is a possibility. There's the probability that growing oil and gas exploration and drilling will continue on or near parts of the NCT, and hikers encountering it will likely be displeased at the noise, smell, truck traffic, and sometimes loss of trail that occurs. Mining or quarrying for ores, minerals, and hard rock is prevalent in some areas, and the state and national forests that host many miles of the NCT are managed for multiple uses, including logging, though hikers rarely enjoy passing through the signs of recent timber harvests or clear-cuts.

Environmental and aesthetic impacts can be severe, but it is not our point here to debate whether or not these practices should be allowable—that's a separate discussion. If impacts are visible, they have been allowed, and hikers might make an effort to better understand these working landscapes— the purposes of the activity, the ways in which impacts on the environment are managed, and the efforts by the NCTA and land managers to mitigate the effects on the trail hiking experience. The result may be a deeper appreciation for the interrelatedness of things as well as for the difficulty in balancing competing and even opposing interests on behalf of the public trust.

The hiking community has very high interest in maintaining the current states of certain working landscapes. For example, when it becomes economically unviable, farmland often converts to housing developments, and most NCT hikers greatly prefer walking along field edges or through woodlots than in the latest "Quail Ridge" or "Fox Hollow" subdivision, where nary a quail or fox will likely be found again. Clear-cut forests are another example. Though it can be difficult seeing a trail once surrounded by mature trees changed to slash piles and sawdust, these areas will be regrown with underbrush within even a year, possibly creating opportunities for berry picking on the trail. Within 15 to 20 years, as the aspens regenerate, the trail will become a haven for grouse and woodcock or support the growth of jack pines, critical habitat for endangered species like the Kirtland's warbler and the Karner blue butterfly. Forest management can be aesthetically displeasing, but the positive value of the ecological diversity it engenders, not to mention the value of the timber and employment opportunities such ventures create, can outweigh the negative value of the temporary disruption of natural beauty.

NCTA chapters are working closely with land managers to build relationships that help mitigate the negative impacts of working landscapes as they occur. Creating buffer zones in clear-cuts is one example; another is routing haul roads or locating drilling pads to ensure and uphold NCT values. In the end, reality necessitates that some portions of the NCT's 4,600 miles traverse working landscapes. Better understanding these areas and their value to local communities—and, in some cases, their importance to NCT preservation—can create a deeper appreciation of the NCT's uniqueness among the National Scenic Trails.

has a series of beautiful and varied waterfalls as well as logging-era and coastal history. There are the deeply incised canyons of the Black River Valley and, of course, glimpses of majestic Lake Superior. More unexpectedly, there is the massive Copper Peak Ski Flying Hill, the only hill for ski flying in the Western Hemisphere and the world's largest artificial ski slide.

This hike begins at a parking area off the Black River National Forest Scenic Byway (Co. Hwy. 513) and totals 3.25 miles. Sights include Great Conglomerate Falls, Potawatomi Falls, Gorge Falls, Sandstone Falls, and Rainbow Falls on the way to delightful Black River Harbor.

Trip Planner

Map: MI-14 (Michigan 14), available from www.northcountrytrail.org
Beginning access: Great Conglomerate Falls parking area (BRF-001)

Nelda Ikenberry had already spent 50 years, off and on, at Black River Harbor when she began to write its history. Her *Stories of a Settlement on Lake Superior's South Shore* weaves tales of trappers, squatters, loggers, fishermen, and miners. Her husband, Gilford Ikenberry Jr., the grandson of early pioneers, had introduced the Iowa farm girl to Black River Harbor in 1950. She remembers, "Who would not be awed with the surrounding forests, the beautiful blue Lake Superior, its lonely beaches, and the marvelous tea-black river cascading down waterfalls behind the cabin!" Before she knew it, she reports, "Everything I touched had a story."

Nelda tells about expert blacksmith Fred Drier (1892–1965). "Trapping was especially important during the Depression, when blacksmith and logger jobs were unavailable," she says. "Fred skinned and sold a large variety of animals such as wolf, coyote, and fox as well as beaver, mink, weasel, skunk, and wildcat. His skill in setting beaver traps involved knowledge of how beaver run to water when trapped, and how to set the trap to provide a quick, clean kill. He could skin a skunk on the trail and quickly have its hide in his pocket without a trace of odor. He knew all the tricks trappers needed to know."

"Fred did a great deal of walking," continues Nelda. "Wearing handcrafted snowshoes and pulling a homemade toboggan, he often found it necessary to walk the wagon road into Bessemer from the Harbor in winter for supplies. One year he walked home fifty miles from Ontonagon along the beach to the Harbor. That required an overnight stay under a driftwood plank in the rain."

Parking: Parking lot
Ending access: Black River Harbor (BRF-002)
Parking: Parking lot
Contact information:
Ni-Miikanaake Chapter, NCTA: nmk@northcountrytrail.org,
   www.northcountrytrail.org/nmk

Trail Guide

From the Great Conglomerate Falls parking area (BRF-001), walk east 0.5 miles to the Black River through the coniferous forest. The most exciting time to visit Great Conglomerate Falls is in spring, when high water roars over a flat bed of conglomerate rock only to be squeezed in a vise of narrow granite walls. However, low-water periods provide delightful opportunities to explore interesting pools. At all times, there is the possibility of sighting bear, fox, coyote, wolf, raccoon, and otter. Spring brings flocks of migrating birds. Eagles nest along the river. Trout enliven the water. With so much wildlife and such a vibrant forest, it is hard to imagine that the whole area (except for small pockets of hemlock and cedar) was completely cutover in the early 1900s.

Follow the NCT downstream along a bluff of hemlock and cedar. Both of these types of trees are in decline here because the numerous deer eat the seedlings necessary for regeneration.

The curious thing about this section of trail is that despite its short length, the waterfalls are each so distinct from each other. Potawatomi Falls, for instance, cascades its water into small pools. Gorge Falls looks as if the river has been squeezed into a narrow slot canyon of conglomerate rock. (Note the bathtub-ring effect below the forest of hemlock and fir.) Rainbow Falls has not only a 30-foot vertical drop but also, almost always, a rainbow. Hike the Rainbow Falls Trail's more than 200 steps to an overlook at the very edge of the action. Rainbow Falls is spectacular in all four seasons, but especially during spring runoff.

Follow the NCT as it crosses the road and parallels it to a junction. A right turn takes hikers 0.5 miles on a side trip to Sandstone Falls, where a 126-step stairway descends to many delightful pools suitable for wading, soaking, and being nibbled by small fish. Continue through the campground until reaching Black River Harbor and its parking lot (BRF-002).

Black River Campground has 40 sites, flush toilets, a host, and occa-

sional bears. It is open from mid-May to October 1. Reservations are not available here, it is first-come, first-served only.

Boat arrivals may wish to moor at Black River Harbor at the mouth of the river, on the shore of Lake Superior. There the Forest Service's harbormaster can accommodate over two dozen boats. Look for migrating mergansers and families of resident river otter.

This hike can be extended eastward by crossing the 210-foot suspension bridge erected by the Civilian Conservation Corps in 1938–39. From there, follow the NCT east to the Porcupine Mountains.

Michigan—Black River Falls

Waypoint Id	Description	Latitude	Longitude
BR-001	Great Conglomerate Falls Parking Area	46.63256	−90.06521
BR-002	Parking Lot	46.66325	−90.05249

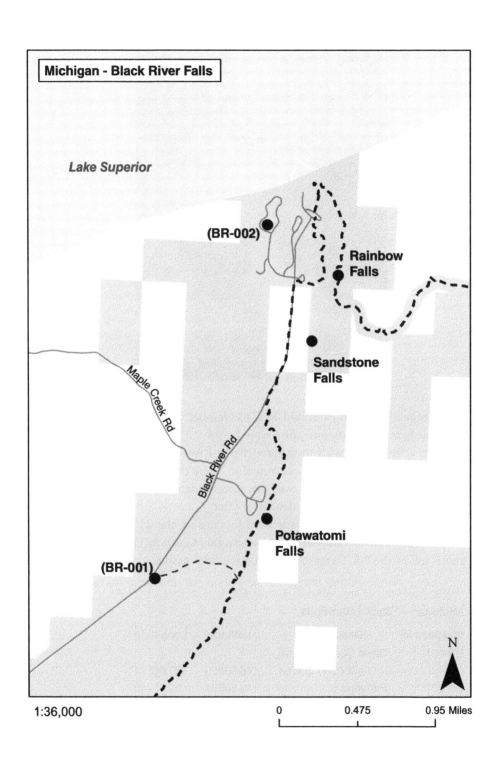

Michigan - Black River Falls

Lake Superior

(BR-002)

Rainbow
Falls

Sandstone
Falls

Maple Creek Rd

Black River Rd

Potawatomi
Falls

(BR-001)

N

1:36,000

0   0.475   0.95 Miles

Wisconsin

Wisconsin proudly lays claim to the highest percentage of completed portions of the NCT and to the longest continuous stretch of trail constructed to meet trail standards. In addition, Wisconsin offers spectacular waterfalls, varied terrain, long vistas, and the ancient Penokee Mountain Range. Weather-wise, expect the first snowfall by mid-November, with most snow melting by mid- to late April. Fall color is best from about the third week of September through the middle of October.

Most of the trail from the Michigan-Wisconsin border to Copper Falls State Park is undeveloped, but some short, spectacular sections do exist, with more becoming available each year. The first real trail segments in Wisconsin pass through Iron County Forest, within the very old and worn-down Penokee Mountain Range. Reaching Wren Falls begin a temporary road walk to Copper Falls State Park, known for its many spectacular waterfalls. From there, follow almost 120 miles of continuous off-road trail that extends westward toward Minnesota. This long stretch is interrupted by only two short road walks. Just beyond the park, a segment of trail extends into the village of Mellen (one of only two trail towns in Wisconsin), where most needed services can be found. At the west edge of Mellen again follow a temporary road walk for 1.8 miles before entering the Chequamegon National Forest.

The Chequamegon section of trail is often credited with giving the NCT its name. Within the forest, the trail passes through the federally designated Porcupine Lake Wilderness and Rainbow Lake Wilderness. Throughout the rest of the forest, observe the parklike open understory. Watch and listen carefully for big bull elk strutting or bugling in the fall, as this part of Wisconsin was chosen to reintroduce a herd of elk.

The NCT exits the Chequamegon National Forest just east of Bayfield County Highway A and enters the Bayfield County Forest—the home of huge red and white pines and several small, pristine lakes. Two nice campsites occur on these small lakes. At South Shore Grade Road, the NCT enters Brule River State Forest. Soon the trail is following the high bluffs overlooking the famous Bois Brule River. Farther west, it follows the Historic Portage (marked by eight stones commemorating explorers, fur traders, and settlers) and passes through the Brule Bog's unique, cedar bog environment on more than 3,900 feet of boardwalk.

Crowshaw Road begins the last of the temporary road walks within the long trail segment. In 1.8 miles, the NCT enters Solon Springs, the other trail town in Wisconsin. Solon Springs offers a full range of services for hikers. Southwest of Solon Springs, pass for more than six miles through the Douglas County Wildlife Area, a pine barrens managed for prairie species. Beyond the open barrens, the trail approaches the St. Croix National Scenic Riverway, where the St. Croix River is paralleled for several miles.

The trail route then passes through long expanses of Douglas County Forest before reaching Pattison State Park. In Pattison, the trail passes Little Manitou Falls, followed by Big Manitou Falls—the highest waterfall in the state. West of Pattison, the trail route again enters Douglas County Forest lands. On reaching the Nemadji River, it follows the high rim overlooking the valley. Beyond the Nemadji, the trail follows the dikes within a large wetland mitigation project area and soon enters Minnesota just south of Jay Cooke State Park.

Wisconsin's Featured Hikes

1. **Wren Falls** (Casey Sag Road to Wren Falls)

2. **Porcupine Lake Wilderness** (Forest Road 213
   [Porcupine Lake Road] to County Highway D)

3. **Historic Portage and Brule Bog Round-Trips**
   (Upper St. Croix Lake trailhead)

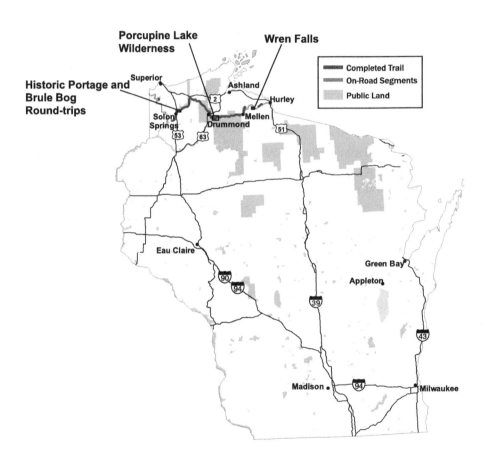

1. Wren Falls (Casey Sag Road to Wren Falls)

Distance: 3.29 miles
Physical difficulty: Easy
Navigation difficulty: Moderate
Highlights: The NCT passes a so-called gold mine whose abandoned shafts and rusting steam boiler are quaint evidence of investor gullibility. Hikers will probably want to invest in a walk, midway through this featured hike, along a very short spur trail to the thrilling vista at the top of a rock outcrop. Payoff comes at the end with pretty Wren Falls. Its solitude, its remoteness, and the dramatic way that it issues from a break in the bedrock are sure to leave a lasting impression.
Visitation: Low
Nearest town: Mellen, WI

This featured hike includes evidence of a classic "gold mine" scam in which, sometime in the late 1800s, crooks peddled shares in a fictitious mother lode to investors, then decamped with the rubes' money. Look along the trail for an old steam boiler and a couple of water-filled mine shafts. Of course, from the NCT's point of view, the real gold is this hike's lovely waterfall, backwoods magic, and occasional, distant views. (Note: Iron County Forest allows camping anywhere, for a maximum of two weeks.)

Trip Planner

Map: WI-01 (Wisconsin 01), available from www.northcountrytrail.org
Beginning access: Casey Sag Road (WRN-001)
Parking: Roadside at trailhead
Ending access: Wren Falls (WRN-004)
Parking: There is no good parking location at the exit trailhead. Hikers are advised to spot a car on Vogue Road (1 mile north on the two-track road). Alternately, they may retrace their steps to the Casey Sag Road trailhead.
Contact information:
WI Regional Trail Coordinator: HQ@northcountrytrail.org

On the building of the Wren Falls segment of the NCT, Bill Menke, the NCTA's regional trail coordinator for Wisconsin, reports, "The Wren Falls segment is not 'remote' compared to some other wilderness or mountainous regions. As trail builders, we had relatively easy access from roads at each end of the 3.4 miles. Our primary difficulty in building the trail stemmed from lack of local volunteers. Iron County Wisconsin's low population density was further complicated by the fact that very few, if any, locals were 'hikers.'

"This segment's construction stretched over a five-year period, beginning in 2007. Our work was shepherded by NCTA's Heritage Chapter, the majority of whose members hail from the Milwaukee area, some five to six hours to the south. To conduct a trail-building work trip, they had to travel a long distance, dedicating at least a weekend to the trip. An additional difficulty was that many of our superannuated 'regulars' felt less capable of wielding heavy trail tools for hours on end.

"So the chapter had to come up with innovative approaches in order to construct this segment. First, the National Park Service office in Madison contracted with the Student Conservation Association for a month-long, high school–aged crew to construct about 1.2 miles of new trail. Early the following summer, NCTA's Brule–St. Croix Roving Trail Crew arrived to lead the chapter in constructing two bridges across deep ravines. And later still that year, the NCTA Heritage Chapter raised funds and contracted with a private trail construction firm to build another 1.5 miles of trail. The remaining amount of tread was located on old, closed, two-track roads and thus required no construction.

"The next year, the chapter contracted with a Minnesota Conservation Corps crew for a week of paid work. The crew constructed three sections of Type 3 puncheon. Later that year, the crew from Brule–St. Croix returned, this time to build two large bridges.

"Last but not least, the easternmost portion of this trail was relocated to avoid erosion caused by the repeated flooding of a small creek. This relocation required a 32-foot-long, clear-span bridge. Once again, with help from Brule–St. Croix, chapter volunteers constructed the bridge over the course of a long weekend.

None of this will be apparent when hikers enjoy this beautiful section of trail. But please remember that the NCT is only possible due to the sweat equity of hikers who valued their experiences so much that they volunteered to give something back and thus 'pay it forward' for the enjoyment of today's hikers as well as future generations."

Heritage Chapter, NCTA: htg@northcountrytrail.org,
www.northcountrytrail.org/htg
Iron County Forestry and Parks Department, 607 Third Ave. N #2, Hurley,
WI 54534; 715-561-2697

Trail Guide

A hundred feet after leaving Casey Sag Road trailhead (WNF-001), hikers are greeted with a beautiful, 34-foot bridge across an unnamed tributary of Gold Mine Creek. The bridge was constructed by volunteers in 2011, and a sign pays tribute to the trail's sponsors. The trail sports wide tread, good blazes, and fine maintenance as it wends its way through the maples to two more, small bridges.

At 0.6 miles, reach a wooded ravine and the aforementioned "gold" mine. Artifacts such as an old steam boiler and a couple of water-filled shafts deteriorate beside the trail.

Pass several more small bridges. At 2.02 miles, a short spur trail (WNF-002), marked by white blazes, leads to the top of a rock escarpment, providing a long-distance vista overlooking the surrounding hills.

Progressing farther west, the trail passes through rolling woodlands, skirts several large and isolated glacial erratic boulders, descends to a 48-foot puncheon boardwalk, and crosses an unmarked jeep road (WNF-003). Follow the trail as it descends and then reaches the jeep road again. Follow the jeep road 50 feet downhill through the alders. Continue to a bridge, cross a marshy creek, and then follow the road north about 300 feet as it parallels noisy Tyler Forks River. Reenter the woods.

Cross a large, grassy opening where alders are encroaching. The trail crosses a wooded hill, parallels the jeep road, passes an NCT sign, and crosses the jeep road again.

Enter the woods and follow the trail along the bluff (and beside the jeep road). The creek narrows into a rocky gorge that becomes the roaring torrent of Wren Falls (WNF-004).

The view from here is notable not only for the classic waterfall but also for the boiling pool of water below it. Note the small cedar trees that seem to grow out of solid rock. Large lichens attest to the aridity of their granite perches, located only a few feet from the violent current.

This isolated waterfall plunges only 21 feet, but its remoteness and narrow chasm make for a dynamic destination for a fun day hike. Return to Casey Sag Road trailhead. Or walk out the potholed waterfall access and turn north on a more well-defined woods road to reach maintained Vogue Road, where a car can be spotted.

Wisconsin—Wren Falls

Waypoint ID	Description	Mileage	Latitude	Longitude
WRN-001	Casey Sag Road	0.00	46.39597	−90.46506
WRN-002	Spur Trail	2.74	46.39480	−90.48252
WRN-003	Unmarked Jeep Road	1.36	46.39446	−90.49994
WRN-004	Wren Falls	3.29	46.39780	−90.50709

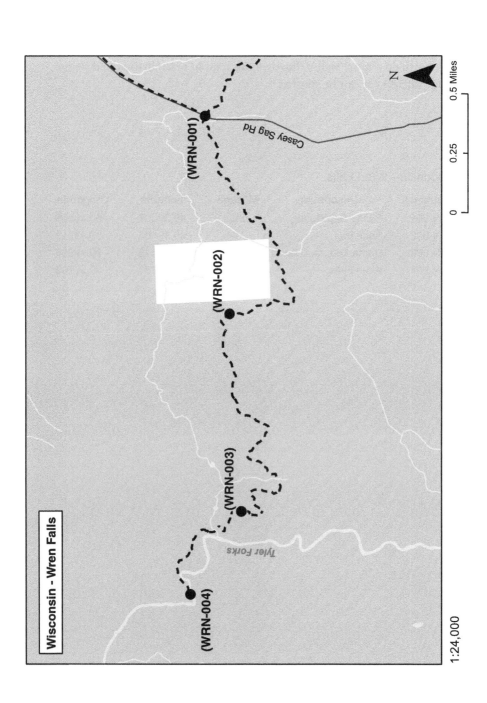

Wisconsin - Wren Falls

(WRN-001)

(WRN-002)

(WRN-003)

(WRN-004)

Casey Sag Rd

Tyler Forks

N

0   0.25   0.5 Miles

1:24,000

2. Porcupine Lake Wilderness (Forest Road 213 [Porcupine Lake Road] to County Highway D)

Distance: 7.14 miles

Physical difficulty: Moderate to difficult. There are some short, moderately difficult climbs. Crossing Eighteen Mile Spring Pond can be difficult during high water. Some beaver dams may be a bit dicey to cross.

Navigation difficulty: Moderate. Chequamegon National Forest's wilderness policy does not permit the NCTA to mark the trail with paint blazes in the Porcupine Lake Wilderness. This lack of blazing makes navigation potentially more difficult for hikers. The trail is well maintained, and rustic wooden NCT signs with pointing arrows are mounted on cedar posts at most confusing intersections.

Highlights: Unusual damage from straight-line winds in 2005; Eighteen Mile Spring Pond; Porcupine Creek; Porcupine Lake; and beaver dams and ponds

Visitation: Light to moderate, depending on the season. However, there is heavy angler traffic all season long on the connector trail and on the NCT to Porcupine Lake.

Nearest town: Drummond, WI

To truly experience the NCT's diversity, wilderness hiking is a must-do. This featured hike in Chequamegon (pronounced sheh-wáh-muh-gun) National Forest is an excellent example. One's navigation skills, ultralight packing ability, and attitude toward bugs will all receive a good test, but prepared hikers knowledgeable about expected conditions will have no difficulty. The reward is an outstanding wilderness hiking experience with the bonus of good fishing possibilities for trout, bluegill, northern pike, and largemouth bass.

In 1984, the US Congress established the Porcupine Lake Wilderness within Chequamegon National Forest. The area features rolling hills to the west and swamps to the east. Its highlight is Porcupine Lake itself, and the best way to see both the wilderness and the lake is on the NCT. Though this is a nonmotorized environment, a day trip allows adequate time to complete this hike. A winter visit on cross-country skis or snowshoes is also highly recommended.

Camping is permitted along the trail as long as campsites are kept at least 100 feet away from the trail and from water. The nearby Two Lakes Campground has a water pump but no showers or flush toilets.

Trip Planner

Map: WI-02 (Wisconsin 02), available from www.northcountrytrail.org
WI Regional Trail Coordinator, HQ@northcountrytrail.org
Beginning access: Forest Road 213 (Porcupine Lake Rd.) (PLW-001)
Parking: Roadside parking at the western wilderness boundary, where the NCT crosses Forest Road 213 (Porcupine Lake Rd.). Alternatively, a connector trail (PLW-002) on the western end of the wilderness (the trail connects to the NCT after it crosses Lake Owen Drive) leaves directly from where campers check in at Two Lakes Campground.
Ending access: County Highway D (PLW-005)
Parking: Off-road parking area at County Highway D at the eastern wilderness boundary
Contact information:
WI Regional Trail Coordinator: HQ@northcountrytrail.org
Chequamegon Chapter, NCTA: che@northcountrytrail.org, www.northcountrytrail.org/che

Trail Guide

Head east from the NCT trailhead (PLW-001) at Forest Road 213 (Porcupine Lake Rd.). This road is also the boundary for the Porcupine Lake Wilderness. A lot of downed trees from the September 2005 windstorm are observable here.

After 0.1 miles, pass the intersection with a connector trail (PLW-002) to Two Lakes Campground, located on Lake Owen and Bass Lake, and a popular spot for loons and fishermen. Turn sharply left at this intersection. The trail passes some huge white pines scattered among the maples, aspen, and balsam firs.

After 0.8 miles, pass a junction with the Eighteen Mile Spring Pond connector trail (PLW-003) coming in from Porcupine Lake Road. Turn right to stay on the NCT. At 1.3 miles, cross Eighteen Mile Creek (either

by fording or by using downed trees). Look northwest from this ford for a faint trail uphill to an informal campsite.

Just after crossing Eighteen Mile Creek, the trail parallels and overlooks Eighteen Mile Spring Pond from a delightful bluff. There is a scenic overlook at the pond's southern end. The trail rolls up and down across wonderful, wooded hills.

Follow beautiful, heavily wooded Porcupine Creek, then cross it on a rustic two-log bridge built in 2007 by the Brule–St. Croix Roving Trail Crew and members of the local NCTA chapter, using primitive skills and techniques—skills that are being lost but are required within wilderness areas. Take a sharp right turn (PLW-004) (the straight path heads back to Porcupine Lake Road and a popular fishing access parking spot). Shortly after crossing the log bridge, arrive at the northern end of wonderfully long Porcupine Lake. There are several primitive, popular campsites, especially on the adjoining hills.

Most of the remainder of the NCT on this hike missed incurring damage from the 2005 storm. From Porcupine Lake, head east along a series of ridges. At an intersection with a large informal campsite on Porcupine Lake, turn left. About midway between the lake and County Highway D will be the first set of beaver dams. Cross on a mixture of short sections of primitive log turnpike and the tops of secondary beaver dams just below the larger dam. These dams are a great demonstration of the engineering abilities of these amazing animals.

About a mile after the smaller beaver dams, reach a large dam (5.3 miles in); the top of this dam is used as trail. Here, wild animals have actually constructed the tread.

Before reaching County Highway D, glimpse marshy West Davis Lake and its connecting bogs (6.75 miles in). East Davis Lake, just beyond County Highway D, has an informal campsite as well as good shoreline access.

Cross the Porcupine Lake Wilderness boundary just before County Highway D (PLW-005). There is a small parking lot at this NCT access point.

To experience the Porcupine Lake Wilderness on a shorter hike, there are options that involve using two connector trails with parking areas along Porcupine Lake Road. Roadside parking is available at a connector trail to Eighteen Mile Spring Pond, and there is a small off-road parking area just north of Porcupine Lake. Consider using one of these connector trails to devise a possible return loop via the very rustic Porcupine Lake Road.

Wisconsin—Porcupine Lake Wilderness

Waypoint ID	Description	Mileage	Latitude	Longitude
PLW-001	Porcupine Lake Road Trailhead	0.00	46.30112	−91.17915
PLW-002	Connector Trail to Two Lakes Campground	0.18	46.29940	−91.17785
PLW-003	18 Mile Spring Pond Connector Trail Junction	0.99	46.29408	−91.16697
PLW-004	Sharp Right Turn	2.88	46.29309	−91.15654
PLW-005	County Highway D	7.14	46.30330	−91.09331

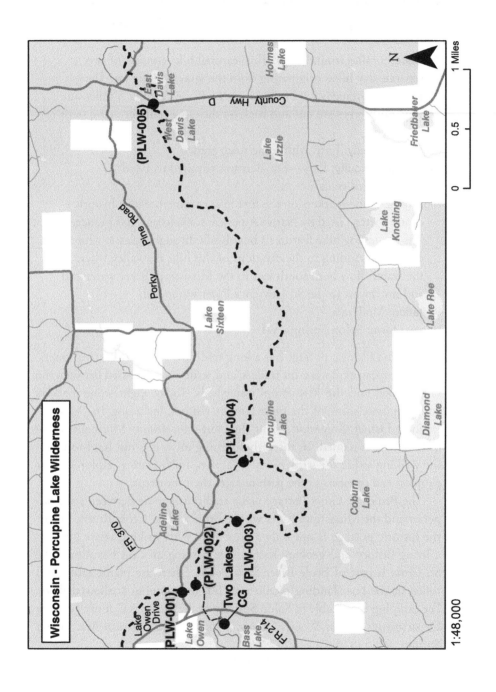

Wisconsin - Porcupine Lake Wilderness

1:48,000

3. Historic Portage and Brule Bog Round-Trips (Upper St. Croix Lake trailhead)

Distance: 9 miles (round-trip). This featured hike consists of two separate day hikes originating from the same parking lot. The Historic Portage is 2.04 miles one way. Brule Bog is 2.5 miles one way. Both hikes are out and back on the same trail, retracing steps to return.

Physical difficulty: Easy, with some steep grades

Navigation difficulty: Easy—but alertness required to avoid unauthorized trails

Highlights: Stone markers on the first hike commemorate a historic canoe portage used by Native Americans, explorers, and pioneers. The Brule Bog hike features a boardwalk through a classic white cedar bog. Adding to the mystique of this hike is a valley where the waters flow both southwest to the Mississippi River watershed and northwest to the St. Lawrence River watershed.

Visitation: Moderate

Nearest town: Solon Springs, WI

Wisconsin's historic portage has a long tradition of use by Native Americans, European explorers, fur traders, and settlers who crossed between the Great Lakes and the Mississippi watersheds. Today, eight stone markers commemorate some of the most famous visitors, including 1679 French explorer Daniel Greysolon, Sieur du Lhut—for whom Minnesota's city of Duluth was named. In the early morning mist, it is not hard to imagine walking stride for stride with voyageurs, missionaries, explorers, first peoples, and pioneers as the path retraces their footsteps.

The Brule–St. Croix Portage was a traditional route between Lake Superior and the Mississippi River via the Brule and St. Croix Rivers. Today, the historic portage is not only a great hike with striking views but also a living history and geology lesson. The parking area on beautiful Lake St. Croix is part of Brule River State Forest. There are picnic tables and toilets at the boat landing/picnic area, but no camping is allowed there. Fee camping is available in Solon Springs, at the Douglas County Forestry Department's Lucius Woods County Park (9231 E. Marion Ave., Solon Springs, WI 54873; 715-378-2219).

Camping is allowed in the Brule River State Forest at designated sites

or by permit. For information, phone Brule River State Forest (715-372-5678) between 8 a.m. and 4 p.m.

The Brule Bog boardwalk is a 0.7-mile, wheelchair-accessible, educational tour of a fabulous white cedar swamp.

Solon Springs was originally called White Birch but was renamed in 1896 in recognition of Tom F. Solon's water-bottling business, the Solon Springs Bottling Company, now long since defunct.

Trip Planner

Map: WI-02 (Wisconsin 02), available from www.northcountrytrail.org
Beginning access: Upper St. Croix Lake trailhead (HP/BB-001)
Parking: Boat landing parking lot at St. Croix Lake
Ending access: Same
Contact information:
WI Regional Trail Coordinator: HQ@northcountrytrail.org
Brule–St. Croix Chapter, NCTA: bsc@northcountrytrail.org,
    www.northcountrytrail.org/bsc

Trail Guide

From the Upper St. Croix Lake parking area's convenient and potable artesian spring, follow the 0.2-mile white-blazed spur trail to its junction with the NCT (HP-002), the beginning of the historic portage trail. Pass a large spring pond that flows into the lake. At County Highway A, there is an NCTA box of informational materials and a large boulder, commemorating the relocating of the trail in 1933.

Sizing up the steep grade that begins the trail, it's not hard to wonder why anyone carrying a canoe and huge load of furs and supplies would pick such a route. Early travelers often valued directness over ease. The trail immediately gives the impression of great age, because it seems to have been worn hip deep, though likely due as much to erosion as to moccasin traffic.

From the top of the bluff, follow the meandering trail along the undulating terrain. It follows the west edge of an escarpment that drops off dramatically farther to the west, affording views of the valley below. This valley was carved by a large torrent of water that drained Glacial Lake Duluth, the predecessor of today's Lake Superior (400 ft. lower), forming the valleys of the Brule and St. Croix Rivers. When the massive glacial flood receded, the springs entering the valley gave rise to two rivers, one flowing north 44 miles to Lake Superior and the other south to the Mississippi. Though today's height of land between the two is a true continental divide, the valley is seemingly so flat that the division of the watershed is almost impossible to discern.

Continue through the birch, balsam, scrub oak, and pine forest to a small boulder with a brass plaque bearing the names of Nicholas and Joseph Lucius and the date 1886 (HP-003). The Lucius brothers were sons of early pioneers in nearby Solon Springs.

Pass seven similar boulders dedicated to significant users of the trail. The boulders are in chronological order, going back in time as the trail heads north. After continuing toward the Brule River past the stone marked "George Stuntz, 1852," encounter beautiful valley views framed by large red pines.

Just beyond the stone marked "Henry Schoolcraft 1820" (HP-004) is a hiker registration box and a simple wooden bench. Many such benches were constructed by Atley Oswald, a charter member of the Brule–St. Croix Chapter of the NCTA. In leaf-off season, this bench affords a beautiful view over several miles of the valley.

Follow the trail as it drops off sharply into a younger forest. At the bottom of the hill, find the stone marked "John Baptiste Cadotte 1819."

Continue along the trail in the shadows of a dense growth of 15- to 20-year-old aspen, birch, and maple for about 350 yards. Entering an older pine and balsam forest, locate the stone marked "Michel Curot 1803"(HP-005).

Ascend another finger of the bluff through conifers dense enough to block direct sunlight, which prevents the buildup of undergrowth. From the top of this promontory, the vast panorama of the Brule Bog opens up. Note the multiple textures and shades of the various forest types.

The trail descends rapidly from the bluff and once again enters a dense tunnel of young timber. After about 100 yards, the trail levels off, and there is an opening where an old two-track trail terminated. Used by trout fishermen, it provided access to the spring-fed pond that lies in the bog a short distance to the west. (The pond is not visible in midsummer but can be seen in leaf-off season.) Since earliest times, this pond has been the subject of controversy regarding the source of both the northeast-bound Brule River and the southwest-bound St. Croix River.

Be careful to follow the NCT via a sharp left turn and not be distracted by the mowed, unauthorized trail on the right. From here on, the trail is relatively level. Follow it along the bog edge through a piney forest. Pass the stone marked "Jonathan Carver 1768" (HP-006). As the bog becomes less visible, walk through a grassy opening that is known for fine blueberry picking in July and August.

About 200 yards beyond large, twin red pines, find the stone marked "Pierre Lesueur 1693" (HP-007). Near here, right on the edge of the bog and 60 feet to the east and a little north, is a fine and clear spring-fed pond.

The remainder of the historic portage portion of this featured hike passes through a dense cover of younger trees that grew up after the destructive hailstorm of August 2000. That storm killed many trees outright and left others dying over time. This area is stocked with abundant blackberry, raspberry, chokecherry, pin cherry, elderberry, and blueberry, along with regenerated aspen, balsam, and birch.

In about 580 yards, reach the stone marked "Daniel Greysolon Sieur DuLhut 1680" (HP-008). Soon afterward, you will come to a two-track trail that branches off from the currently drivable logging road about ten yards to the right. This old road leads to an uncut "island" in the valley that was logged about 20 years ago. A side jaunt on this grown-over trail is rewarded by a small, clear stream, the humble beginnings of the mighty Brule River.

Continue along the portage trail for another 180 yards to a small opening, a remnant of the old Beaupres homestead. From there, in 400 yards, hikers come face-to-face with a routed wooden sign that points the way to the spot where the original users of the portage loaded their heavy packs into canoes to begin traveling the waters of the Brule River.

The end of the portage is less than 100 yards along a narrow, somewhat muddy track through heavy alder, willow, and meadowsweet brush. At an open grass and sedge bog, the spot is marked by a nine-inch, round-topped wooden post (HP-009).

This is the east branch of the Brule River. Take a few minutes to look around and ponder the relief the voyageur must have felt at being able to put his burden down. Though this winding, shallow stream doesn't look like much, in a few miles, it will become a foaming, roaring torrent tumbling toward Lake Superior.

Retrace your steps back to the Upper St. Croix Lake trailhead to conclude the first day of this featured hike.

The second day of the hike begins at the same trailhead (HP/BB-001). Follow the trail to the same junction located about 30 feet up from County Road A. Turn left and head west on the NCT. Follow it 0.3 miles to the Brule Bog boardwalk.

The boardwalk portion of the trail begins at St. Croix Creek (BB-002), where there is a bench. The boardwalk totals 0.7 miles and was built entirely by the Brule St. Croix Roving Trail Crew and members of the NCTA's local chapter. After crossing St. Croix Creek, travel through a cedar bog, crossing a small island in the middle. Continue through an ash bog, following the second section of boardwalk.

At the end of the second section of boardwalk, approaching County Road P, turn right on an upland trail that is actually an elongated island. Follow this upland portion until the trail veers off left toward the unseen bog and, in 500 feet, paved County Road P (BB-003).

Crossing County Road P, enter the longest and most pristine section of the bog and follow the boardwalk through the royal ferns and spongy sphagnum moss. In the month of June, look for lady slippers. A long passage through a stand of black spruce is a perfect example of the small, slow-growing conifer that dominates northern North America.

At an abandoned beaver dam, look for joe-pye weed and boneset. Cross an open area of quaking aspen on the edge of the vast bog. A mile after crossing County Road P is Catlin Creek Campsite (BB-004) , which has a fire ring, another of the many Oswald benches, and a wilderness-style latrine (200 ft. across the trail). Continue to follow the trail, soon crossing Catlin Creek (a good water source) on a small bridge, built in 2011 after a large aspen fell directly on and destroyed the previous bridge. Continue parallel to the winding creek along the trail, which is nicely benched into the steep hillside, until reaching Crowshaw Road (BB-005).

Retrace your steps to the Upper St. Croix Lake trailhead.

Wisconsin—Historic Portage and Brule Bog Round-Trips

Waypoint ID	Description	Mileage	Latitude	Longitude
HP/BB-001	Upper St. Croix Lake			
	Trailhead	0.00	46.37923	−91.77905
HP-002	Junction with NCT	0.20	46.38115	−91.77619
HP-003	Lucius Stone	0.43	46.38326	−91.77290
HP-004	Schoolcraft Stone	0.67	46.38488	−91.76863
HP-005	Curot Stone	0.91	46.38608	−91.76428
HP-006	Carver Stone	1.25	46.38880	−91.75825
HP-007	Lesueur Stone	1.51	46.39058	−91.75376
HP-008	DuLhut Stone	1.75	46.39304	−91.74968
HP-009	End of the Portage	2.04	46.39618	−91.74696
Waypoint Id	**Description**	**Mileage**	**Latitude**	**Longitude**
HP/BB-001	Upper St. Croix Lake			
	Trailhead	0.00	46.37923	−91.77905
BB-002	St. Croix Creek/Boardwalk	0.58	46.38581	−91.77196
BB-003	County Road P	1.13	46.39175	−91.77131
BB-004	Catlin Creek Campsite	2.20	46.39563	−91.78918
BB-005	Crowshaw Road	2.50	46.39404	−91.79221

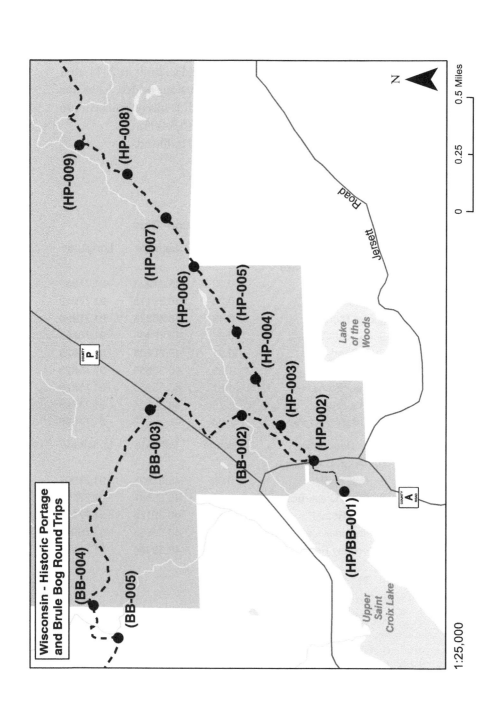

Wisconsin - Historic Portage
and Brule Bog Round Trips

(HP-009)

(HP-008)

(HP-007)

(HP-006)

(HP-005)

(HP-004)

(HP-003)

(HP-002)

(BB-003)

(BB-002)

(BB-004)

(BB-005)

(HP/BB-001)

COUNTY P ROAD

COUNTY A ROAD

Lake
of the
Woods

Upper
Saint
Croix Lake

Jersett Road

N

0   0.25   0.5 Miles

1:25,000

Minnesota

From the leisurely Lakewalk of downtown Duluth to the rugged Sawtooth Mountains and the gentle Laurentian Divide, the NCT offers a cache of contrasting hiking experiences in Minnesota. Historic landmarks include the remnants of iron mining along the Mesabi and Vermilion ranges, as well as Paul Bunyan's logging era. Native American historic sites abound, as does plentiful wildlife, including such Great North Woods icons as moose, whitetail deer, black bears, Canada lynx, timber wolves, and bald eagles.

The NCT enters Minnesota near Jay Cooke State Park, where the Superior Hiking Trail also begins. This famous 300-mile trail takes hikers first through the city of Duluth before heading northeast, following the ridgeline of Minnesota's scenic North Shore. Reaching the end of the Superior Hiking Trail, near Grand Portage National Monument, the NCT then heads west, following the aptly named Border Route Trail, 65 miles paralleling the US-Canada border. At the end of the Border Route Trail, at the famed Gunflint Trail (Cook Co. Hwy. 12), the NCT picks up the Kekekabic Trail (the "Kek"), which heads 41 miles west toward Snowbank Lake, northeast of Ely. Both the Border Route Trail and the Kek traverse the million-acre Boundary Water Canoe Area Wilderness and should be attempted only by experienced backpackers or backcountry travelers, due to the wilderness conditions found there.

From Snowbank Lake Road trailhead, the NCT hiker must road walk into Ely and either continue road walking southwest to Grand Rapids or hike the Mesabi Trail, an incomplete multiple-use trail traversing the Mesabi Iron Range to Grand Rapids. Leaving Grand Rapids, another road walk heads southwest to Remer, where a long, contiguous NCT segment begins, including the 70-mile NCT segment within the Chippewa National Forest heading west toward Walker.

Leaving "the Chip" west of Walker, the NCT enters Hubbard County and the Paul Bunyan State Forest, traverses the scenic Itasca Moraine landscape, and comes close to Akeley and Lake George. Upon reaching Itasca State Park, the NCT is "in the neighborhood" of the acknowledged headwaters of the Mississippi River at Lake Itasca and historic Douglas Lodge, both of which can be reached via side trails. West of Itasca, the NCT turns south and follows the Laurentian Divide before reaching the end of the completed foot trail within Tamarac National Wildlife Refuge. South of Tamarac, the route takes a road walk toward Frazee, Vergas, Maplewood State Park, Pelican Rapids, and Fergus Falls before turning west and heading toward the Red River and North Dakota. The original route entered North Dakota at Breckenridge-Wahpeton.

The **combined 400 or so miles** of the Superior Hiking, Border Route, and Kekekabic Trails constituting Minnesota's Arrowhead Region have been informally considered part of the NCT for some time. Yet there still remains the small matter of full congressional authorization in order for what's known as the "Arrowhead Re-route" to become official. This reroute replaces a roughly 100-mile stretch of the NCT's route between Jay Cooke State Park (south of Duluth) and the existing NCT segment in the Chippewa National Forest near Remer. This part of the NCT route has not attracted much volunteer or agency interest in the last 30 years, because it would require building and maintaining 70 to 80 miles of wetland boardwalk. The alternative Arrowhead route includes almost 400 miles of existing, contiguous, volunteer-maintained hiking trails offering superb hiking experiences among world-class scenery and wilderness. Another 100 to 150 miles of new trail will need to be built from the edge of the Boundary Waters Canoe Area Wilderness near Ely southwest to the existing NCT segment within the Chippewa National Forest. More information and updates on this issue may be found online at northcountrytrail .org/get-involved/advocacy/arrowhead-re-route/.

The three existing trails in the Arrowhead Region are maintained by separate nonprofit trail organizations that publish guidebooks and maps and organize volunteer projects. Though highly recommended, featured hikes on these trails are not included in this book. The Superior Hiking Trail is thoroughly laid out in *Guide to the Superior Hiking Trail,* published by the Superior Hiking Trail Association (218-834-2700; www.shta.org). The 65-mile-long Border Route Trail is well described in *The Border Route Trail Guide,* published by the Border Route Trail Association (info@borderroutetrail.org), www.borderroutetrail.org. Information on the Kekekabic Trail is available from info@kek.org and by writing to the Kekekabic Trail Club (309 Cedar Ave. S, Minneapolis, MN 55454).

Minnesota's Featured Hikes

1. **Milton Lake Esker** (FR 2324 to Milton Lake Public Access)

2. **Wetland Wonders** (State Highway 200 to State Highway 84)

3. **Shingobee-Anoway** (County Road 50 NW trailhead to Shingobee Recreation Area trailhead)

4. **The Itasca Moraine Chain of Lakes** (Nelson Lake to County Road 4)

5. **Itasca State Park** (US Route 71/South Entrance trailhead to State Highway 113/Gartner Farm trailhead)

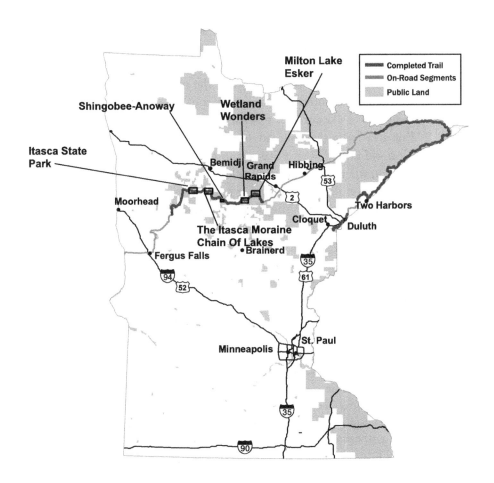

1. Milton Lake Esker

Distance: 2.9 miles (round-trip)
Physical difficulty: Moderate
Navigation difficulty: Easy
Highlights: The west end of this trail threads its way atop an esker, which is a narrow ridge formed by glacial streams. The esker contains towering red and white pines, and it delivers views of surrounding lakes and wetlands. Though nearby Remer's population is only 372, the town can provide everything that NCT hikers typically want except all-you-can-eat buffets.
Visitation: Low
Nearest town: Remer, MN

Fans of Milton Lake Esker are divided on how best to enjoy it. Some hikers love the springtime sound of drumming ruffed grouse. Other visitors prefer the esker's fall foliage. Local NCTA volunteer Katie Blau most enjoys snowshoeing the esker, especially when the old growth pines are beautifully adorned with snow. Her favorite part of the trail is where it becomes a cave or tunnel-like corridor formed by snow-laden spruce trees.

This area has a rich railroad and logging tradition. For instance, the 100-year-old city of Remer has a restored Soo Line depot, along with a railroad car, where visitors can enjoy learning about local history. For trivia buffs, the Lower 48's largest nesting population of bald eagles, about 150 nesting pairs, is located in the Chippewa National Forest.

Trip Planner

Map: MN-09 (Minnesota 09), available from www.northcountrytrail.org
Beginning access: Milton Lake public boat access (MLE-001), located at the end of Forest Road 2324 (Milton Lake Dr. NE), approximately 6 miles from Remer
Parking: There is plenty of parking available at the public boat access.
Ending access: Retrace steps back to the lake's public boat access.
Contact information:
MN Regional Trail Coordinator: HQ@northcountrytrail.org
Arrowhead Chapter, NCTA: arw@northcountrytrail.org, www.northcountrytrail.org/arw

Trail Guide

At Milton Lake public boat access (MLE-001), first walk 200 feet up the NCT, coming to a junction with a side trail and a latrine on the left, then a second side trail on the right, and then a delightful little campsite.

The esker is a distinct ridge, topped with towering old-growth red pines and white pines. Lower down the slope is a mix of cedars, balsam firs, spruces, poplars, birches, and red and white oaks. As you walk the trail's wide tread, enjoy the unexpected feeling of elevation in an otherwise flat countryside.

Follow the trail to a nearby, unnamed pond and its ancient-looking beaver lodge. Because the esker trail is at least 50 feet or more above the surrounding forest floor, it provides a grand viewing platform for this pond's lily pads in summer and for its deer, coyote, wolf, and hare tracks in winter.

After 0.3 miles, the trail leaves the ridge/esker and continues along a two-track path. Sugar maples, poplars, and balsam firs begin to dominate the surrounding vegetation. Pass an enormous swamp, the springtime home to many kinds of nesting ducks.

The remainder of this hike consists of a gently rolling woods pathway. Pass through a "spruce tunnel," where the long alley of evergreens foretells cold, northern winters.

Upon reaching Forest Road 2321B (MLE-002) hikers can either re-trace steps back to Milton Lake or extend the hike along the gently rolling woods pathway 0.63 miles farther east to Forest Road 2321B, where there is a nice parking area.

Minnesota—Milton Lake Esker

Waypoint Id	Description	Mileage	Latitude	Longitude
MLE-001	Milton Lake boat landing	0.00	47.13440	−93.93450
MLE- 002	FS 2321B	1.45	47.12785	−93.91805

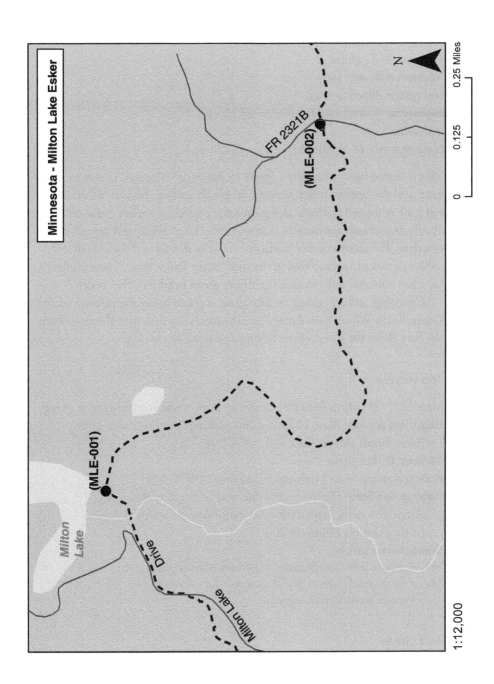

Minnesota - Milton Lake Esker

Milton Lake

(MLE-001)

Drive

Million Lake

FR 2321B

(MLE-002)

N

0   0.125   0.25 Miles

1:12,000

2. Wetland Wonders (State Highway 200 to State Highway 84)

Distance: 6.42 miles
Physical difficulty: Easy
Navigation difficulty: Easy
Highlights: Several stands of large red pines
Visitation: Low
Nearest town: Longville, MN

This featured hike is literally a "walk in the park." The trail is easy to navigate, and the terrain is flat, verging on gently rolling. Several tall stands of red pine whisper invitingly along the way. Providing variety between these stands are mixed hardwoods, a few ponds, large bogs, and several mini-marshes. The charm of this landscape is in the details and the overall atmosphere of sylvan repose. Trail maintainer Brian Pavek says, "I love wetlands on a hot summer day because their lime green brightens the woods."

Canoeing and kayaking are also great ways to enjoy the portion of the Great North Woods near Longville. The locals say they love floating down the Boy River for its excellent fishing and wildlife viewing.

Trip Planner

Map: MN-09 (Minnesota 09), available from www.northcountrytrail.org
Beginning access: State Highway 200 parking area (west side of Boy River, south side of the road) (WW-001)
Parking: Parking area
Ending access: State Highway 84 trailhead (WW-004)
Parking: On State Highway 200 just west of the Boy River. An alternative is the larger, off-road parking area located 0.1 miles further east on Highway 200.
Contact information:
MN Regional Trail Coordinator: HQ@northcountrytrail.org
Star of the North Chapter, NCTA: stn@northcountrytrail.org, www.northcountrytrail.org/stn

Trail Guide

Follow the NCT west from its parking area (WW-001) at State Highway 200. Immediately cross a private access to an inholding. Be sure to notice a huge fallen tree on the left side of the trail. The tree is 30 inches in diameter, and its bark is beautiful, moss-covered, and deeply furrowed.

Though the trail starts in a mixed hardwood forest, a stand of large red pines appears within a half mile. Next, on the right, is a vast bog growing up in small tamaracks. The trail hugs a ridge along the edge of the bog and then enters a mixed hardwood forest.

After crossing East Macemon Road (WW-002) (a connector road to State Hwy. 200), there is another large, parklike stand of red pines.

There are more delightful wetlands to come, even a separate wetland on either side of the trail at one point. Note the beaver lodge on the right.

Cross West Macemon Road (another connector to State Hwy. 200) to soon reach another wetland on the left. Continue through a mixed hardwood forest. There is a nice bridge along the way. Go past the signs that indicate hikers are leaving Chippewa National Forest.

After passing a large opening in the woods, reenter the Chippewa National Forest. Note the large pond on the right with a campsite just to the left. Eventually, the trail makes a sharp right just before four large, round wooden posts. Soon, there will be a sizable pond and a beaver lodge to the right.

Cross County Road 126 (WW-003), yet another connector with State Hwy. 200. Walk through a stand of spruce trees followed by an area full of aspen saplings. The trail next transits a mix of aspen saplings and large red and white pines.

Skirt a very large bog on the left, and pass through another stand of red pines. Soon, the trail reaches the trailhead at State Highway 84 (WW-004). Look slightly to the right to see the NCT parking area across the road.

Minnesota—Wetland Wonders

Waypoint ID	Description	Mileage	Latitude	Longitude
WW-001	State Highway 200 Parking Area	0.00	47.04452	−94.11138
WW-002	East Macemon Road	1.44	47.04283	−94.13776
WW-003	Cross County Road 126	5.77	47.04133	−94.20406
WW-004	State Highway 84 Trailhead	6.42	47.04347	−94.21521

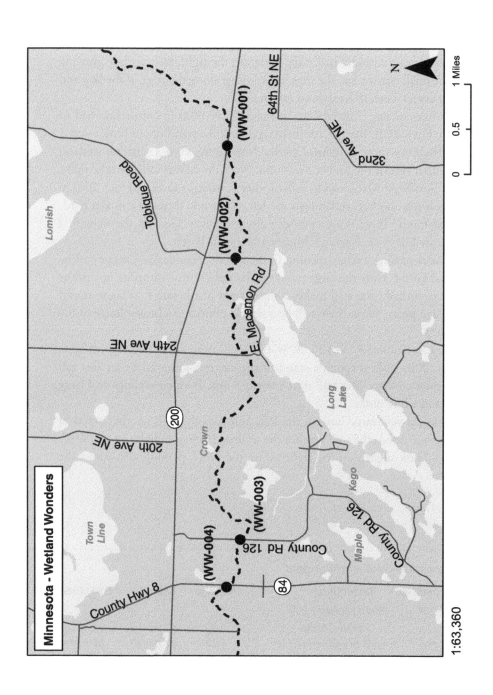

Minnesota - Wetland Wonders

Lomish

Tobiano Road

(WW-001)

(WW-002)

64th St NE

32nd Ave NE

E. Macemon Rd

24th Ave NE

200

20th Ave NE

Crown

Long Lake

Town Line

County Hwy 8

(WW-004)

(WW-003)

County Rd 126

84

Kego

Maple

County Rd 126

N

0   0.5   1 Miles

1:63,360

3. Shingobee-Anoway (County Road 50 NW trailhead to Shingobee Recreation Area trailhead)

Distance: 3.46 miles
Physical difficulty: Moderate
Navigation difficulty: Easy
Highlights: Pine forests, Anoway Lake Bridge, scenic Shingobee River Valley, and the historic Shingobee Winter Recreation Area
Visitation: Medium
Nearest town: Walker, MN

Hikers will enjoy a lovely woods walk that ends at a former downhill ski area first developed by a German immigrant in the 1930s. The Shingobee River Valley is a great place to learn about wild rice and its traditional harvest by Native Americans. Native food, summer and winter fun, and great scenery make this featured hike a year-round delight.

Trip Planner

Map: MN-09 (Minnesota 09), available from www.northcountrytrail.org
Beginning access: County Road 50 NW trailhead (SA-001)
Parking: Parking area with kiosk and NCT sign
Ending access: Shingobee Recreation Area trailhead (SA-005)
Parking: Parking area at trailhead
Contact information:
MN Regional Trail Coordinator: HQ@northcountrytrail.org
Itasca Moraine Chapter, NCTA: itm@northcountrytrail.org,
    www.northcountrytrail.org/itm

Trail Guide

The parking area at the County Road 50 NW trailhead (SA-001) boasts a kiosk and an NCT sign. Instead of immediately following the road, the trail ascends to the power line and parallels the road 0.1 miles north before beginning to utilize gravel County Road 50 NW. Follow that road downhill to its bridge over the Shingobee River, then across the magnificent marshland to where the NCT heads west on the road's subsequent long rise.

Turn left where the trail enters a diverse forest of spruce, balsam fir, bigtooth aspen, quaking aspen, basswood, birch, green ash, and red oak. Follow the trail, as it contours the slope above the marsh and river, to a wooden bridge (SA-002). The distance from the County Road 50 NW parking lot to the wooden bridge is 1.7 miles.

Cross the wooden bridge within sight of Anoway Lake. The surrounding fir-clad ridges provide a dark contrast to the feathery, young tamaracks and pointy cattails in the nearby marshes. Contrast their greens with that of the wild rice plants standing en masse beside the somnolent channel. Follow the mossy, grassy trail away from the river up into a stand of balsam fir, where there is a junction with a ski trail. Turn right and follow the trail through a large stand of red pines. In 0.2 miles, the trail reaches a campsite (SA-003), equipped with a picnic table.

At a nice, grassy meadow, spacious enough for at least a half-dozen tents, there is a wooden cross marked "Mile 15, In Memory of Harry Jennings Crockett." It commemorates the sudden death by heart attack of a runner in the annual North Country Marathon.

The trail becomes a wide, northeasterly and northerly, woodsy track. Turn left off the grassy boulevard onto a narrow track heading west, pass-

---

Minnesota is famous for wild rice, sometimes called "the caviar of grains." Less well-known is that this grain actually comes from a species of grass and is not closely related to the familiar white and brown Asian rice. Wild rice, sometimes called Indian or Canada rice, is an annual and grows in the shallows of freshwater lakes and streams primarily in the northern Great Lakes region of the United States, as well as in the Canadian Prairie Provinces.

An integral part of Native American cultures in these regions, the traditional harvest of wild rice typically involves bending the stalks of ripe seed heads over a canoe's gunwale and tapping them with a threshing stick, knocking the grains into the bottom of the canoe. The process can be ritualized; often, the size of the threshing sticks (called knockers) and the manner of their use is strictly prescribed.

The centrality of wild rice among indigenous cultures is indicated by the language usage. For one example, derivatives of the Objibwe word *manoomin*, meaning "good berry," are used in the names of such places as Menominee, Manitoba, Minnesota, and Mahnomen.

Traveling through northern Minnesota, those seeking a true NCT experience will find wild rice as iconic as the loon and the North Star.

ing a peekaboo view of Recreation Lake. At the grassy junction (SA-004), go straight ahead.

Just before reaching State Highway 34, leave the NCT and go straight ahead for a mile on a connector (ski) trail to the parking area at the Shingobee Recreation Area trailhead (SA-005). After some ups and downs parallel to Highway 34, the connector trail will go to Shingobee Hill, where there was formerly a rope tow for skiers. Nowadays, nonprofit groups may reserve the old Shingobee Chalet (for free use) from the Chippewa National Forest. For more information, contact Shingobee Recreation Area, Chippewa National Forest, Walker Ranger District (201 Minnesota Ave. E, Walker, MN 56484; 218-547-1044).

Minnesota—Shingobee-Anoway

Waypoint ID	Description	Mileage	Latitude	Longitude
SA-001	County Road 50 NW Trailhead	0.00	47.02908	−94.59573
SA-002	Wooden Bridge	1.83	47.03765	−94.62362
SA-003	Campsite	2.25	47.03814	−94.62873
SA-004	Grassy Junction	2.67	47.04111	−94.63154
SA-005	Shingobee Recreation Area Trailhead	3.46	47.03672	−94.64342

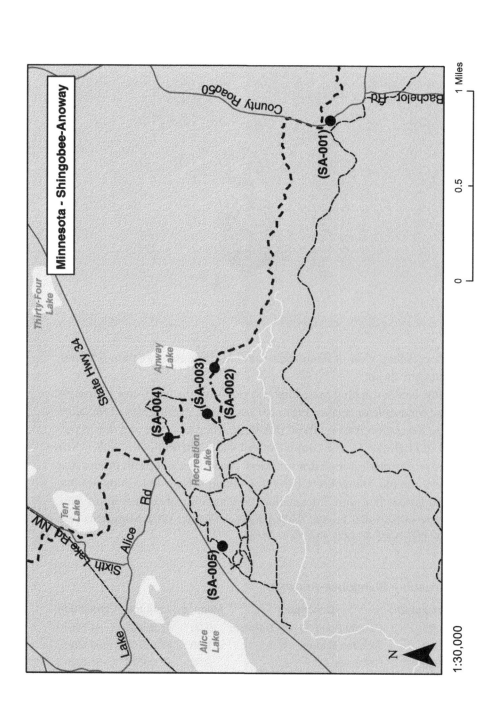

Minnesota - Shingobee-Anoway

1:30,000

4. The Itasca Moraine Chain of Lakes (Nelson Lake to County Road 4)

Distance: 10.32 miles
Physical difficulty: Easy
Navigation difficulty: Easy
Highlights: Old logging railroad grades, numerous lakes, restful overlooks, and a side trail to Nelson Lake Campground
Visitation: Medium
Nearest town: Lake George, MN

This 10-mile featured hike between Nelson Lake and Hubbard County Road 4 is known for the more than 25 kettle lakes that formed when humongous glacial ice blocks were trapped and covered by sands, rocks, and soils. They melted, creating large, often kettle-shaped depressions—hence the term "kettle lake."

Ponds along the way are at their liveliest in early spring, when snow remains late in shady spots. Spring peepers and other chorus frogs, fol-

lowed by wood frogs and then leopard frogs, greet the early spring hiker. Understanding the geomorphology of glacially formed lakes, like Nelson Lake, enhances the hiking experience but is not requisite for a successful hike. Nelson Lake features a 1.4-mile lake-encircling loop trail and inviting campsites. Camping is available by self-registration and costs $14 per night. The campsites are managed by Lake Bemidji State Park.

Trip Planner

Map: MN-10 (Minnesota 10), available from www.northcountrytrail.org
East access: Nelson Lake Boat Landing trailhead (ITM-001)
Parking: Boat access parking lot
West access: County Road 4/Halvorson Forest Road trailhead
  (ITM-008)
Parking: Parking area located immediately off Halvorson Forest Road
Contact information:
MN Regional Trail Coordinator: HQ@northcountrytrail.org
Itasca Moraine Chapter, NCTA: itm@northcountrytrail.org,
  www.northcountrytrail.org/itm

Trail Guide

From the Nelson Lake trailhead (ITM-001), take the connector trail along the west side to reach the south shore of the lake. Continue around the lake and turn off the Nelson Lake loop trail onto the blue-blazed NCT. Go west on the trail toward County Road 91. Pass aspen, oak, birch, maple, and mixed mature pine forests.

About 0.5 miles west of Nelson Lake on the south side of the trail, there is a pond with plenty of nearby black spruce and tamarack. At a nice stand of paper birch, cross another trail (ITM-002). Continue through a corridor of aspen, chokecherries, and alders whose new growth is evidence of recent logging. Just before reaching County Road 91, there is a pond on the north side of the trail. Note the beaver crossing between the higher-water bog on the left and the unnamed lake on the right.

After crossing County Road 91 (ITM-003), pass through a stand of young aspens as the trail meanders westward. Go left about 100 feet and reenter the woods. Cross another beaver dam that has backed up a small lake.

Near pretty Robertson Lake, follow the trail west through a logged-off area to a junction of two skid roads. Descend via a corridor through heavy brush to another unnamed lake. From a large oak tree at the top of the rise, there is a lovely (though brushy) view of this classic kettle lake. A bit farther, the trail turns west through a stand of young aspens, eventually descending to Crappie Lake. Look for bald eagles in the treetop snags around the lake.

The trail follows a "sprinkle road" southward to a favorite location among fishermen, Island Lake. In the early 1900s, logging in this area was often done in winter. Horses pulled tanks of water mounted on sledges, sprinkling the water to make ice roads. Horse-pulled sleds then hauled logs

Henry Schoolcraft (1793–1864) was a geographer, explorer, and Indian agent who wrote pioneering ethnographic studies of Native Americans. His early explorations of the upper Midwest were legendary, and the places he named along the way bear witness to the legacy of his prodigious efforts throughout the region. In 1820 and again in 1832, he sought to determine the geographic headwaters of the Mississippi River. Fond of creating place-names by mixing Latin and Indian syllables, he denominated his source of the Mississippi River as "Itasca" (a name meaning "true head" and formed by joining two Latin words) and thus named Itasca Lake.

Bruce Johnson of the Itasca Moraine Chapter of the NCTA believes that pinpointing the exact source of the mighty river is less important than appreciating the area's magnificent environment. Johnson says, "While I hike this trail, my senses soak in the surrounding natural environment. From moss and wildflowers to huge oak and pine, from insects and butterflies to minnows and frogs along the water's edge, from birds, mice, mink, fox, bobcat, beaver, deer, and bear to possibly timber wolves: they are all here, and I am passing through their domain."

Johnson continues, "I relish a good backrest tree to sit down beside or to snuggle up against. One of my favorites is along this part of the trail. While relaxing at such moments, I scarcely know the time of day or the day of the week. I feel beyond relaxed and content, especially since I know that I helped build this trail."

out of the woods via these ice roads from one lake to the next and eventually to a stream that floated them down to the waiting sawmills.

Forty feet before the lake (ITM-004), follow the trail to the right. Wind through the mature forest around the north and west sides of the lake to another "sprinkle road" on the southwest corner. This flat, straight, former ice road connects to Upper Teepee Lake. Follow the shore as the trail ascends to a bench with a 180-degree view of the scenic, 12-acre lake.

Soon the trail leaves the Paul Bunyan State Forest at the Teepee Lakes "land bridge" and enters Hubbard County land. Follow the trail to the right, and cross the Teepee Lakes land bridge, with Lower Teepee Lake on the south and Upper Teepee Lake on the north. This 300-yard land bridge is also a county snowmobile trail. The trail meanders along the west side of Lower Teepee Lake to a fine picnic spot on a point.

Soon the trail turns west and crosses an ATV trail (ITM-005). Continuing west through a mature forest, the trail skirts around gentle hills, avoids bogs, and generally loses elevation. Follow the trail past Spur Lake, where there is a small cabin on the northeast shore. Reach and cross a new, informal logging road (ITM-006).

Continue hiking, and soon pass between two mature Norway pines before crossing Steamboat Pass Road. From that road, the trail goes northwest for 3.0 miles to the County Road 4/Halvorson Forest Road trailhead. Going west, the trail passes through a stand of young aspens and then makes a turn at two mature Norway pines. The trail turns again at a hilltop stand of birch trees and then heads back into young aspens, followed by mature northern hardwoods. Cross a saddle and pass a tamarack bog located on the south side of the trail. Pass more bogs.

Pass a pond on the south side of the trail, and reach a junction with a side trail that leads to a backcountry campsite (ITM-007) overlooking the west side of the pond. Amenities at the campsite include three improved tent sites, a latrine, a fire ring, and a bench with a table. From the campsite, follow the trail northward to a black spruce bog that soon segues to a tamarack bog.

At a north-facing slope, the trail reaches a large bench. The mature forest will give way to a logged-over area of regenerating aspen. Mature forest will then transition to another old logging railroad grade. The trail passes a pond , climbs a steep hill, and contours along the edge of the slope.

Turn west into a mature forest and pass two large deer hunting stands (one is jokingly labeled the Lake George Hilton Annex) before descending into a stand of young aspens. Soon, road noise may be heard from the traffic on Hubbard County Road 4. In a few minutes reach the County Road 4/Halvorson Forest Road trailhead (ITM-008) and the end of this hike.

Minnesota — The Itasca Moraine Chain of Lakes

Waypoint ID	Description	Mileage	Latitude	Longitude
ITM-001	Nelson Lake Boat Landing trailhead	0.00	47.15766	−94.84099
ITM-002	Trail Crossing	1.18	47.15703	−94.85596
ITM-003	Co. 91	2.43	47.15697	−94.87708
ITM-004	Island Lake	4.19	47.16160	−94.90322
ITM-005	ATV trail	6.29	47.14354	−94.92075
ITM-006	Steamboat Pass Road	7.34	47.14656	−94.94086
ITM-007	Backcountry Campsite	8.53	47.15475	−94.95900
ITM-008	Co.4/Halvorson Forest Road Trailhead	10.32	47.16621	−94.98096

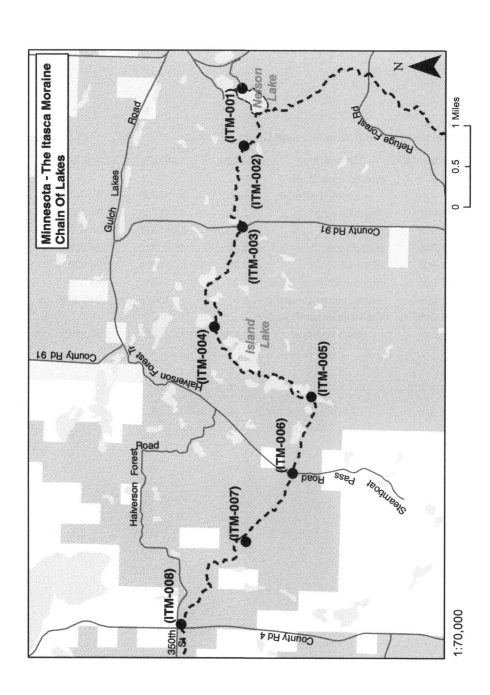

Minnesota - The Itasca Moraine
Chain Of Lakes

(ITM-001)
(ITM-002)
(ITM-003)
(ITM-004)
(ITM-005)
(ITM-006)
(ITM-007)
(ITM-008)

Nelson Lake
Island Lake

Gulch Lakes Road
Refuge Forest Rd
County Rd 91
County Rd 91
Halverson Forest Tr
Halverson Forest Road
Steamboat Pass Road
County Rd 4
350th St

N

0   0.5   1 Miles

1:70,000

5. Itasca State Park (US Route 71/South Entrance trailhead to State Highway 113/Gartner Farm trailhead)

Distance: 6.36 miles
Physical difficulty: Easy
Navigation difficulty: Easy
Highlights: Scenic lakes, "headwaters" of the Mississippi River,
old-growth pine and hardwood forests, and wildlife
Visitation: Medium
Nearest town: Park Rapids, MN

Many people refer to Itasca State Park as Minnesota's national park. The reason for this becomes very clear on this featured hike, located at the southern end of the park. Of this segment, 2.8 miles coincide with the Eagle Scout Trail, maintained by the park. NCTA-maintained portions sport only minimal blazing, at the park's request.

Along the trail, 11 lakes are visible—Lakes Niemada, Sibilant, Iron Corner, Gilfillan, Lashbrook, Hernando De Soto, Mikenna, Morrison, Horn, Bogus, and Augusta. Other attractions include old-growth forests and abundant wildlife.

Rich in history and natural beauty, the Mississippi River headwaters are also steeped in controversy. The mighty river extends 2,252 miles to the Gulf of Mexico and drains 41 percent of the continental United States. Finding its source was one of the great stories of exploration in the 19th century. In fact, the true source is still a point of debate. Some think that Hernando De Soto Lake is the source of the Mississippi River.

Trip Planner

Maps: MN-10 (Minnesota 09), available from
www.northcountrytrail.org
Beginning access: South Entrance trailhead (ISP-001) on County
Highway 122 (just off US Rte. 71)
Parking: Located at trailhead; requires state park permit
Ending access: Gartner Farm trailhead, 0.6 miles north on 540th
Avenue from the junction of State Highway 113 and Kueber Road
(ISP-011) (NOTE: At the Hwy. 113 junction, Kueber Rd. goes
south and 540th Ave. goes north; they are the same road)

Parking: Located at trailhead; requires state park permit
Contact information:
MN Regional Trail Coordinator: HQ@northcountrytrail.org
Laurentian Lakes Chapter, NCTA: llc@northcountrytrail.org,
     www.northcountrytrail.org/llc
Itasca State Park: www.dnr.state.mn.us/state_parks/reservations_campsite.html

Trail Guide

From the NCT kiosk at the park's South Entrance (ISP-001) on County Highway 122, follow the spur trail 0.1 miles south to a bearing tree at the junction with the east-west NCT. Turn west and walk downhill to an unnamed eutrophic pond. Follow the trail through a typical mix of red pine, white pine, birch, oak, and aspen.

Pass a nameless pond that is almost entirely filled in and another that is half filled in, on the way to the next named body of water, Sibilant Lake. The trail descends from the Sibilant Lake Overlook in a grove of red pines. Pass a quaking bog, where the surrounding water encloses the central tippy "land."

Continue through the old-growth forest past several more unnamed lakes. Pass between three closely spaced white pines—a small feature typical of the subtle beauty to be found here. There are many other examples, such as the glowing light on cattail leaves at sunset. Consider as well the contrast between the whiteness of the paper birches and the stateliness of neighboring red pines.

Reach a junction (ISP-002) with the Ozawindib Trail. Originally named the Lind Saddle Trail, it was located and paid for in 1899 by Minnesota's governor John Lind to traverse the southern part of the then-new Itasca State Park. Look for one of the Saddle Trail's original, concrete mileposts.

Turn left on the broad Ozawindib Trail. After 0.1 miles, the trail jags right and becomes the Eagle Scout Trail. On this section, there are state park signs only—there will be no blue blazes. Follow the trail past the Iron Corner Campsite (ISP-003), located on a little peninsula with lovely lakeshore views. The campsite features a fire ring, a tent site, and water from the lake. A state park permit and reservation is required to camp at this site.

Follow the trail west through a predominantly hardwood forest. Gilfillan Lake is another lovely, conifer-ringed jewel. Next, arrive at a round, deep lake named Lashbrook. At the junction (ISP-004) with the Deer Park Trail, continue straight on the Eagle Scout Trail.

When the De Soto Trail is reached, continue straight along Hernando De Soto Lake. Note that use of the Adirondack-style shelter (ISP-005) is restricted to picnicking. This well-situated shelter faces the grand Hernando De Soto Lake and is backed up by Picard Lake. It is a welcome rest spot for hikers, skiers, and snowshoers.

Pass the "Detour to Nicollet Trail"(ISP-006), and cross a height of land to an enchanting view of a small island through a screen of red pines and jack pines. The trail crosses a narrow, potentially wet connection between lakes. At the Nicollet Trail junction (ISP-007), turn left and continue along Hernando De Soto Lake. Immediately pass the rotting remains of the De Soto Cabin, surrounded by basswood trees and then the beautiful Hernando De Soto Lake campsites (fee, reservations required). Continue paralleling Hernando De Soto Lake, and cross a portage trail between it and Mikenna Lake.

Pass the portage (ISP-008) between Hernando De Soto and Morrison Lakes. Walk along an esker ridge to the east of a tamarack bog. This area suffered much damage during a 2010 tornado, which downed many large old-growth pines.

The trail passes between Horn and Morrison Lakes. At a spot between the two lakes, turn left (ISP-009) on a grassy woods road; follow it west for 0.9 miles through a mixed forest of predominantly red pines. At the junction (ISP-010) with the parking spur road, go left (south) 0.3 miles to the Gartner Farm trailhead (ISP-011) and the end of this NCT segment (0.6 miles north of the junction of Hwy. 113 and 540th Ave.).

Minnesota—Itasca State Park

Waypoint Id	Description	Mileage	Latitude	Longitude
ISP-001	South Entrance	0.00	47.15459	−95.15064
ISP-002	Ozawindib Trail	1.19	47.15461	−95.17030
ISP-003	Iron Corner Campsite	1.36	47.15175	−95.17072
ISP-004	Deer Park Trail Junction	3.32	47.14976	−95.20591
ISP-005	Shelter	3.67	47.15179	−95.21148
ISP-006	Detour to Nicollet Trail	3.87	47.15058	−95.21414
ISP-007	Nicollet Trail Junction	4.04	47.14964	−95.21833
ISP-008	Portage	4.60	47.14934	−95.22780
ISP-009	Turn Left	5.19	47.14968	−95.23678
ISP-010	Junction with Parking Spur	6.10	47.14876	−95.25460
ISP-011	Gartner Farm Trailhead	6.36	47.14476	−95.25502

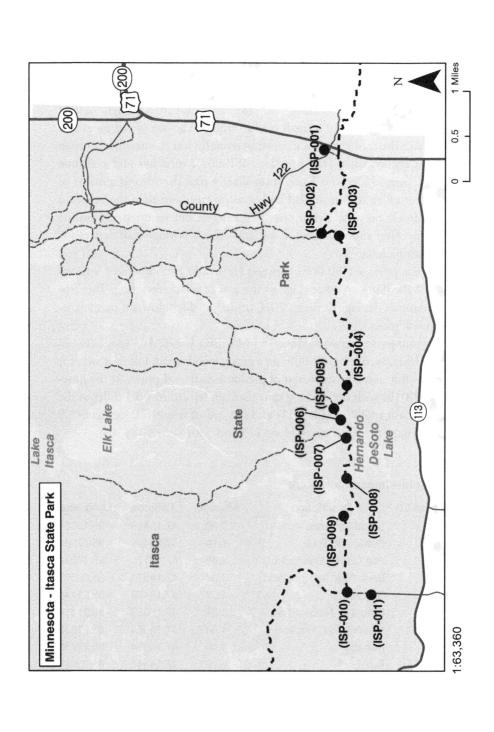

North Dakota

NCT hikers on North Dakota's "Big Sky" prairies will find unique experiences, unlike any other on the NCT. Expansive vistas and rolling landscapes seem to go on forever, contrasting the more intimate trail features back east. Then, there is the wind. Whether hiking in the relatively moist eastern part of the state or the more arid west, the wind will be constant. Other hurdles include the immense distances and some of the most extreme weather encountered in any of the NCT's seven states. North Dakota's highest recorded temperature is 121°F (49°C) at Steele on July 6, 1936, and the lowest recorded temperature is −60°F (−51°C) at Parshall on February 15, 1936. Wise hikers are alert for hail, tornados, blizzards, droughts, floods, and thunderstorms.

The ranch culture of the Flickertail State has the feel of small-town America and a very low statewide population density. The NCT in North Dakota showcases the vastness of the northern Great Plains. Along the trail, hikers will encounter patches of remnant prairie, pothole wetlands, the bottomland forest of the Sheyenne River, grazing cattle and buffalo, and row crops (of canola, sunflower, wheat, and sugar beets), plus rolling, glaciated hills. Local features include grain-hauling railroads, ghost towns, Native American archaeological sites, and a booming economy based on agriculture, lignite coal, crude oil, and natural gas extraction. Crops cover the flatter eastern North Dakota, while grasslands predominate in the hillier west.

North Dakota has such a widely dispersed population, accustomed to such immense distances, that local folks don't tend to think much about recreational walking. The state doesn't have much of a hiking culture. Its small population (less than a million) and the preponderance of private land help to explain why only a little more than half of North Dakota's projected 475 NCT miles have been completed. The very active volunteers in eastern North Dakota are making mighty strides each year; hopefully their enthusiasm will infect mid-Dakota and generate more volunteers to help build and maintain the trail heading west to the Lake Sakakawea State Park terminus.

Starting at the Red River of the North at Wahpeton, North Dakota, the NCT heads north for Fort Abercrombie State Historic Site. Originally built in 1858, this reconstructed army fort from the era of the fur trade was once known as "the Gateway to Dakota Territory." From Fort Abercrombie, the route heads west to the Sheyenne National Grasslands (a unit of the larger Dakota Prairie National Grasslands administered by the US Forest Service), the largest remnant of tallgrass prairie still in public ownership. Within the grasslands, the NCT meets up with the Sheyenne River, North Dakota's longest river and a major tributary to the Red River of the North. The NCT route follows the Sheyenne closely for most of its path across North Dakota. Stops along the way include Sheyenne State Forest (where you can hike to North Dakota's only waterfall), Fort Ransom State Park, Clausen Springs Recreation Area, Valley City, Lake Ashtabula, New Rockford Canal, and Lonetree Wildlife Management Area. West of Lonetree, the NCT follows the McClusky Canal to Lake Audubon National Wildlife Refuge and then, at Lake Sakakawea, crosses Garrison Dam to the western terminus at Lake Sakakawea State Park.

North Dakota's Featured Hikes

1. **Sheyenne National Grasslands** (round-trip)

2. **Sheyenne State Forest** (round-trip)

3. **Lake Ashtabula** (West Crossing NCT kiosk to County Road 19)

4. **Lonetree Wildlife Management Area** (Coal Mine Lake Campground to Jensen Campground)

5. **Lake Sakakawea State Park** (access road off State Highway 200 to LSSP Visitors Center)

1. Sheyenne National Grasslands (round-trip)

Distance: 6.9 miles (round-trip)

Physical difficulty: Easy

Navigation difficulty: Generally moderate; easy when the easily visible gravel tread is not covered by snow. The entire segment is marked with four-by-four cedar posts that are branded with the NCT emblem.

Highlights: The NCT traverses rare habitats of tallgrass prairie and oak savannah. An elevated lookout site provides panoramic views that demonstrate visually the stunning beauty of the great American tallgrass prairie. Best of all, in spring, summer, and fall, there are always one or more plants that are about to bloom.

Visitation: Low

Nearest town: Lisbon, ND

The Peterson field guide *The North American Prairie* (a good resource for flower identification) describes the Sheyenne National Grassland as "a wildflower oasis." This astonishing place is the most extensive tallgrass prairie in public ownership. However, don't be surprised to see lots of cattle, which, along with sheep, still feast on the wildflower paradise.

Please remember to close all gates. All fences crossing the trail have "horse gates," which are easily opened and normally close automatically.

There are no facilities in the National Grasslands other than an occasional stock "tank" (a man-made, livestock-watering pond). Bring water and all other supplies that might be needed. Be prepared for possible ticks (not Lyme disease–carrying deer ticks), mosquitoes, and poison ivy. There are no poisonous snakes in eastern North Dakota.

Forest Service rules for minimum-impact camping mean that no-fee, backcountry camping is available anywhere near the trail. The agency is planning to create a developed campground near the east trailhead and three overnight campsites along the NCT. Mountain bikes and horses are allowed on this part of the NCT.

The best times to see wildflowers are June and August. The western prairie fringed orchids typically bloom during a 10-day period around July 10 when a single four-foot-high plant can sport two dozen white blossoms. Sheyenne National Grassland is almost the only place where you can see this extremely rare beauty.

Trip Planner

Map: See guidebook map.
Beginning and ending access: Large parking area at 147th Avenue SE/
County Road 53 (SGL-001)
Contact information:
ND Regional Trail Coordinator: HQ@northcountrytrail.org
Dakota Prairie Grasslands Chapter, NCTA: dpg@northcountrytrail.org,
www.northcountrytrail.org/dpg
Sheyenne National Grasslands, 701 Main St., PO Box 946, Lisbon, ND
58054; 701-683-4342
More information: Camping, RV parking, a museum, a stockade wall,
and three blockhouses are available on the Minnesota/North
Dakota border at Fort Abercrombie State Historic Site, (PO Box
148, Abercrombie, ND 58001; 701-553-8513).

Trail Guide

This featured hike begins at a parking area (new in 2011) at County Road
53 (147th Ave. SE) (SGL-001). Lift the spring-controlled "horse gate"
and walk the NCT 0.3 miles, paralleling the road. The trail then heads
southeast into the prairie.

The trail winds its way generally eastward through burr oak and wetlands. Pass Site Post 17, where there is a typical stand of burr oak beside
a savannah showing the ill effects of overgrazing. If this sandy soil were
in healthier condition, there would be more native grasses, such as sand
bluestem, prairie sandreed, porcupine grass, blue grama, and Junegrass.

Note that at Site Post 18, the trail was thoughtfully located along the
north side of the oak groves to provide shade for hikers. Pass some of the
ponds that dot the landscape. Isolated oaks lend a parklike feeling to the
peaceful scene. Ducks float on the water. Wildflowers wave in the breeze.

At Site Post 19, look for a savannah and oaks. The long stands of
cottonwoods on the southern horizon were introduced by farmers. The
peachleaf willows at the nearby wetland are probably native, but much of
the vegetation is not. This area was once heavily farmed (70 farms have
disappeared) and overgrazed.

At 0.2 miles beyond Site Post 20, you will reach a signed junction. Take
a right off the trail and climb up the steep ridge to the top of Lookout

Hill (SGL-002). The Forest Service removed its fire lookout tower here decades ago. Look straight south to see farms on the horizon. The flats to the southeast are prime habitat for prairie chickens. Late April hikers get to hear the frenetic booming of the chickens' mating ritual. To the north is the seemingly endless hardwood forest of the Sheyenne River bottomland. The trail is at the edge of dune country, where the dunes give way to flat savannah. Retrace your steps to return to the starting point.

North Dakota—Sheyenne National Grasslands

Waypoint ID	Description	Mileage	Latitude	Longitude
SGL-001	Parking Area	0.00	46.47503	−97.34327
SGL-002	Lookout Hill	3.45	46.47631	−97.29515

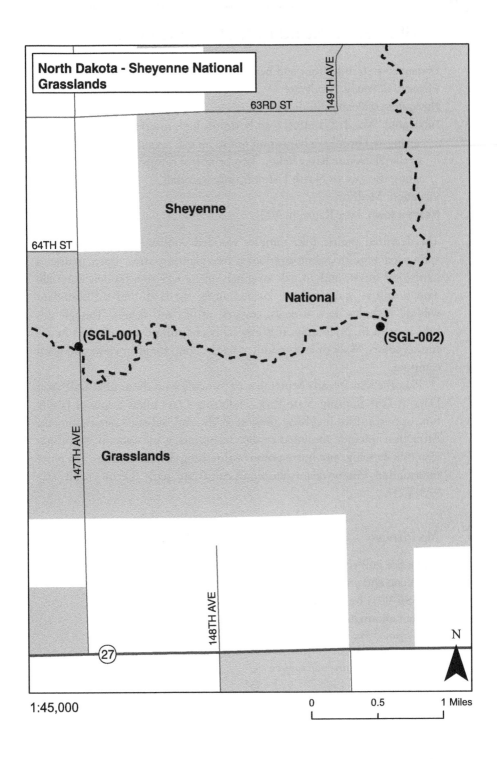

North Dakota - Sheyenne National Grasslands

149TH AVE

63RD ST

Sheyenne

64TH ST

National

(SGL-001)

(SGL-002)

147TH AVE

Grasslands

148TH AVE

27

N

1:45,000

0   0.5   1 Miles

2. Sheyenne State Forest (round-trip)

Distance: 4.56 miles (out and back)
Physical difficulty: Moderate
Navigation difficulty: Moderate
Highlights: Wooded coulees, river bottoms, high meadows leading to spring-fed brooks, a hardwood forest, an oak savannah, and views of the Sheyenne River Valley. Two primitive campsites are located along the way to North Dakota's only waterfall.
Visitation: Medium
Nearest town: Fort Ransom, ND

This featured prairie hike samples wooded coulees and river bottoms, spring-fed brooks, scenic overlooks, tree-planting areas, open prairie, a hardwood forest, and an oak savannah on its way to a hidden waterfall. Two primitive campsites are located along the trail, and the abundant wildlife includes deer, turkeys, coyotes, mink, and fishers. Though this hike is great in any season, it is especially charming when cloaked in autumn's colors. Walk or cross-country ski this loop for great views and good camping.

Plan the hike in early September to coincide with the annual Sodbuster Days at Fort Ransom State Park. Sodbuster Days offers a mix of family fun, opportunities involving pioneer skills, and old-time entertainment. Attractions include mounted cavalry reenacters, a pie auction, Scandinavian folk dancing, and horse-powered threshing demonstrations. For more information, visit www.fortransomnd.com/state_park_8.html or call 701-973-4331.

Trip Planner

Maps: See guidebook map.
Beginning and ending access: Sheyenne State Forest trailhead (SSF-001) on County 121 1/2 Ave.
Contact information:
ND Regional Trail Coordinator: HQ@northcountrytrail.org
Sheyenne River Valley Chapter, NCTA: srv@northcountrytrail.org, www.northcountrytrail.org/srv
Fort Ransom State Park: 701-973-4331
Sheyenne State Forest, 6824 State Hwy. 32, PO Box 604, Lisbon, ND 58054; 701-683-4323

Trail Guide

This featured hike begins just south of the Sheyenne River's renovated, single-truss Martinson Bridge. The trailhead (SSF-001) is located at the parking area's kiosk. Turn right at an abandoned farm and ascend a dirt track for 0.1 miles.

Turn right and walk through a wooden NCT arch. Cross a ravine and climb into a meadow overgrown with oak, ash, and thistle. The hilltop offers a grand view of the Sheyenne River Valley, a glacial meltwater trench formed by the flow from northern glacial lakes south into Glacial Lake Aggasiz.

After a dip into another oak and ash forest, follow the NCT as it crosses the open prairie. This grand aerie delivers expansive 270-degree prairie views. Descend through a patch of sumac into the next deep forest. Curve through another meadow. Drop into the shade-giving oaks. At the stock ford, there is a steel bridge (SSF-002) for hikers. The trail parallels an un-named creek, weaving through cover vegetation and openings.

Mineral Springs Campsite (SSF-003) features a fire ring, a picnic table, a spring, and a large, flat, grassy site sheltered by tall cottonwood trees and eroded bluffs. The distance from the Martinson Bridge parking area to Mineral Springs Campsite totals 1.6 miles.

Continue north as the trail maintains elevation around the base of a wooded hillside. Pass under a picturesque colonnade of cottonwoods. Follow what was once a woods road, continuing to contour around the hill. Cross the small steel bridge over an unnamed creek at a fine, grassy potential campsite.

Continue another 400 feet (crossing a tributary's steel bridge) to the only waterfall in North Dakota. The woodsy seclusion of this waterfall (SSF-004) on a small tributary of the Sheyenne River makes up for what the falls may lack in stature.

The nearby campsite facilities consist of a fire ring and a picnic table. Stately oaks and basswoods provide as fine a place for contemplation as anyone could wish. The sounds of the waterfall lull you to sleep at night. From Mineral Springs Campsite to the falls totals 0.6 miles.

This hike currently ends at the waterfall. To complete it, reverse direction and return the 2.2 miles to the Martinson Bridge trailhead.

North Dakota—Sheyenne State Forest

Waypoint ID	Description	Mileage	Latitude	Longitude
SSF-001	Sheyenne State Forest Trailhead	0.00	46.50261	−97.87818
SSF-002	Steel Bridge	1.38	46.50084	−97.89370
SSF-003	Mineral Springs Campsite	1.60	46.50317	−97.89416
SSF-004	Waterfall	2.28	46.50326	−97.90134

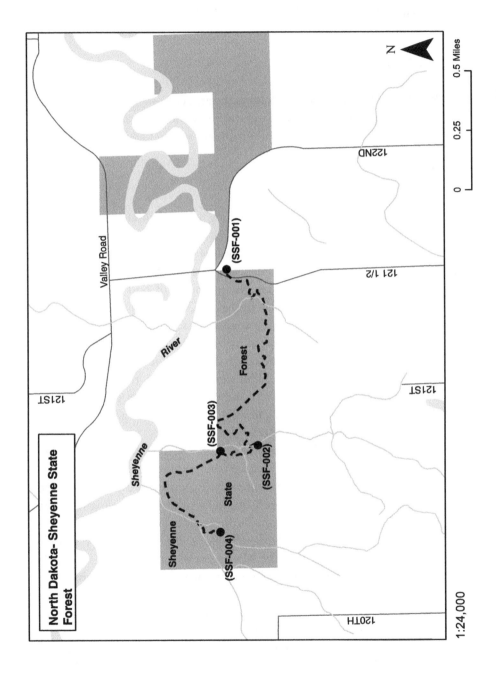

North Dakota- Sheyenne State Forest

(SSF-001)

(SSF-003)

(SSF-002)

(SSF-004)

Sheyenne

River

Valley Road

121ST

Forest

State

Sheyenne

121 1/2

121ST

122ND

120TH

N

0   0.25   0.5 Miles

1:24,000

3. Lake Ashtabula (West Crossing NCT kiosk to County Road 19)

Distance: 4.31 miles
Physical difficulty: Moderate
Navigation difficulty: Easy
Highlights: This featured hike follows the attractive shoreline of Lake Ashtabula, an impoundment of the Sheyenne River, and winds around Baldhill Creek, a major tributary stream known for its wildlife.
Visitation: Medium
Nearest town: Valley City, ND

Located along the shores of a 27-mile-long reservoir, this featured hike provides a great introduction to the natural environment of the 200-foot-deep, glacially formed Sheyenne River Valley. The glacial till soil here is flavored with many boulders and gravel deposits. The north and east facing slopes and ravines constitute miniature environments of burr oak, green ash, box elder, cottonwood, and quaking aspen. On the drier west- and south-facing slopes, there are a variety of prairie grasses and herbaceous plants.

Look for raccoon, mink, beavers, muskrat, coyotes, red foxes, fox squirrels, striped skunks, and white-tailed deer. Birdlife includes the iconic white pelican, sharptail grouse, Hungarian partridge, ringneck pheasant, double-crested cormorant, western meadowlark, Canada goose, northern shoveler, mallard, canvasback, gadwall, red-tailed hawk, goshawk, Swainson's Hawk, and American kestrel.

There is much useful information about North Dakota birding at the North Dakota Birding Society website (www.ndbirdingsociety.com/). Several local birding guides, available for hire, specialize in finding both eastern and western birds for makers of life-lists who are traveling to North Dakota. Search for North Dakota birding guides online.

The hike includes several pastures along the north side of Baldhill Creek. At the Wieland Wildlife Management Area, look for sagebrush, yucca, and prickly pear cactus. The cottonwood is its characteristic tree. Along pastures and rolling steppes are fir, ash, willow, many types of wildflowers, and even prickly pear cactus. Cattle may be seen, sometimes occupied with cooling themselves in the water.

The Army Corps of Engineers maintains excellent developed campgrounds at both the west and east sides of the West Crossing Bridge on County Highway 21(118th Avenue SE).

Trip Planner

Maps: ND-104 (North Dakota 104), available from:
northcountrytrail.org

Beginning access: West Crossing NCT kiosk, 0.25 miles south of the
West Crossing Bridge on County Highway 21 (118th Ave. SE)
(ASH-001)

Parking: Parking lot with informational kiosk

Ending access: County Road 19 (115th Ave. SE) (ASH-003)

Parking: There is room for several vehicles at the Baldhill Creek
trailhead.

Contact information:

ND Regional Trail Coordinator: HQ@northcountrytrail.org

Sheyenne River Valley Chapter, NCTA: srv@northcountrytrail.org,
www.northcountrytrail.org/srv

US Army Corps of Engineers: 701-845-2970

Trail Guide

This featured hike begins at the West Crossing NCT kiosk, 0.25 miles
south of the West Crossing Bridge on County Highway 21 (118th Ave.
SE) (ASH-001). Walk downstream (southwest), keeping the cattails on the
left and looking for wrens, finches, redwing blackbirds, and so on. Keep a
birding guide available to help with identification. On the right are meadows bordered by dramatic bluffs. Listen for kingbirds and other species.

The terrain changes to a dry steppe characterized by sagebrush, lichen-
covered rocks, prickly pear cactus, and, at dawn and again in the evening,
the aerobatic flying of noisy nighthawks. After crossing a creek with large
rocks (ASH-002), the trail heads south toward the lake before turning to
the west to follow along impounded Baldhill Creek (which enters the lake
from the west.) The NCT generally hugs the shores of the creek (lake) all
the way to the road, leaving Corps land and crossing some privately owned
land (be sure to follow all the posted rules). After a total walk of 5 miles,
this NCT segment ends at County Road 19 (ASH-003), just north of the
bridge over Baldhill Creek. Across the road is Wesley Acres Bible Camp.

North Dakota—Lake Ashtabula

Waypoint ID	Description	Mileage	Latitude	Longitude
ASH-001	West Crossing NCT Kiosk	0.00	47.15802	−98.01397
ASH-002	Creek Crossing	1.39	47.15893	−98.02713
ASH-003	County Road 19	4.31	47.14926	−98.06746

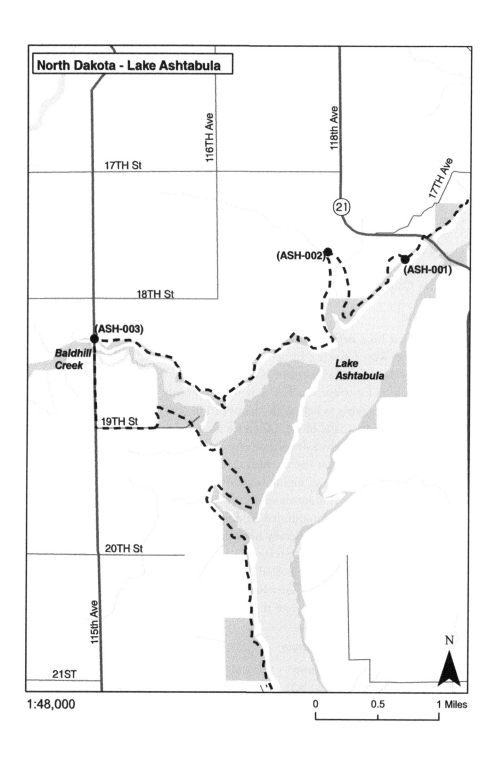

North Dakota - Lake Ashtabula

116TH Ave

118th Ave

17TH Ave

17TH St

21

(ASH-002)

(ASH-001)

18TH St

(ASH-003)

Baldhill
Creek

Lake
Ashtabula

19TH St

20TH St

115th Ave

21ST

N

1:48,000

0   0.5   1 Miles

4. Lonetree Wildlife Management Area (Coal Mine Lake Campground to Jensen Campground)

Distance: 5.33 miles
Physical difficulty: Easy—a fairly level hike characterized by prairie grasslands
Navigation difficulty: Easy
Highlights: Lakeshore hiking, beautiful prairie, and historic features such as historic teepee rings. Both Coal Mine Lake and Jensen Campgrounds offer vault toilets, picnic tables, fire rings, and nonpotable, fresh water.
Visitation: Low
Nearest town: Harvey, ND

In central North Dakota, the Lonetree Wildlife Management Area consists of 33,000 Bureau of Reclamation acres (within which there is a 1,000-acre national wildlife refuge administered by the US Fish and Wildlife Service). The Lonetree Wildlife Management Area is managed by the North Dakota Game and Fish Department.

In the 1930s, the Civilian Conservation Corps built the Coal Mine Lake Dam on the Sheyenne River. Nowadays, the NCT follows the pretty shores of Sheyenne and Coal Mine Lakes between two of the three Lonetree Wildlife Management Area campgrounds. The area offers opportunities to see plentiful waterfowl, upland game, and other prairie species, such as white-tailed deer and moose, all within the context of scenic views, historic teepee rings, and a delightful campground situated in a grove of large cottonwood trees.

Teepee rings were created when Native Americans used rocks to hold down the outer portion of their portable homes. After people broke camp, their rings of rock remained as indications of where the teepees had been. Such teepee rings are only found on tracts of native prairie that have never been broken for cultivation. Part of the challenge of finding them is to discover their locations in lush vegetation.

Trip Planner

Maps: ND-109 (North Dakota 109), available from www.northcountrytrail.org

East access: Coal Mine Lake Campground (LT-001) (off 21st Ave. NE)
Parking: Campground parking lot
West access: Jensen Campground (LT-004) (off 16th Ave. NE)
Parking: Campground parking lot
Contact information:
ND Regional Trail Coordinator: HQ@northcountrytrail.org
ND Game & Fish Department: 701-324-2211

Trail Guide

Beyond the Coal Mine Lake Campground (LT-001) and next to the water, the NCT heads west past wildlife food plots planted on the Wildlife Management Area. The trail then follows the north shore of shallow Coal Mine Lake. The coal seam giving rise to the lake's name is sometimes visible across the water on the south shore. About every fourth year, the land is cut for hay, which explains the large, round hay bales spread across the flat meadows. After following the north shore of the lake for 2.5 miles, note the re-created expanse of native grasses to the right.

Next, the NCT uses a minimally maintained gravel road for 0.5 miles to reach the south shore of Sheyenne Lake. (Though Coal Mine Lake and Sheyenne Lake are both shallow parts of the Sheyenne River, they are referred to by different names.) Turn left at the road junction (LT-002). Follow the NCT across the man-made causeway, which, during extended wet periods in certain spots, may be under several inches of water. The NCT will then curve northwest, then southwest toward Teepee Ring Hill, which is visible in the distance. During the spring and autumn migrations, thousands of waterfowl fill the air and marshes.

Turn right at the end (LT-003) of the 150-yard second causeway. Follow the NCT toward a lone clump of willow trees. Walk toward and then climb northwest through virgin prairie to a prominent hill.

Teepee Ring Hill delivers excellent views of the surrounding prairie and nearby lakes. Even better, close observation finds scattered stones denoting the sites where Native Americans erected their teepees atop this hill. This historic campsite offers superb views, reliable water, and a constant breeze to give relief from any insects.

Continue west 0.5 miles downhill to State Highway 14. After crossing the highway, head southwest, with the final 0.5-mile section characterized by prairie grasslands and wildlife enhancements, such as tree plantings. Chinese elms, self-seeded from trees planted by early settlers, indicate pioneer homesites. The hike ends at the Jensen Campground (LT-004).

The Jensen Campground is a large meadow at a former farmstead. The campground's well dates back to the pioneer Jensen family that lived there for decades among the cottonwoods. Richard Jensen recalls, "My great grandfather Peder M. Stafslien came from Coon Valley, Wisconsin, and homesteaded that land in 1901. He named his farmstead Gryta, which is Norwegian for "kettle," because it was in the valley between two hills. It was last occupied by Peder Stafslien's grandson Duane Jensen in September 1985. Duane had lived there from the time he was 4 years old until he retired at 65, operating it as a small grain/cattle/dairy farm. I believe that the buildings were razed in 1986."

North Dakota—Lonetree Wildlife Management Area

Waypoint ID	Description	Mileage	Latitude	Longitude
LT-001	Coal Mine Lake Campground	0.00	47.67836	−100.13834
LT-002	Road Junction	2.42	47.69285	−100.18523
LT-003	End of Causeway	3.17	47.69298	−100.19737
LT-004	Jensen Campground	5.33	47.69572	−100.23941

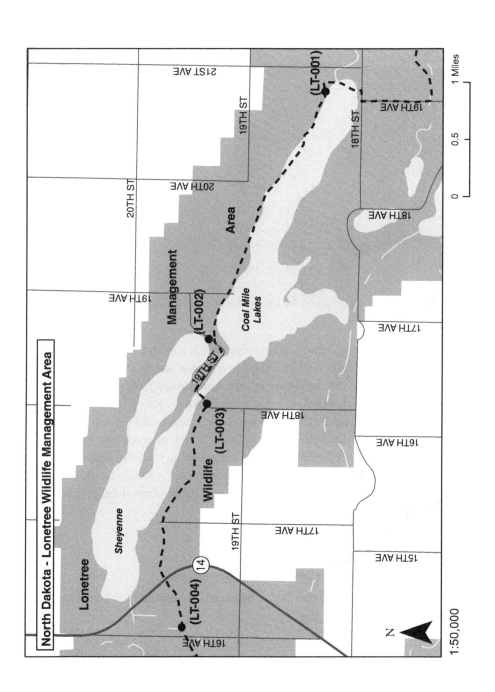

North Dakota - Lonetree Wildlife Management Area

5. Lake Sakakawea State Park (Access road off State Highway 200 to LSSP Visitors Center)

Distance: 1.5 miles
Physical difficulty: Easy
Navigation difficulty: Easy
Highlights: Hike from the Garrison Dam to the western terminus of the NCT.
Visitation: Medium
Nearest town: Pick City, ND

This featured hike offers the opportunity to stand at the extreme western end, or terminus, of the NCT. It samples some classic wide-open spaces of Lewis and Clark country, now transformed by a vast lake. In the 1950s, the Garrison Dam's impoundment of the Missouri River created a 368,000-acre, 178-mile long reservoir. In addition to camping, fishing, boating, birding, and panoramic views, Lake Sakakawea State Park also offers two small sleeping cabins, rented out from mid-May through the end of September.

Trip Planner

Map: See guidebook map.
Beginning access: Access road's shoreline parking lot (SAK-001)
Ending access: Lake Sakakawea State Park Entrance Station Center (SAK-005)
Contact information:
ND Regional Trail Coordinator: HQ@northcountrytrail.org
Lake Sakakawea State Park, PO Box 732, Riverdale, ND 58565;
    701-487-3315; lssp@nd.gov, www.parkrec.nd.gov/parks/lssp/lssp.html

Trail Guide

Park at the little turnaround beside the lake at the access point (SAK-001). Raise the lift gate and follow the interpretive markers to the gravel road, following it to the SST ("sweet-smelling toilet"), a total of 0.1 miles.

    Continue west along the mowed NCT, up into the small ash and chokecherry trees. Continue up across open meadows, and cross a seasonal trickle in a small draw. At a junction with the White-Tail Trail (SAK-002), turn left to descend on the NCT through ash thickets and grassy openings.

At a junction with the Shoreline Trail (SAK-003), continue on the NCT past the bench. Shortly afterward, at the Overlook Trail junction, turn right (near a spring) on the NCT.

Turn left on the NCT at another Shoreline Trail junction (SAK-004). (A right turn on the Shoreline Trail would go to the state park's large, developed, fee campground and boat launch.) At another junction with the Overlook Trail, turn right on the NCT. The Lake Sakakawea State Park Entrance Station Center (SAK-005) is within sight. Continue walking to it, the end of this NCT segment, and, thus, the western terminus of the NCT. Look for the sign marking the NCT's western terminus, about 50 feet before the Visitors Center.

North Dakota—Lake Sakakawea State Park

Waypoint ID	Description	Mileage	Latitude	Longitude
SAK-001	Access Point	0.00	47.50885	−101.43973
SAK-002	White-Tail Trail Junction	0.83	47.51478	−101.44816
SAK-003	Shoreline Trail Junction	0.96	47.51638	−101.44884
SAK-004	Second Shoreline Trail Junction	1.25	47.51971	−101.45070
SAK-005	Lake Sakakawea State Park Entrance Station Center	1.50	47.51959	−101.45339

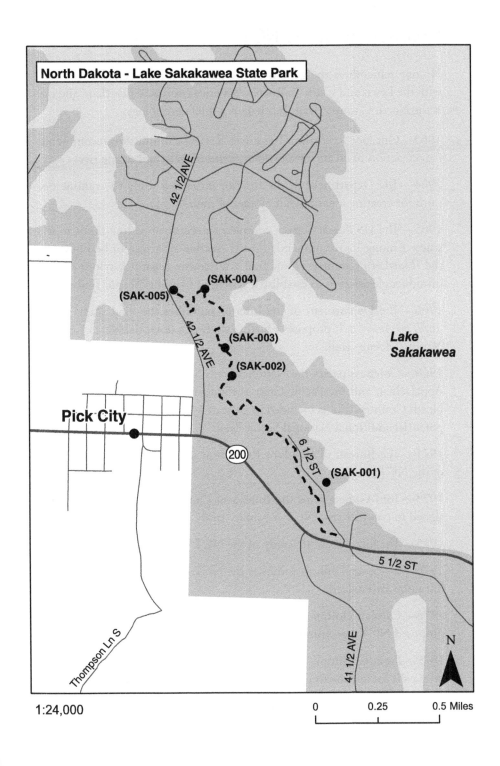

North Dakota - Lake Sakakawea State Park

42 1/2 AVE

(SAK-004)
(SAK-005)

42 1/2 AVE

(SAK-003)
(SAK-002)

Lake
Sakakawea

Pick City

200

6 1/2 ST

(SAK-001)

5 1/2 ST

41 1/2 AVE

N

Thompson Ln S

1:24,000

0   0.25   0.5 Miles

Chronology of the NCT

No one remembers the genesis of the idea to link the Appalachian Trail with the Lewis and Clark Trail across America's northern heartland and call it the North Country Trail. But here is a brief chronology.

1963—Outdoor Recreation Resources Review Commission recommends federal action to create nationwide systems of trails and scenic rivers.

1964—The Department of the Interior initiates a study to examine options for creating a nationwide system of trails.

1965—The US Forest Service completes a report providing input to the study. Among its recommendations is creation of a trail to be known as the "Northern Country Trunk Trail"; Wisconsin senator Gaylord Nelson introduces legislation to establish a system of National Scenic Trails.

1966—The Department of the Interior publishes the final study report *Trails for America.* It proposes a further study of a potential North Country National Scenic Trail.

1968—Congress passes the National Trails System Act and identifies the Appalachian and the Pacific Crest as the first National Scenic Trails. The North Country Trail is included in a list of 14 trail routes to be studied as potential additional National Scenic Trails.

1971—The Bureau of Outdoor Recreation initiates the feasibility study of the NCT.

1973—Tom Gilbert joins the Bureau of Outdoor Recreation and is assigned to complete the NCT feasibility study.

1975—The final feasibility study of the NCT is published.

1976–79—Several bills to authorize the NCT are introduced in Congress, but none are enacted.

1978—Carolyn Hoffman hikes (and bikes in Ohio) the entire route of the proposed NCT, becoming the first person to do so.

1979—President Jimmy Carter's annual Environmental Message to Congress calls for authorizing the NCT. Lance Feild, president of the International Backpackers Association, persuades Senator William Cohen (ME) and Representative William Whitehurst (VA) to introduce a bill authorizing a North Country National Scenic Trail.

1980—The Cohen-Whitehurst bill is amended into another parks and recreation bill and passes. On March 5, President Carter signs Public Law 96-199 authorizing the NCT. Administration of the trail is assigned to the National Park Service.

1981—Tom Gilbert begins writing the plan for the NCT. Lance Feild organizes the North Country Trail Association, with its first meeting in White Cloud, Michigan, where the new organization accepts donation of a historic school house to serve as its national headquarters.

Winter 1981–82—The first issue of the *North Country Trailblazer* newsletter is published.

1982—The National Park Service completes and publishes the *Comprehensive Plan for Management and Use of the North Country National Scenic Trail.*

1983—The first 673 miles of the NCT are certified as official, entitling them to be marked with the official trail emblem.

1987—Rerouting the NCT in Northeastern Minnesota's Arrowhead Region is first suggested and discussed.

1989—The NCTA publishes Wes Boyd's *Following the North Country National Scenic Trail,* the first book giving information about hiking the entire trail.

1991—Byron and Margaret Hutchins publish their guide *Certified Sections of the North Country Trail.*

1992—The number of the NCT's "certified" miles of trail crosses the 1,000-mile threshold.

January 1995—The NCTA newsletter is named the *North Star.*

1995—The NCTA opens its first office, in Grand Rapids, Michigan.

1996—The National Park Service publishes *A Handbook for Trail Design, Construction, and Maintenance,* by Bill Menke, to standardize the work done by all trail partners and create a "thread of continuity."

1998—The number of the NCT's "certified" miles of trail crosses the 1,500-mile threshold; the National Park Service and the Forest Service agree on a "Desired Future Condition" statement concerning trail management, primarily on National Forest lands. (The NCTA joins in signing a memorandum of understanding in 1999.)

1999—The NCTA publishes the first of a new series of hiking maps for the trail.

2000—The NCT is named 1 of 16 National Millennium Trails by the White House. The only other National Scenic Trail so honored is the Appalachian Trail. NCTA membership crosses the 2,000 threshold.

2001—The NCTA office moves to Lowell, Michigan.

2004—The NCTA publishes *Hikeable Segments of the North Country National Scenic Trail;* NCTA membership crosses the 3,000 threshold.

2004—The National Park Service completes the study *Northeastern Minnesota Route Assessment* and recommends changing the route to follow the Superior Hiking, Border Route, and Kekekabic Trails and other new routes (the Arrowhead Re-route).

2005—The NCTA, the National Park Service, and the New York Department of Environmental Conservation initiate a planning and alternatives study to select a route through Adirondack Park.

2007—The NCTA hosts the Partnership for the National Trails System's biennial National Scenic and Historic Trails Conference in Duluth, Minnesota.

2011—The NCTA wins the Hertzog Award for Best Friends Organization, Midwest Region, National Parks Service.

Many thanks to Tom Gilbert for compiling this chronology.

Bibliography

Brower, J. V. *Itasca State Park: An Illustrated History.* St. Paul, MN: McGill-Warner, 1904.

Cayuga Trails Club. *Guide to Hiking Trails of the Finger Lakes Region.* 12th ed. Ithaca, NY: Cayuga Trails Club, 2011.

DuFresne, Jim. *Backpacking in Michigan.* Ann Arbor: University of Michigan Press, 2007.

DuFresne, Jim. *Porcupine Mountains Wilderness State Park: A Backcountry Guide for Hikers, Backpackers, Campers, and Winter Visitors.* 2nd ed. Holt, MI: Thunder Bay Press, 1999.

Dwyer, Tom. *A Guide to the Allegheny National Forest.* University Park, PA: Penn State University Press, 2001.

Eberhart, M. J. *Trekking the North Country Trail.* Franklin, NC: Thirsty Turtle Press, 2009.

Fernandez, Kathleen M. *A Singular People: Images of Zoar.* Kent, OH: Kent State University Press, 2003.

Folzenlogen, Robert. *Hiking Ohio: Scenic Trails of the Buckeye State.* Glendale, OH: Willow Press, 1990.

Freeman, Rich. *Take A Hike: Family Walks in New York's Finger Lakes Region.* Englewood, FL: Footprint Press, 2006.

Funke, Tom. *50 Hikes in Michigan's Upper Peninsula.* Woodstock, VT: Countryman Press, 2008.

Gieck, Jack. *A Photo Album of Ohio's Canal Era, 1825–1913.* Kent, OH: Kent State University Press, 1988.

Hamka, Terry. *The Copper Mines of Ontonagon County.* Jackson, MI: Copperlady Press, 2011.

Hansen, Eric. *Hiking Michigan's Upper Peninsula.* Guilford, CT: Globe Pequot Press, 2005.

Hutchins, Byron, and Margaret Hutchins. *The North Country Trail in Pennsylvania.* Rockford, IL: Hutchins Guidebooks, 1991. Rev. ed. 2002.

Ikenberry, Nelda B. *Black River Harbor: Stories of a Settlement on Lake Superior's South Shore.* Ironwood, MI: printed by the author, 2009.

Jamison, James K. *The Mining Ventures of This Ontonagon Country.* Ontonagon, MI: printed by author, [1950?].

Jenkinson, Clay S. *Message on the Wind.* Reno, NV: Marmarth Press, 2002.

Jones, Stephen R., and Ruth Carol Cushman. *The North American Prairie.* New York, NY: Houghton Mifflin Harcourt, 2004.

Kudelka, Scott R. *Fort Ransom and Beaver Lake State Parks.* Cambridge, MN: Adventure Publications, 2008.

Kudelka, Scott R. *North Dakota's Best Hiking Trails.* Cambridge, MN: Adventure Publications, 2010.

Mason, Philip P., ed. *Schoolcraft's Expedition to Lake Itasca: The Discovery of the Source of the Mississippi*. East Lansing: Michigan State University Press, 1993.

Mitchell, Jeff. *Hiking the Allegheny National Forest: Exploring the Wilderness of Northwestern Pennsylvania*. Mechanicsburg, PA: Stackpole Books, 2007.

Modrzynski, Mike. *Hiking Michigan*. Helena, MT: Falcon Press, 1996.

Nerburn, Kent. *Neither Wolf nor Dog: On Forgotten Roads with an Indian Elder*. Novato, CA: New World Library, 1994. Rev. ed., 2002.

Norris, Kathleen. *Dakota: A Spiritual Geography*. New York, NY: Houghton Mifflin, 2001.

North Country Trail Association. *Hikeable Segments of the North Country National Scenic Trail*. Lowell, MI: North Country Trail Association, 2003.

Plank, Lisa Barker. *Images of America: Lowell*. Mount Pleasant, SC: Arcadia, 2010.

Pond, Robert J. *Follow the Blue Blazes: A Guide to Hiking Ohio's Buckeye Trail*. Athens: Ohio University Press, 2003.

Ramey, Ralph. *Fifty Hikes in Ohio*. 2nd ed. Woodstock, VT: Backcountry Publications, 1997.

Storm, Roger E., and Susan M. Wedzel. *Hiking Michigan* 2nd ed. Champaign, IL: Human Kinetics, 2009.

Strickland, Ron. *Pathfinder: Blazing a New Wilderness Trail in Modern America*. Corvallis: Oregon State University Press, 2011.

Sundquist, Bruce, Carolyn Yartz, and Jack Richardson. *Allegheny National Forest Hiking Guide*. 4th ed. Pittsburgh, PA: Allegheny Group, Sierra Club, 1999.

Superior Hiking Trail Association. *Guide to the Superior Hiking Trail: Linking People with Nature by Footpath along Lake Superior's North Shore*. Two Harbors, MN: Ridgeline Press, 2007.

Townsend, Chris. *The Backpacker's Handbook*. 4th ed. New York: McGraw-Hill, 2012.

Weaver, Will. *The Last Hunter*. St. Paul, MN: Borealis Books, 2010.

Weaver, Will. *Red Earth, White Earth*. St. Paul, MN: Borealis Books, 1986.

Index

Adams, Charles F., 140
Adams Fly Festival, 140
Adirondack Mountain Club (ADK), 25;
    Onondaga Chapter, 25
Adirondack Mountains, 3, 21, 22;
    Adirondack Blue Line, 21; "forever
    wild" designation, 2; NCT route in,
    211
Adirondack Park, 21
Adirondack Park Agency, 21, 22
Agates, 163
Allegany State Park, 24, 43, 44, 45, 46
    (map), 47
Allegheny Mountains, 3
Allegheny National Forest, 47, 50, 51, 52
Allegheny Plateau, 74, 85
Allegheny Reservoir, 4, 47, 50
Allegheny River, 3
American Discovery Trail, 75
Appalachian Trail, 1, 4, 5, 6, 9, 23, 66, 85
Arnold, Benedict, 22
Ash Cave (OH), 85, 86, 88
Atlantic Ocean, 3

Backpacker's Handbook, The, 14
Backpacking in Michigan, 108
Baker Trail, 47, 57
Barry State Game Area, 107, 111, 112,
    114, 115 (map)
Beaver Creek State Park, 76, 77, 78, 80
    (map)
Bemidji State Park, 222
Bessemer Ranger District, 181
Big Creek State Forest and Park (OH), 74
Big Two-Hearted River, 149
Birch Grove Schoolhouse, 117, 122, 123
Birch Grove Trail Loop, 122, 124, 125
Black River Harbor, 181, 183, 184, 185,
    186 (map)
Blau, Katie, 210
Boardman River (MI), 139, 140, 143
Border Route Trail, 8, 207, 208
Border Route Trail Association, 9, 208
Boundary Waters Canoe Wilderness Area,
    3, 207, 208

Bowman Lake Loop, 127, 128, 129
    (map)
Brule Bog, 187, 200, 201, 203, 204, 205
    (map)
Brule River State Forest, 187, 200, 201
Brule–St. Croix Portage, 200
Brule–St. Croix Roving Trail Crew, 191,
    197, 204
Buckeye Trail, 3, 8, 73, 81, 85, 87, 90,
    91, 94, 97, 101
Buckeye Trail Association, 9, 15, 73, 81,
    85, 102
Bunyan, Paul, 207
Bureau of Reclamation, 245
Burr Oak State Park, 74
Butler County (PA), 48

Cadotte, John Baptiste, 203
Calumet (MI) Pasty Fest, 167
Canal Era, 75
Canals: Erie (NY), 4; Miami and Erie
    (OH), 4, 75; Ohio and Erie (OH),
    76, 78, 79, 81, 82; Sandy and Beaver
    (OH), 74, 77, 78, 79
Carver, Jonathan, 203
Chappel, Ed, 127
Chequamegon National Forest, 187, 195
Chief Noonday, 111
Chippewa National Forest, 207, 208,
    210, 215
Civilian Conservation Corps, 86, 113,
    122, 124, 185, 245
Clarion River, 47, 56, 57, 58, 59
Clausen Springs Recreation Area, 232
Clear Creek State Forest (PA), 56, 58
Compass, 18
Conkle's Hollow State Nature Preserve
    (OH), 86
Conservation Trail (NY), 43, 44
Consumer's Energy, 137
Continental Divide National Scenic Trail,
    4, 6
Cook Forest State Park, 47, 49, 56, 57,
    58, 60 (map)
Copper Country State Forest, 108

Copper Falls State Park, 187
copper mining, 173
Copper Peak Ski Flying Hill, 183
Copper Range (MI), 172
Cornwall, Great Britain, 167
Cox, Josh, 102
Craig Lake State Park, 108
Crown Point, 3, 21, 22
Curot, Michel, 203
Curtiss, Glenn, 39, 40
Curtiss Museum, 39
Cuyahoga Valley National Recreation
    Area, 73

Davis Hollow Cabin, 61, 63, 64 (map)
Dayton, OH, 3, 75, 76, 94, 96, 98, 100
    (map)
Dayton Peace Accords, 98
Deeds Point MetroPark (OH), 94, 95, 98
Department of the Interior, 30
"Desired Future Condition," 30
Dogwood Trail, 78
Dollar Lake parking area, 139, 140, 145,
    146 (map)
Drier, Fred, 183
DuFresne, Jim, 108
Duluth, MN, 3, 200, 207

Eastern terminus extension, 5
East Fork State Park (OH), 75
Edmund Fitzgerald, 4, 162
End to Enders (E2E), 6
EPIRB (Emergency Position Indicating
    Radio Beacon), 19

Fallasburg County Park, 107, 116, 119
Federated Garden Clubs, 124
Feild, Lance, 122
Finger Lakes, 3, 4, 25, 35
Finger Lakes Trail, 8, 16–17, 21, 25, 32
    (sidebar), 33, 38, 39, 43, 44
Finger Lakes Trail Conference, 8, 13, 15,
    32, 34, 38, 43, 44
Five Rivers Fountains of Light, 97, 98
Five Rivers MetroParks, 75, 95
Flood of 1913, 98
Foothills Trail Club, 43, 44

Fort Abercrombie State Historic Site
    (ND), 231, 235
Fort Custer National Cemetery, 107
Fort Ransome State Park (ND), 232, 238
45th Parallel, 150
French and Indian War, 22

Garrison Dam (ND), 249
Gilfillan, Merrill, 73
Girty, Simon, 77, 103
Gitche Gumee, 149, 162
Glacial Lake Duluth, 202
GPS, 13, 15
"Grandma" Gatewood, 73, 85, 86
Grand Portage National Monument, 207
Great Black Swamp, 75, 101
Great Chicago Fire, 128
Great Conglomerate Falls, 181, 183, 184,
    185, 186 (map)
Great Depression, 86, 127
Great Lakes Shipwreck Museum, 162
Great Miami River Recreation Trail, 75
Green Mountain Boys, 22
Green Mountain Club, 23
Green Mountains, 23
Grey, Zane, 4
Greysolon, Daniel, Sieur du Lhut, 200,
    203
Guernsey Lake Campground, 139, 140,
    146 (map)
Gulf of Mexico, 4
Gunflint Trail, 207

Halliday, Len, 140
Hammondsport, NY, 38, 39, 41
Hass, Tim, 163
Hell's Hollow, 49, 61, 64, 65 (map)
Hemingway, Ernest, 4, 140, 149
Henry County Park District, 101
Henry's Mills, 49, 50, 51, 52, 55 (map)
Hiawatha National Forest, 108
Hickory Hill Camping Resort, 38
Historic Portage, 187, 200, 205 (map)
Hocking Hills (OH), 74, 85, 90
Hocking Hills State Park/Forest, 76, 85,
    86, 88, 89 (map)
Hodenpyl Dam, 130, 131, 137

Hudson River, 3, 4
Huffman Prairie Flying Field, 94, 96

Ikenberry, Nelda, 183
Independence Dam State Park, 101, 102
Iron County Forest, 187, 190
Iron Range (MN), 3
Itasca Moraine, 207, 221, 225 (map)
Itasca State Park, 207, 227, 230 (map)

James, Mabel, 43
Jay Cooke State Park (MN), 188, 207, 208
Johnson, Bruce, 223
Jordan River, 147, 148
Jordan River National Fish Hatchery, 147, 148
Jordan River Pathway (loop trail), 107, 147, 150, 151 (map)

Kalkaska, MI, 139
Kekekabic Trail, 8, 207, 208
Kekekabic Trail Association, 9
Kekekabic Trail Club, 208
Kellogg Bird Sanctuary, 112
Kent Co (MI) Fairgrounds, 116
Keweenaw National Historical Park, 173
King Milling Co., 116
Klos, Keith, 53

Labrador Hollow State Unique Area, 25, 26, 27, 28
Lake Ashtabula, 232, 242, 244 (map)
Lake Audubon National Wildlife Refuge, 232
Lake Champlain, 3, 4, 5, 21, 22
Lake Huron, 4
Lake Michigan, 4
Lake Sakakawea, 3, 232, 249
Lake Sakakawea State Park, 3, 5, 231, 249, 250, 251 (map)
Lake Superior, 4, 108
Lake Superior Shoreline hike, 161, 164 (map)
Lake Superior State Forest, 108, 164
Laurentian Divide, 207
Laurentian Shield, 3

Leatherstocking Region, 21
Leave No Trace, 10
Lesueur, Pierre, 203
Lewis, Yankee Bill, 111, 112
Lightfoot, Gordon, 4, 162
Lind, John, 228
Little Beaver Creek Wild and Scenic River, 74, 77, 79
Little Miami River Water Trail, 75
Little Miami Scenic Trail, 75
Little Presque Isle Point State Recreation Area, 168, 169
Little Smokies (OH), 90
Loda Lake Wildflower Sanctuary, 122, 124, 125
Lonetree Wildlife Management Area, 232, 245, 248 (map)
Longfellow, Henry Wadsworth, 162
Long Trail, 23
Lowell, MI, 107, 116, 121 (map)
Lowell State Game Area, 107, 116, 118
Lucius, Nicholas and Joseph, 202
Ludlow, Israel, 98

Mackinac Bridge (Big Mac), 4, 107, 108, 153
Mackinaw State Forest, 107, 147
Maine Junction, VT, 23
Manistee National Forest, 13, 107, 122, 123, 127, 128
Manistee River Loop, Trail, 13, 107, 108, 130, 131, 132, 133, 134, 136, 138
Maps, 13
Marietta, OH, 74
Marquette, MI, 108, 166, 167, 171 (map)
Maumee River, 103
Maumee Valley Heritage Corridor, 101
McClusky Canal, 232
McConnells Mill State Park, 48, 61, 62, 63
McCormick Tract Wilderness Area, 108
Mellen, WI, 187, 190
Menke, Bill, 191
Mesabi Range, 207
Mesabi Trail, 207
Meyerholtz Park, 101, 103

Miami and Erie Canal, 75, 98, 101, 103
Miami Conservancy District, 97, 98
Michigan Department of Natural
    Resources (DNR), 113, 114, 148, 157
Michigan Recreation Passport, 154, 157
Michigan SEEDS of Adventure Day
    Camp, 132
Middlebury, VT, 23
Middleville, MI, 107, 111, 112, 114, 115
Middleville State Game Area, 116
Milford, OH, 75
Milton Lake Esker, 210, 213 (map)
Minnesota Arrowhead Re-Route, 208
Minnesota Conservation Corps, 191
Mississippi River, 3, 200, 207, 223, 227
Missouri River, 3, 249
Mitchellsville Gorge, 24, 38, 39, 42 (map)
Mohawk Valley (NY), 3, 21
Moraine State Park, 48, 61, 62
Morgan, John Hunt, 77
Morgan Hill State Forest, 25
Muskallonge Lake State Park (MI), 108,
    161

National Cash Register Co., 98
National Museum of the United States
    Air Force, 94, 96
National Park Service, 5, 9, 17, 20, 32,
    96, 107, 117, 191
National Park System, 108
National Trails Act of 1968, 1
National Trails System, 1, 4, 5, 21
NCT Trail Town, 66
Neal, Theresa, 157
Nelson Boundary Blue, 16
New York Department of Environmental
    Conservation, 25, 27, 34; Region 7
    office, 25; Region 8 office, 32
1982 comprehensive plan for NCT, 21
Nomad, Nimblewill (M. J. "Eb"
    Eberhart), 6, 31
North American Prairie, The (Peterson
    Field Guide), 234
North Country National Scenic Trail:
    authorization, 1; length, 1
North Country Trail Association, 52, 63;
    about, 6–8, 107, 122; chapters, 47;

citizen stewards of, 113; headquarters,
    8, 107, 117; website, 2, 15
North Country Trail Association,
    Allegheny National Forest Chapter,
    51, 53
North Country Trail Association,
    Arrowhead Chapter, 210
North Country Trail Association, Brule–
    St. Croix Chapter, 201, 202
North Country Trail Association,
    Chequamegon Chapter, 196
North Country Trail Association, Chief
    Noonday Chapter, 112, 113
North Country Trail Association, Clarion
    Chapter, 56, 57, 58
North Country Trail Association, Dakota
    Prairie Grasslands Chapter, 235
North Country Trail Association, Grand
    Traverse Hiking Club Chapter, 140,
    145
North Country Trail Association, Great
    Trail—Sandy and Beaver Canal
    Chapter, 78
North Country Trail Association, Harbor
    Springs Chapter, 152
North Country Trail Association,
    Heritage Chapter, 191, 192
North Country Trail Association,
    Hiawatha Shore-to-Shore Chapter,
    157
North Country Trail Association, Itasca
    Moraine Chapter, 222, 223
North Country Trail Association, Jordan
    Valley 45° Chapter, 147
North Country Trail Association,
    Laurentian Lakes Chapter, 228
North Country Trail Association, NCT
    Hikers Chapter, 166
North Country Trail Association, Ni-
    Miikanaake Chapter, 184
North Country Trail Association, Peter
    Wolfe Chapter, 172, 173
North Country Trail Association,
    Sheyenne River Valley Chapter, 238,
    243
North Country Trail Association, Spirit of
    the Woods Chapter, 127, 128, 131

North Country Trail Association, Star of the North Chapter, 214
North Country Trail Association, Superior Shoreline Chapter, 161, 163
North Country Trail Association, Wampum Chapter, 48, 66
North Country Trail Association, Western Michigan Chapter, 116, 117, 122
North Dakota Birding Society, 242
North Dakota Game and Fish Department, 245, 246
Northern Michigan University, 166, 167
Norwich Mine, 174

Ohio and Erie Canal Towpath Trail, 81, 82, 84 (map)
Ohio Historical Society, 74
Ohio River, 3, 74, 75
Ohio to Erie Trail, 75
Oil and gas: history of, 52; impacts of, on NCNST, 50
Old Man's Cave (OH), 85, 86, 87
Old Victoria (MI), 108, 172, 173, 179, 180 (map)
Old Victoria Restoration Site, 172
Onondaga Loop, 24, 25, 29 (map)
Onondaga Trail, 25, 27
Oswald, Atley, 202
Ottawa National Forest, 108, 174, 181
Outdoor Recreation Resources Review Commission (ORRRC), 21

Pacific Crest National Scenic Trail, 4, 9
Pacific Northwest National Scenic Trail, 6
pasty, 167
Patterson, John H., 98
Paul Bunyan State Forest, 207, 224
Pavek, Brian, 214
Pennsylvania State Game Lands, 47; State Game Lands Number 95, 47; State Game Lands Number 148, 48, 69; State Game Lands Number 285, 48, 67
Penokee Mountain Range, 187
Pere Marquette State Forest, 107, 139
Pictured Rocks National Lakeshore, 3, 108, 156

Pittsburgh, 3
Porcupine Lake Wilderness, 195, 196, 198, 199 (map)
Porcupine Mountains (MI), 3
Porcupine Mountains Wilderness State Park, 108, 174, 181
Presque Isle City Park, 108

Rachel Carson Trail, 47
Rachel Carson Trails Conservancy, 57
Red Plaid Nation, 2, 5
Red River of the North, 231, 232
Revolutionary War, 21, 61, 82, 103
Rocky Mountains, 5
Rogue River State Game Area, 107
Ron Strickland's Ten Hiking Essentials, 18

Sand Lakes Quiet Area, 139, 141, 142
Sandy and Beaver Canal Association, 77
Saratoga, 21
Sawtooth Mountains, 207
Schoolcraft, Henry, 202, 223
Scurry, Ed, 58
Sea-to-Sea Route, 75
seiche, 163
Seneca Lodge (Watkins Glen), 31, 36
Serpent Mound (OH), 74
Shawnee, OH, 74
Shawnee State Forest, 3, 74, 75, 76, 90, 93 (map)
Shawnee State Park, 90, 91
Sheyenne Lake National Wildlife Refuge, 245
Sheyenne National Grasslands, 232, 234, 237 (map)
Sheyenne River, 231, 232, 236, 239, 242, 245
Sheyenne State Forest, 232, 238, 241 (map)
Shingobee hike, 217, 220 (map)
Shingobee Recreation Area, 217, 219
Shore-to-Shore Equestrian Trail, 139, 143, 144
Skurka, Andrew, 14
Slippery Rock Creek/Gorge, 48, 61, 62
Snaketown, 76, 101, 102, 105 (map)

Society of Separatists of Zoar, 81
Solon Springs, 188, 200
St. Croix River National Scenic Byway, 188
St. Ignace, 108
St. Lawrence River, 4, 200
Sterling Marsh, 127
Straits of Mackinac, 3
Student Conservation Association, 48, 191
Stuntz, George, 202
Sturgeon River Gorge Wilderness Area, 108
Sugar Hill State Forest, 24, 30, 31, 32, 37 (map)
Superior Hiking Trail, 3, 8, 207, 208
Superior Hiking Trail Association, 9, 208
Susquehanna River, 3, 4

Tahquamenon Falls, 4, 108, 156, 158
Tahquamenon Falls Brewery, 156, 159
Tahquamenon Falls State Park, 108, 156, 157, 160 (map)
Tahquamenon River Trail, 156, 158, 160 (map)
Tamarac National Wildlife Refuge, 208
Tar Hollow State Forest (OH), 74
Ticonderoga, 21
Tinker Falls, 25, 27
trail blazes, 16
trail register, 15, 67
Traverse City, 139, 146 (map)

Underground Railroad, 4, 74
United States Mine, 177
United States Navy, 5, 22
Universal Trans Mercator (UTM), 13
Upper Peninsula (MI), 3
Upper Vondegreen Trail, 78, 79
US Army Corps of Engineers, 242, 243

US Fish and Wildlife Service, 147, 148, 245
US Forest Service, 52, 124, 234, 236
Utsumi, Prof. Santiago (MSU), 112

Valley City (ND), 232
Valley of the Giants, 107, 139
Vermilion Range, 207
Vermont, 5, 6, 23

Wabash Cannonball, 4, 75
Wampum Hike, 49, 66, 71 (map)
War of 1812, 101
Washington, George, 48
Watkins Glen State Park, 24, 30, 31, 32, 35 (map)
Wayne National Forest, 3, 74
Western terminus extension, 5
Wetland Wonders hike (MN), 214, 216 (map)
Wetmore Landing (Lake Superior), 166, 169
wild rice, 218
Wilderness State Park, 107, 152, 154, 155 (map)
Wisniewski, Greg, 102
W. K. Kellogg Biological Station (MSU), 112
Wood, Wallace D. "Wally," 32
working landscapes, 181, 182
Wren Falls, 187, 190, 191, 192, 194 (map)
Wright, Wilbur and Orville, 96, 98
Wright-Patterson Air Force Base, 94, 96, 98

Yankee Springs State Recreation Area, 107, 111, 112, 114, 115 (map)
Yooper, 107

Zoar, OH, 74, 76, 81, 82, 83, 84 (map)

Printed and bound by CPI Group (UK) Ltd, Croydon, CR0 4YY

13/04/2025

14656506-0001